MICROSC..

WORD BIBLE

A Deep Dive into Microsoft Word's Latest Features with
Step-by-Step Practical Guide for Beginners & Power Users

Robinson Cortez

TABLE OF CONTENTS

xiv

CHAPTER ONE
WORD ROUTINE

In this chapter, we'll begin by looking at the Microsoft screen, gaining an overview of everything we'll be looking at on the screen so you can begin to recognize some of the options available to you. You will get an overview of some of the features inside of Microsoft Word and grasp some of the languages we'll be using throughout the book.

The First Step

Before you even think of getting any job done in Microsoft Word, you should know this very important part which is how you can get it up and running on your computer. Without further ado, let's see how you can get Microsoft Word entirely for free. First, you'll see how you can get Word on the web, and secondly, you'll know how to install Word on your pc also entirely for free. Well, let's jump on the PC.

From The Web

You can get Microsoft Word for free on the web by going to the website **office.com**. Once you land on office.com there are three different options. If you already have a Microsoft account, let's say you use skype or you've used office before, chances are you already have an account and you could simply **sign in**.

If you don't have a Microsoft account, don't worry, you can also **sign up** for the free version of Office by clicking on the **sign up for the free version of office** link as shown below and this will prompt you to set up a new Microsoft account.

There's also a third option over here to "**Get Office**". This brings you to a marketing website where you can purchase Office.

So, you go ahead and sign in. Once you click on sign in, **office.com** gives you free access to Microsoft word; not only do you get Microsoft Word, you can also get Excel, PowerPoint, and a whole bunch of other very powerful apps but for this book, we're focused on Word. Over on the left-hand side to kick off a new Word document you can click on the "**Create**" icon and right up at the top you can start a new Word document.

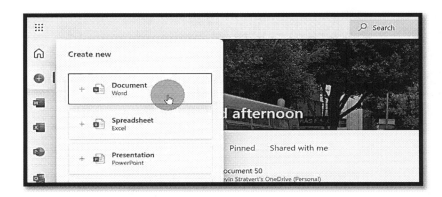

Also, if you go down here you can click on the Word icon and this drops you to the Word start page. Here too you can also start a new document or you could jump into one of the available templates or browse for more templates.

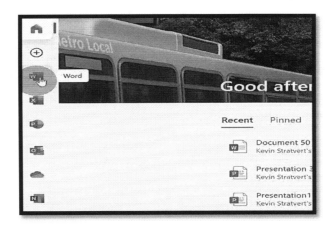

Once you've been using Word on the web, you'll be able to get back to all of your recent documents down below. Back on office.com, let's say that you have a Word document that you had started on your computer or you started working on it somewhere else and now you want to work on that document on the web. Well, you can easily get a document from your computer or maybe a flash drive and send this to the web. How do you do this? All you need to do is simply get your document and then drag and drop it onto office.com.

You'll see a blue highlight appear and once you release it, here you see that it automatically uploads it for you and if you wait a moment this will automatically open it in Word.

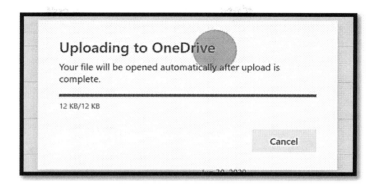

This has now opened this document in word and although you're working on a document using Word online that doesn't mean you can't take that document and get it back onto your computer. Up in the top left-hand corner under the File menu, there's the option to **"Save as"** and when you click on that, you can save a copy online under any name you want.

Also, right down below there's the option to download a copy to your computer; you could take a document, upload it, work on it using Word online, and then you can download a copy again to your computer, and not only can you **download a Word document** you could also **get a PDF** and an **ODT**. You might be wondering why you would ever want to install Office when you could use Word on the web. Well, with Word on the web you have to be online. Also, it's missing some of the functionality that you find in the desktop app but it has the functionality that you're likely going to use most often. For Example, the Table of contents is now available on the web.

Also, one thing that might surprise you is that the web has some functionality that the desktop version of Word does not have. Here for example, under the home tab if you go over to **"Dictate"**, you can take an audio file and have Word online transcribe that for you; that's not something you could do on the desktop.

An even easier way that you can access Word on the web if you're on a Windows 10 or 11 computer is if you have Windows 10 or 11 and it includes an app called **Office**. To access this app simply go down to the taskbar, click on **"Search"** and then type in **"Office"**.

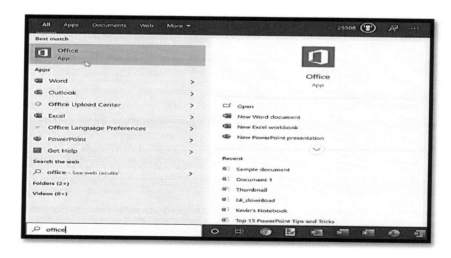

You'll see the best match appear for the Office app, you go ahead and click on that. This opens up the Office app and it looks very familiar to what you just saw on Office.com.

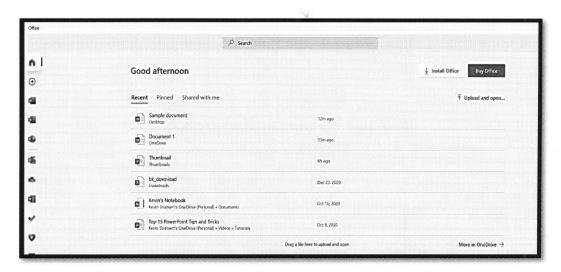

Here too you can access Word the same way. In the top left-hand corner once again, you can click on the "**Create**" icon and here you could kick off a blank new Word document. Also, if you click on the Word icon on the left-hand side this will bring you to the Word start page, and just like before you could kick off a new document, jump into one of these templates and you can also get back to recent documents.

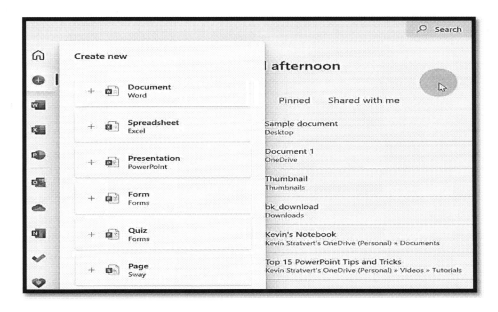

This is one more way to access Word on the web. One of the very nice features is that down here on your taskbar you'll see the Office icon, if you right-click on this you can get back to recent documents, PowerPoint, Excel files, and you can also kick off a new document directly from here so you don't even have to open the app to kick off a new word document.

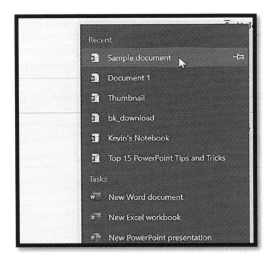

Switching On Your Desktop

Now that we've looked at how you can get Word on the web entirely for free, let's see how you can **install Office** on your desktop. First, let's look at the approach that you can use if you're a student, a teacher, or an administrator at an educational institution. Head over to the URL below.

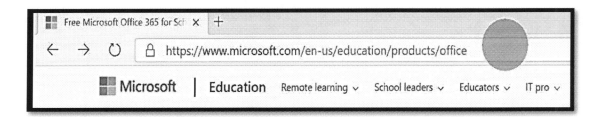

Once you land on this page, you can type in your school email address below, and once you finish typing in your email address click on "**Get started**" to see if you're eligible to download and install Office for free.

After you type in your email address, it'll ask you if you're a student or a teacher, so select the one that you are and when you finish signing up for your account, once again you'll land on the website that we saw earlier and that's office.com.

If you're eligible on office.com, in the top right-hand corner you'll see an option to **install Office**. When you click on this you can then install all of the Office 365 apps; it includes things like Outlook, and OneDrive for business, and here you get Microsoft Word.

Now if you don't like using Word on the web and you're not a student or a teacher (so you don't qualify for the education deal), you can still get Word on your computer entirely for free and you're going to use something called **Microsoft Rewards** to get Microsoft Word for free.

You might be wondering what Microsoft Rewards are and how this will help you get Microsoft Word. Well, Microsoft Rewards is a program that Microsoft created to reward you for using Microsoft products, which means the more you use Microsoft products, the more points you get, and then you can redeem different things with those points. For example, you could get Microsoft Word but you could also get all sorts of other things like gift cards from many different retailers.

To get to Microsoft Rewards head to the URL below.

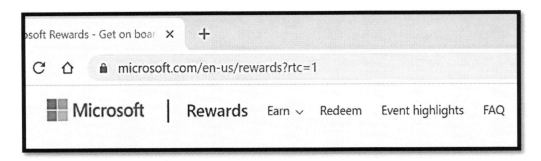

Here you could either sign up for free (if you don't yet have a Microsoft account), but if you already have a Microsoft account you can go ahead and click on sign in.

After you've signed in you might be wondering how you earn points. There are three different ways that you can earn points. The first way to earn points is to search on **Microsoft Bing**; simply head to **bing.com** and then you can type in your search query. The second way to earn points is to search using Bing on your phone; here you're going to type in a word, click on search, and once again you just earned even more points. The third way to earn points is to use the **Edge** browser when you're searching on bing.com. Those are the three different ways that you could earn points and if you want a quick reminder of how you could earn points on the Bing rewards homepage, over on the right-hand side you can click on the option that says Points breakdown.

Here you'll see how many points you've earned daily and how many potential points you can earn. You can earn up to 270 points per day or about 120 per year and that's more than enough to buy Microsoft Word.

If it feels painful to have to earn all of these points, think of it this way: you likely already search on the web anyway and so if you just make Bing part of your daily habit of searching on your pc and searching on your phone, you're going to start accruing points very quickly and you're going to get word and lots of other things entirely for free. After accumulating your points over some time, you can redeem your points. On the left-hand side, you'll see a tab that says "**Redeem**".

Click on that and within this page, on the left-hand side, click on **Shop**.

Within Shop you'll see all different types of gift cards that you can redeem with your Microsoft points. Here, for example, you can get an Xbox gift card, you can get Skype credit, and below that, you can shop with different retailers. To get Microsoft word for free you're going to redeem either a gift card at Target or Walmart.

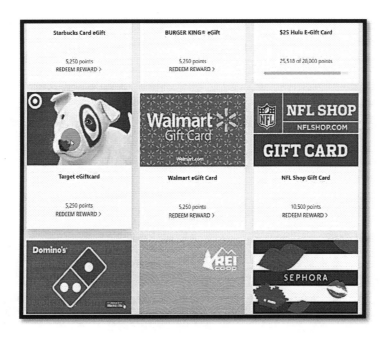

If you're in a market where there is no Walmart and there is no target, there should be local retailers in your market where you can get a gift card, and then you can use that gift card to purchase Office. Once you pick up your gift card with either Walmart, Target, or whoever the retailer is in your local market, you can search for Microsoft 365, and here you can get a personal version of Microsoft 365. This gives you access to Word along with all of the other Microsoft 365 applications. The only downside with Microsoft Rewards is that it's currently not available in all markets. If you're in a market that doesn't support Microsoft Rewards, well, unfortunately, this technique won't work for you but hopefully, some of the other techniques will work and you'll be able to use Word entirely for free.

Starting Word

So how do you start Word on your computer? Well, there are a couple of options. First, if you have the icon already pinned to your taskbar, you can click on that button.

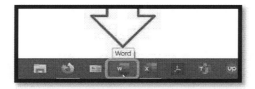

If you don't see this down there, you can go over here to the search bar and type "**Word**", it should appear up there, and you can click on that icon.

A Blank Document

When you first launch Word, you'll be confronted with the home page, which displays a list of recent documents in the main body of the screen. They're all displayed under here; you can just double-click on any of them to open that document.

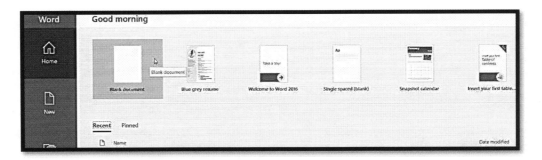

This is a convenient way to quickly access files you've recently worked on. So that's a little bit of information on how to access recent documents, but what we want to focus on here is how to create a blank document, and if you look just above that Recent list, the first thing you'll see is a Blank document. It's quite simple; just choose "**Blank document**" to make a new one. But before we do that, let's have a look at some of the other options you have in this area for creating new documents. If you don't want a blank document, you may create one based on a template, and Word provides a variety of different templates to choose from.

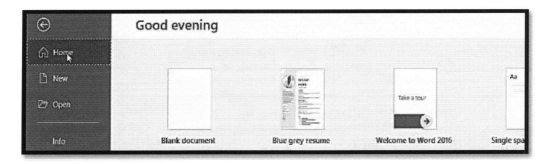

Now, if you've never used a template before and aren't sure what they are, it's just a good starting point; for example, if you know you need to create a resume or some meeting notes, you can search for a specific template related to a resume or meeting notes, and it will already have a lot of the information or layout that you need for that particular document. You can see some templates at the top here, and if you click on the "**More templates**" link, you can go through and take a look at some of the templates that are available for you to use. There are a lot of them in here, and they're worth checking out if you've never been into this section before.

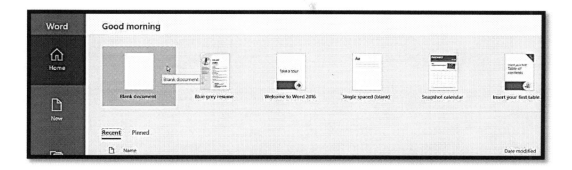

If you're looking for something extremely particular, such as a resume, you can enter it in, click the magnifying glass, and it will search the templates, bringing up a list of all of those Resume templates. If you find one you like, you can just click on it and begin working on it.

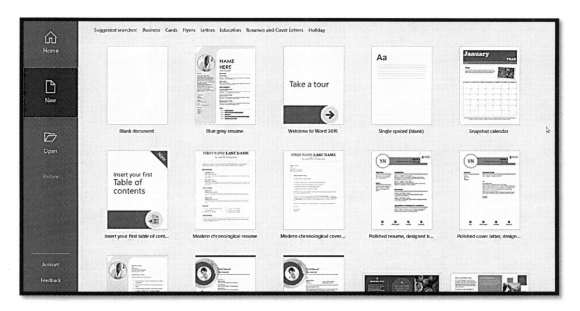

You can just pick a Blank document if you don't want to utilize a template. So now we've generated a blank document, the first thing you should notice is that if you look up to the top of the screen, you'll see what we refer to as the **Title bar**, which currently states Document 1, indicating that this document hasn't been saved yet.

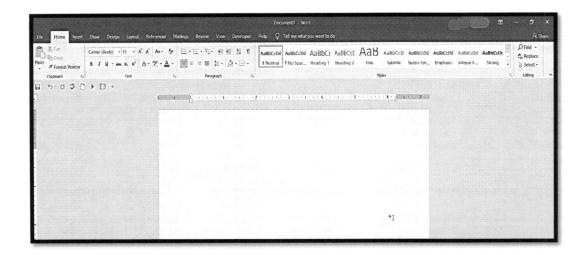

You'll see that when you create a new blank document, the default name is document 1, 2, or 3, and so on, just be aware of that since you'll notice this change when we save this document later.

Ribbons and Tabs

Home, **Insert**, **Layout**, **View**, **Draw**, **Mailings**, **Review**, **Developer**, and **Help** are some of the tabs on this screen.

What you see on your computer may alter somewhat from what we have here, depending on which of these tabs you have selected, but in general, you will see these tabs running across the top, and what these tabs contain or what we refer to as **Ribbons,** which contain all of the commands that you require. If you click on the home tab, for example, you'll see the home ribbon, which has all of the commands that run across the top of the screen, and these commands are generally organized into their appropriate ribbons. The commands that you use the most are found on the home ribbon, and we'll go over some of them later in this chapter, but just know that they're ordered logically with their respective commands. Before we go any further with these ribbons, it's worth noting that if you're on the home ribbon, you'll notice that the commands are organized into groups; for example, we have **Clipboard**, **Font**, **Paragraph**, and **Styles**. At the bottom of each of those groups, you'll see a little downward arrow, and if you click that, you'll find more advanced options or more options related to that group, so just be aware that you're not limited. If it has a drop-down arrow, you'll most likely discover some more complex commands in there if you click on it.

Inside Word

Once you're inside Microsoft Word, you have a lot of options here. The first option is to start with a blank document, which is most likely what you want to do. You also have several options over here on the left. You have the **home screen**, **New**, **Open**, **Account**, **Feedback**, and **Options**.

Home is selected by default. Under the "**Recent**" tab are recent documents that have been opened. Under the "**Pinned**" tab is any document that you want to open often, these will be very frequently used files, and the way you get them in the pinned list is by going to "**Recent**" and clicking on the pin icon right there, then when you go back to the home button, go back to the Pinned tab and you will see that document now resides under the Pinned list. "**Shared with me**" will be any documents that have been shared with you over OneDrive. If you go to

"**New**", you can either select a blank document or you can look through all of the templates down here that Microsoft Word has provided for you. These templates allow you to quickly begin a resume, a calendar, or a lot of other frequently used documents such as brochures and reports.

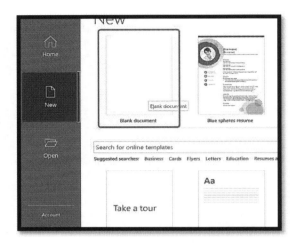

If you go to the **Open** menu, you can see a lot of files that you have opened recently, more so than you can see on the home screen. If you go to **Browse**, you'll be able to find a document on your computer. And if you go to **OneDrive**, you'll be able to see any kind of documents that you've shared with everyone else, or people have shared with you.

The **Account** menu tells you information about your Microsoft Office subscription and gives you different options for setting defaults for Microsoft Word

The Backstage View

It's worth mentioning that the **backstage view** is available in all Microsoft Office programs; for example, if you're using PowerPoint, Excel, or even Outlook, you'll see a backstage view. You might be curious as to where it is and how to get to it. To put it simply, it's the **File** tab at the top.

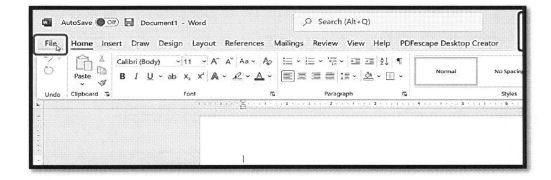

If you go to **File**, you'll see the backstage view, which is where you'll see all of your document's mini-tasks. So, starting with the menu that runs along the left-hand side, we can see that it's divided into a few divisions. We have three icons in the top section: Home, New, and Open. If you click on "**Home**," you'll be sent to the home screen, which we'll discuss in more detail later.

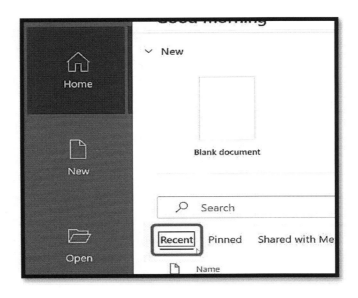

Then there's "**New**," which is where you'd go if you wanted to make a new document, either a blank one or one based on an existing template.

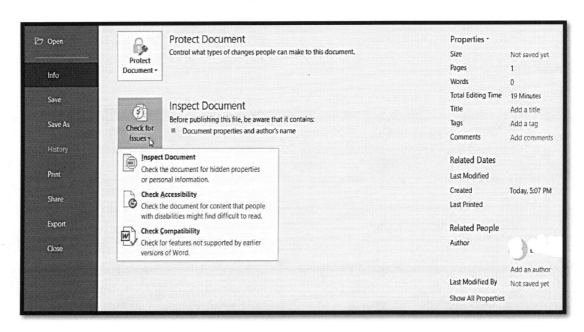

There's also "**Open**," which is where you'd go if you wanted to open a fresh file or one, you'd saved somewhere.

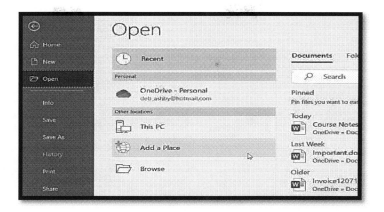

In the "**Info**" section, you'll find all of the details about the document you're now working on. If you haven't saved your document or it doesn't have any content in it yet, there isn't much information to show you about it in this section. You'll discover all the attributes on the right-hand side, and you'll see that these will alter if you start doing some of those things.

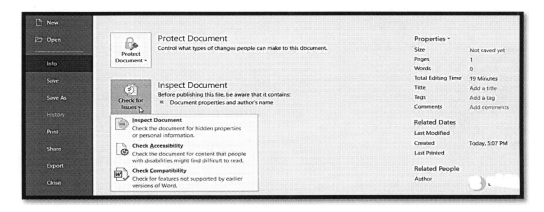

For the document above, you can see that it now says the document isn't saved, that it has one page and zero words, and that it tells us how long we've been in that file. We could go through and add a title and tags to help with searching. So just keep in mind that if you're seeking information regarding the file you're currently working on, this is a good place to start. If we return to the left-hand side, we'll find some more items that we may utilize in our document. The first option is "**Protect Document**," which allows you to limit the types of changes that others can make to your document. So, if you're sharing this document with others, say, if you've sent it to a client, a coworker, or someone else on your team, you can have some control over what they can do with it; for example, you can apply some editing restrictions if you want, and that's where you'll find all of those kinds of options, which we'll go over in more detail later.

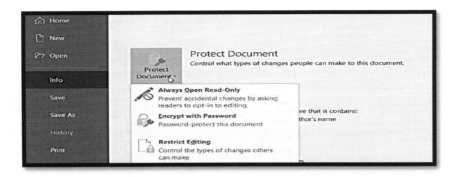

We then have an "**Inspect Document**" option, which allows you to inspect or conduct a quick check on your document once you've done it to ensure that it has some features that make it available to others and that there are no incompatibility issues. This means that if you're using Word 2024, you should be aware that someone you're sharing the document with might be using an older version of Word, so it's worth pointing out or highlighting in your document or figuring out which elements they won't be able to see because some functionality in 2024 isn't available in older versions.

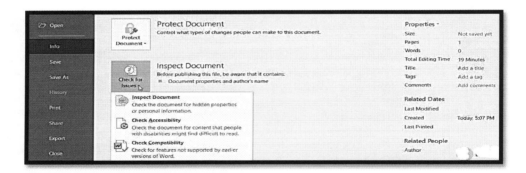

Let's imagine a new typeface was released in 2024, and you used it in your document; if you shared it with someone who doesn't have that version of Word, they might not be able to see the font you chose, and the same is true for other things. It's always a good idea to check if your document is compliant and makes any necessary adjustments before sending it out, and you can do that by clicking the "**Inspect Document**" option. We also have a section called "**Manage Document**," where you may go back and recover unsaved versions of your document. We've probably all done it at some point: begun typing forgot to save, and then quit the program, believing we'd lost everything. One of the nice things about Word 2024 is that it saves your documents automatically. If you had prior versions, they will appear on this "Manage Document" screen, and you may click to restore them. This is a lifesaver, so make a mental note of where that button is located.

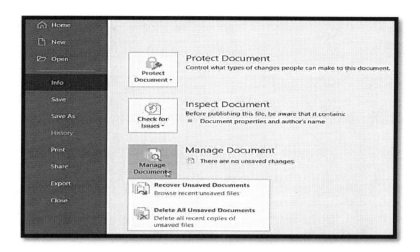

Then there's "**Save**" and "**Save As**" beneath that. These two operate in a somewhat different manner. You'll notice that when you click "**Save**," you must first save your document before you can use it. If you click "**Save**" right now, it will take you to the "**Save As**" region and ask you where you want to save your document because you haven't done so yet. If you'd already saved your work and merely wanted to save some modifications, you could just click the "**Save**" button, which will appear to do nothing but save the changes to the file name.

The difference between the two is that one is used to save a document that has previously been saved as a name, while the other is used to pick a folder and save a document for the first time. You'll now be able to find past revisions of your work in the "**History**" section. Then there's "**Print**," which does exactly what it says on the tin. If you've written a beautiful document and want to print it, you can come in here, choose your printer, and see all of your printing options.

There is a "**Share**" option in this section that will allow you to share your document in a variety of ways. You have the option of emailing it, saving it to the cloud and sending a link to individuals, presenting it online, or even posting it to a blog. When it comes to sharing, there are numerous alternatives.

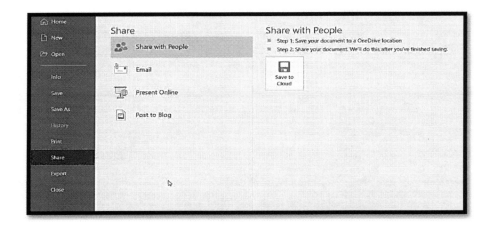

23

You should use "**Export**" primarily if you want to **create a PDF file**. If you've never used a PDF before, it's essentially a version of your document that's very difficult to modify, so if you want to secure your document or don't want people to be able to simply go in and alter it, it's always worth saving or producing a PDF of it before sending it.

There is a lot of software available these days that allows users to alter PDF files, but in general, if you want to add an extra layer of security, producing a PDF is a good option, and this is where you would go. Finally, at the bottom of the page, there is a "**Close**" button that will close your document. Our third and final piece is at the bottom. We have the "**Account**," which simply displays information about your account, including personal information and the Office version you're using.

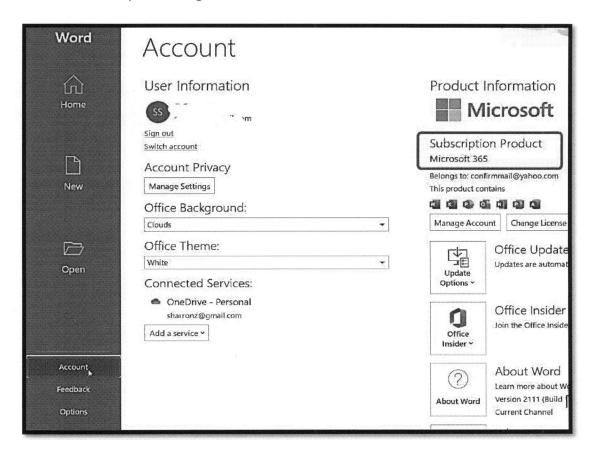

We have a "**Feedback**" button, if you want to be helpful and provide Microsoft with some useful feedback, you can utilize it.

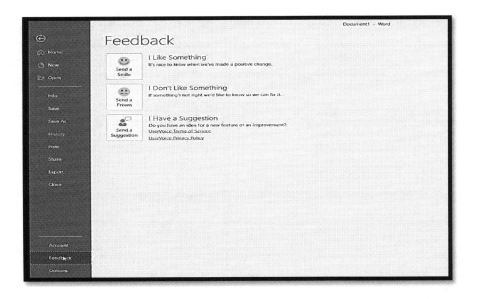

Finally, there's the "**Options**" section, which we'll go over in-depth later, but it's where you'll find all of the little things you can set as defaults and small modifications you can make to how Word works in general for you and how it is specific to use. This will allow you to personalize the way your Word version functions, and there are a lot of options here.

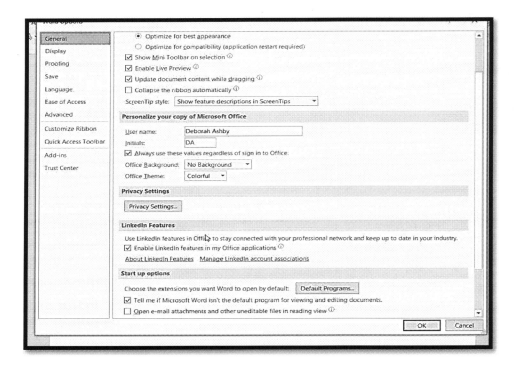

One other thing you'll notice in this backstage view is the **back arrow** at the top, which does exactly what you'd expect it to do: it returns you to the document you were in.

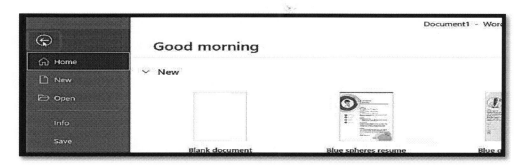

Now, let's go back to Microsoft Word

The Home Tab

If you click the home tab, you will see that the **home ribbon** comes up, and you have a lot of options here. Now if you have some text in your Word document and you would like to be able to see this closer up, you can go to **View**, **Zoom**, and change this so that you can see closer up what you are doing with all of these options on the home tab.

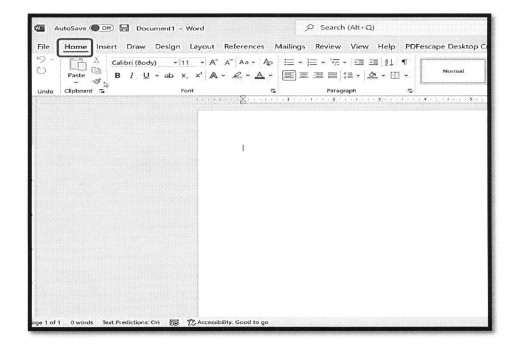

Back to the Home tab, if you double click with your mouse on any word, you will select the entire word. Here you can **bold**, **italicize**, or **underline** your text. You can also use the **strike-through** option. If you're editing someone else's paper but you want to leave what they had originally put in the text, you can use the strike-through. You can also **change the color** of your font; you can **highlight** all of your text and **center** it, **right-justify** or **left-justify** it. You can also **change the spacing** when you have **paragraphs** right here. You can **add bulleted points**, and **number points** and you can even make this an **outline** if you have multiple lines on here. With the **Indent** button, you can indent or you can out-dent. You can also **highlight** your text. Over here on the right side, you can **dictate** a new sentence if you would like. These are some of the options in the home ribbon.

The Insert Ribbon

In this tab, there are a couple of options we should review. First of all, in Word, you can **insert a table** of information so that all of your rows and columns are lined up and are formatted well.

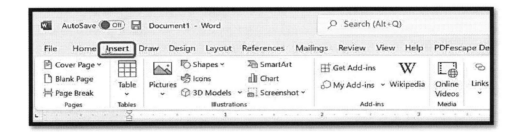

Clicking on the **Pictures** tab allows you to **insert a picture**. You can insert pictures from your device; you can use stock images, or even get pictures online and into your document. There are a couple of other things you can insert including **Shapes**, **Icons**, **Screenshots**, **Online videos**, **Links**, **Symbols**, and **Equations**, among others. You can also **insert the page number** on your document by going to the button on top of the page, whatever your preferences are for page number, and then you can make your page number be on the left, center, or right.

The Layout Ribbon

On the Layout, you can **change the margins of your page**. The normal setting is 1inch all around but you can also customize those margins and make them whatever size you would like by hitting "**Customize**".

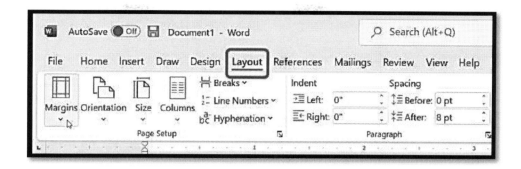

You can **change the orientation of your page** from Portrait to landscape.

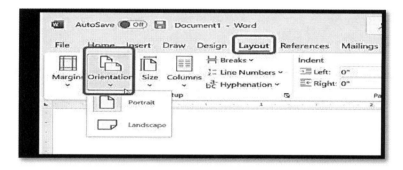

You can also **change the size of your paper** here.

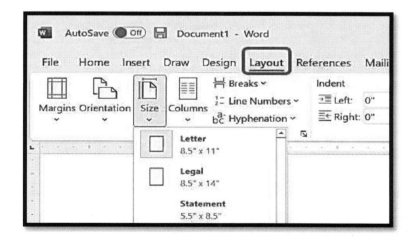

Here's one that is used often; sometimes you may want to **insert a page break** and have information print on a different page. What you would do is go to "**Breaks**" and hit "**Page**".

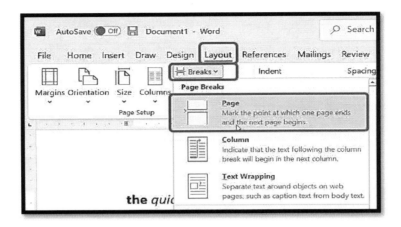

If you scroll down, you will see that the page break is right there. Sometimes that's very useful when you have one sentence appearing at the bottom of a document that you would prefer for it to go onto the next page. But be careful with that because, as you add words to your page, the page break will remain in place, and your text may spill over onto another page, yet leave the page break and it might not look right.

The Review Ribbon

There are some options here that are very useful when you are working with Microsoft Word. Let's say you want to make your paper a little more exciting and you have a word in your document that you don't like and you would like to use something more emphatic. if you double-click on the word and go up to "**Thesaurus**", you can now see different words that could be used to replace that word.

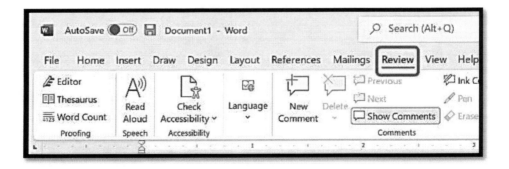

If you click on the new words and insert any of them, you can see that you have now replaced the synonym with the initial word.

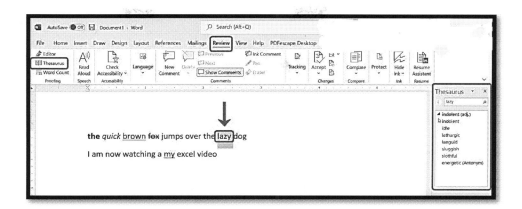

You can also click on "**Word count**" and see how many words you have on this page. In the Status bar, you can see how many words you have on your page as well.

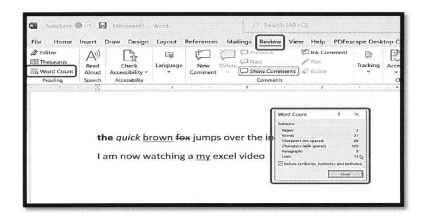

The View tabs

On the View tab, you can **zoom** in and out of the document that you are working with.

You can also pick "**Multiple**" to see how many pages you have within your document and get a rough idea of what it's going to look like when you print it out. You can also **switch windows** to any other document you may have opened at this time, or for a shortcut on that you can press **Alt + Tab** on your keyboard and switch between word documents as well. To go back to the regular view that you've been working with, click "**One Page**", click on **zoom**, and go back to your regular view.

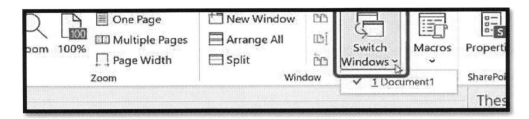

What if You Can't Remember All of These?

One more thing you should note is up there in the "**Search**" **bar**. This is true for all Microsoft Office applications.

If you can't remember one of the commands we went over and you click in here and type a word, you will see it right up here. With that, instead of having to search for the ribbon, you can type in the command of what you would want to do until you get a little more familiar with the environment inside of Microsoft word

Changing the View of your Document

This is where we'll find our views, all the way over on the right-hand side. This is just a quick way of switching between views, and these buttons correspond to how you're now looking at your document. As you can see, the first one is Read Mode, and switching to it provides you with a fresh perspective on your paper. It removes almost everything on the screen except your document, allowing you to see more clearly what you're looking at. This is useful if you're trying to read a document. The Print Layout view is the next one we have; it's the one you'll be in by default, and it's the one you'll be in most of the time when you're working on your papers. The Web Layout view is the next one. So, if you're creating something for the web, or if you want to incorporate things like HTML code, you'd go into this Web Layout view and create your document that way.

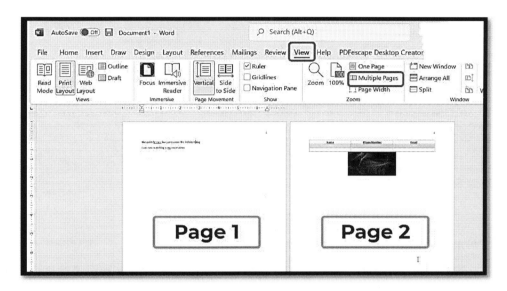

That's Not All

We have what we term the **Quick Access Toolbar** found directly beneath the ribbons, and this toolbar contains a few different commands that you can configure. Its entire purpose is to provide you with quick access to the commands that you use the most frequently, which will differ widely from person to person based on what you do in your everyday work.

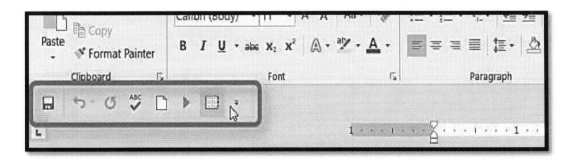

If you click the drop-down at the bottom, you'll notice that you have a lot of alternatives for adding to that fast access toolbar. The ones that are currently checked are already in the toolbar, but you can add any of the ones listed here if you want. Alternatively, if you want a command that isn't mentioned here, you can browse for **more commands** and choose something to add to the Quick Access Toolbar from there.

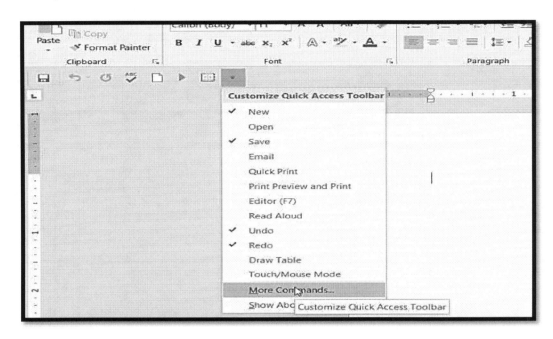

Moving to the top of your document, you'll notice a **ruler** running across the top and a ruler running down the side. On this top ruler, you might notice some small triangles in the little block at the bottom. It says Left indent, Hanging Indent, and First Line Indent when you hover over it, and this helps you align the text in your document; so be aware of the ruler and the Indent functionality in there.

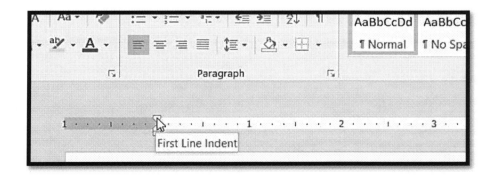

33

The **Status bar** is located at the bottom of the screen, and on the left-hand side of the status bar is some general information about our documents. You can see from the image above that we're in section 1 and on page 1 of 1. We presently have no words in the document, and it also indicates that our language is set to English (United States), but these will undoubtedly alter as we begin to add content.

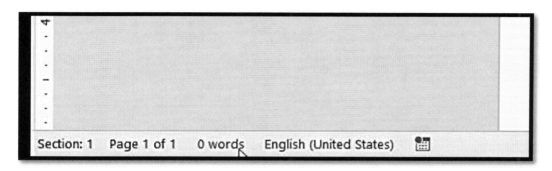

It's also worth mentioning that the View ribbon at the top can also be used to access various options, such as **views** and **zoom**. You can see in the first group that we have our layouts, as well as a couple of extra views and some zoom possibilities.

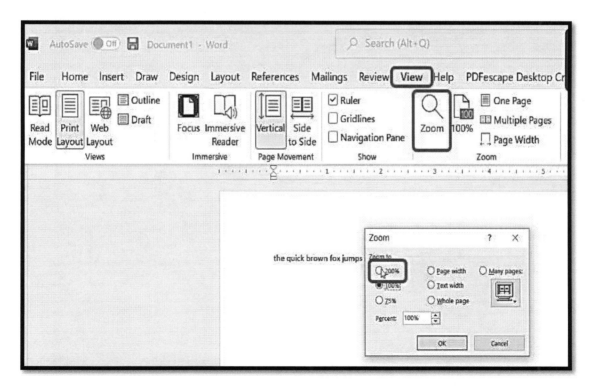

The **Scroll bar** on the side of the Word screen is the last thing to mention. So, you can go up and down, and if you have more pages, you'll be able to scroll through all of them.

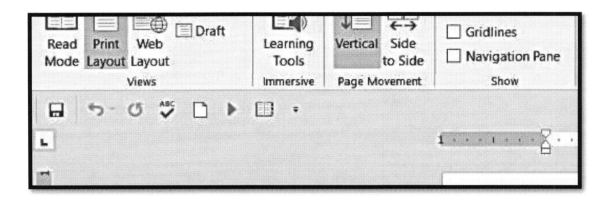

So that's a summary of what you're looking at on your Word screen right now, and hopefully, that's gotten you a little bit more familiar with the terminology we'll be using throughout this book, and it's a nice foundation for us to leap off into our following chapters.

CHAPTER TWO
TYPING MASTERY

In this chapter, we'll look at how to get started typing, some of the minor things you'll notice when you start typing your first documents, and several keyboard shortcuts that will help you out while you're typing.

What Happens When You Type?

There are a few things to keep in mind when typing your first document. We'll look at these things to familiarize you with the typing interface, which will help you prevent mistakes and make typing easier and more enjoyable.

The Margins

You'll notice that the cursor is flashing, but it isn't flashing directly at the page's left-hand edge. This is because there is a left margin of approximately an inch in there, and you can see that as you start typing, all of your text will start coming out there.

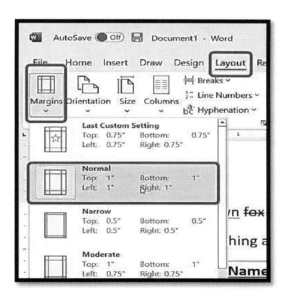

So, after typing a basic line, if you continue typing when you reach the end of a row, you won't need to hit the enter key to move on to the next line; it will automatically wrap as you type, you can just keep typing and it will wrap itself around, eliminating the need to hit enter at the end of a line. If you want to force a line break, for example, if you were on a line and wanted to do anything on the following line, you can hit the enter key, which will take you down to the next line and allow you to continue typing.

Capitalizing the First Letter

Another thing to keep in mind is that if you start typing a sentence at the beginning of a line and don't capitalize the initial letter, Word will capitalize it for you. So, if you just start typing, you'll notice that it has capitalized it for you without you having to go back and change it. This is because of Word's autocorrect feature, which recognizes certain words and changes them for you, making your life much easier. In the following chapters, we'll go over a lot of the autocorrect settings.

Colorful Underlines Explained

There are a few more things to keep in mind

If you misspell a word, you'll notice a red squiggly underline, which indicates that you've made a mistake with that word. So, you can hover over the word and right-click your mouse to bring up a menu of possibilities, and more often than not, the term you're looking for will be among them. If it isn't, you'll have to go in and manually make the change.

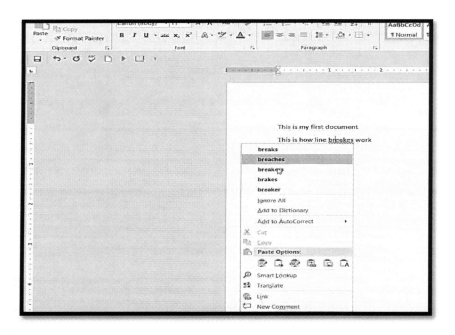

If you add a comma and/or a double space to a sentence, Words will detect a problem. There's a grammatical issue, and this type of error is fairly common, especially when you're working quickly. You might accidentally type a comma, or hit the spacebar twice, but you can see now with the double underline that if you right-click it tells you how to rectify it.

Unknown Words?

When you misspell a word, you can right-click and add the word to the dictionary. There will be times when your sort of word is the name of someone or a place. Word doesn't always recognize things like that and will tell you it's spelled incorrectly when it isn't; it's just not recognized by Word.

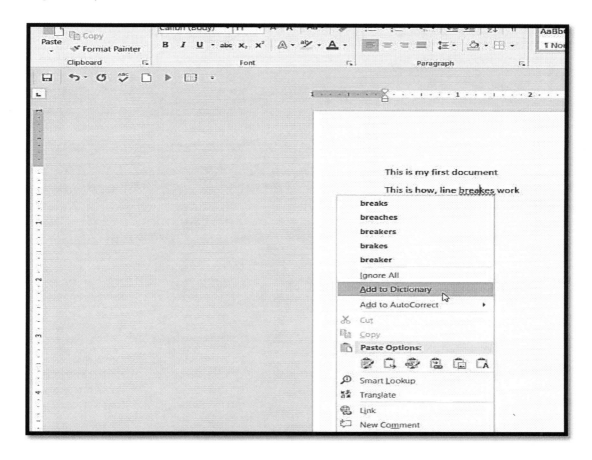

If you, have it, you can pick "**Add to Dictionary**," and it will add the word to the Word dictionary, ensuring that it does not register as a spelling problem the next time you type it. So, keep that in mind, and all of these options are available from the right-click menu.

Switching Between Documents

If you want to create another blank document, simply go to **File**, "**New**," then "**Blank Document**." If you check up in the title bar, you'll see that it now says Document 2. This means that your original document hasn't been closed; it's just been moved beneath the one you're currently working on. There are a couple of options for switching between the two documents, or in this example, switching back to the original. You can access your Word icon by hovering your mouse over it in the bottom status bar. If you have the Word icon pinned to your toolbar, you can see both of your documents and choose which one you wish to work on. As a result, you can return to Document 1 at any time.

You may also go to the View ribbon and select "**Switch Windows**," which will display a list of all of your open documents. You can go back to Document 2 once more. Being able to flip between any or all of the documents that you have open is quite convenient.

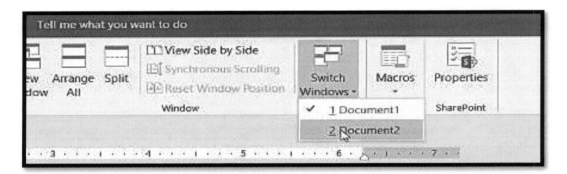

Closing Your Document without Closing Word

If you want to close your document, you can do it quickly and conveniently. A word of caution: if you look right up in the upper right-hand corner, you'll see a large cross icon that states "**Close**," which will close Word completely, so be wary of that.

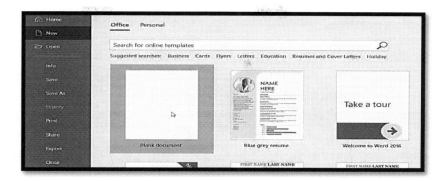

Note: You can just go to file and select "**Close**" if you only want to close one file.

Some Useful Keyboard Shortcuts

Here, you get to see some Microsoft Word keyboard shortcuts; the ones that are found to be most useful.

Your Familiar Commands

To begin, let's review some of the most commonly used keyboard shortcuts, which are **Ctrl + C**, **X**, and **V** for **Copy**, **Cut**, and **Paste**, respectively, as well as **Ctrl + Z** to **undo** a mistake and then **Ctrl + Y** to **redo** whatever you've undone. Those are some basic keyboard shortcuts that everyone should be familiar with; they can be used in nearly any program, but let's look at the most useful Microsoft Word keyboard shortcuts.

Quick Save and Print Commands

The first is "**quick save**," and we all know the importance of saving frequently. It's a good idea to save whenever you make substantial changes, but instead of having to remove your hand off the keyboard and go up to the Save button, you can simply hold **Ctrl** and tap **S (Ctrl + S)** to do a quick save. There's a similar shortcut for printing quickly. Holding **Ctrl** and tapping **P (Ctrl + P)** brings up the print choices, which you can adjust if desired, before clicking Print. So, **Ctrl + S** and **Ctrl + P**, are some good easy time savings.

Spelling and Grammar Check

The **F7** key is yet another simple keyboard shortcut. The **spelling** and **grammar check** can be accessed by pressing F7.

The Navigation Command

Ctrl + F is another Microsoft Word keyboard shortcut that you may find useful. The **Find panel**, also known as the **Navigation panel**, appears when you click this. So, you can type a word into the navigation search box and it will try to find it in your document. This is especially useful if you're working on a large document, such as a research paper, a master's thesis, or something similar, and you've got thousands of words. If you make a mistake, such as using incorrect terminology in your paper, and you want to find all instances of the mistake, you can simply type in the word and it will find all instances of that mistake.

Text Formatting

The following three keyboard shortcuts are for text formatting. When you're typing in Microsoft Word, every time you take your hands off the keyboard, you're wasting time and losing efficiency. To aid with this, three keyboard shortcuts eliminate the need to come up here and click bold, italics and underline. To underline or italicize text, press the Ctrl key and tap U (Ctrl + U). As soon as you begin typing, you'll see that the content is underlined. Hold Ctrl and hit U again to stop the highlighting; nothing will be underlined now. **Ctrl + B** create bold text, and **Ctrl + I** similarly create italicized text. Of course, if you don't undo "bold," your italics will be bolded and italicized, so remember to turn off the italics; the same goes for underlining and bold.

Automatic Page Break

Automatic page break is another useful Microsoft Word keyboard shortcut. Everyone has gone into Word, placed the cursor where they want a page to stop, and then tapped enter numerous times to transfer the rest of the text down to the next page at some point. That is completely unnecessary; you don't need to press enter fifteen times to get your text to the correct location. Instead, if you wish to finish a page, break it, and start a new page below, simply hold the **Ctrl** key and touch **enter**; the page will be broken, and the new page will begin below.

The Repeat Command

F4 is another helpful Microsoft Word keyboard shortcut. What is the purpose of F4? Whatever you've done recently will be **repeated**. If you touch the F4 key after you've tapped "delete" or "backspace" a few times, it will continue to delete. If you press F4, anything you were doing at the time will be continued. Another example: if you type the phrase "Hello" followed by a space, then press F4, it just repeats the word you just wrote.

The Return Command

Shift + F5 is the next keyboard shortcut. Holding down the Shift key and pressing F5 returns you to the last location where your cursor was. So, let's say you want to copy a paragraph from the bottom of a page and paste it at the top of it. You'll highlight the text or sentence, copy it with Ctrl + C, and then hold **Shift** and hit **F5** to return to where you last had your cursor, where you can now paste in that sentence or word with Ctrl + V.

Extending Your Highlighted Texts

The "**Shift + Left arrow**" and "**Shift + Right arrow**" keys are also handy. Remember that a double-click on a word highlights the word, and a triple-click on a word highlights the phrase or paragraph, depending on the application you're using, which is quite beneficial if you want to copy the entire paragraph or word. But what if you're dragging or double-clicking and want to enlarge the highlighted text before copying it? If you hold down the Shift key and then press the right arrow key, the highlighted text will extend to the point where you want it to stop and you can now copy and paste it. You won't have to click and drag to get exactly what you want; simply double-click the initial word, hold Shift, then press the right arrow to stretch it as far as you like. The left arrow returns you to the previous position and expands to the left, however in Microsoft Word, this is a highly helpful keyboard shortcut.

Duplicating your Format

Then there's **Ctrl + Shift + C**, which performs what? It duplicates the formatting rather than the text. So, let's assume you've set up your document with the layout you want, and you'd like to duplicate it elsewhere. You select the formatting you wish to copy, hold Ctrl, Shift, then hit C, and the formatting is copied. Now you go down and highlight the area where you want to paste the formatting, and if you hold **Ctrl**, **Shift**, and hit **V**, it copies the formatting rather than the words. There are many more Microsoft Word keyboard shortcuts available, but these are the most commonly used. Now that you know how to get started with Word, we've gone over all of the fundamentals that will serve as a wonderful springboard and a solid basis for moving on to some of the more advanced options, which we'll begin to explore in the next part.

CHAPTER THREE
EDITING YOUR DOCUMENT

In this chapter, we'll explore how you can make your text look presentable and easy to read. We'll be focusing on non-printing characters and what we mean by non-printing characters is that there are some characters that you can't see, such as space and enter tab, and we'll show you how to make them visible so that you can work with your document a little bit better. We'll also look at line spacing and how to modify it while typing in your manuscript. As we proceed, we'll look at paragraphs and other components that you will come across as you type in Word. To edit text, you have to **select** it first. Just **click** and **drag** on it as you need or hold down the Shift key and move the **insertion point** character per character with the arrow keys. You can also double-click on any word to select it quickly or click once from the left to select entire lines.

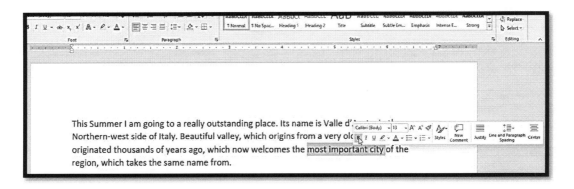

At this point, you can edit text with the dialog box showing up or the home tab above. You can **adjust font family**, **size**, **style**, **change the font color**, **add highlighting** or apply amazing effects, including **outline**, **shadow**, or **reflection**. Hover over these to get a quick preview before applying any.

Working with characters that aren't printable

If you start with a blank document, the first thing you'll do is set it up. So, you'll start by typing a word or a sentence, then pressing the Enter key, which will move you down a line. You might come across the **tab key** on your keyboard when working on your document, which will offer you a little bit of space in there, and what the tab does is that it pauses at the half-inch point on the ruler, so you can press tab many times and it will travel half an inch across the page each time. The advantage of utilizing tabs rather than putting in a lot of space to get your cursor where you want it is that everything will be lined up, so if you go beneath and start typing something, pressing the tab key will jump you precisely underneath where the tab was in the above line. So instead of tapping the spacebar over and over to move your text along, it's a lot easier to line things up. So just keep in mind that you have those tabs while you're working on a document, and you'll see how to alter them and create your custom tabs later so things line up where you want them to line up on the page.

A couple of things to keep in mind while typing: you'll notice that as you get to the end of these sentences, it just wraps around; you didn't have to hit Enter or insert a line break to get it to wrap around to the next line, which is perfect; you'll also notice that you may have a little squiggly line under some texts; if you right-click and look at your options, the top line is probably what you want. After typing, you'll realize that you've used some tabs and that there are some spaces in there that you can't see. "Well, I don't need to see the tabs and spaces," you might say, but it's sometimes quite important, and you'll see some examples of why in a moment, plus there's a feature in Word called the **Show/hide** button that will display all of those non-printing characters. When you go to the paragraph group on the home ribbon, there's a little object that looks like a paragraph marker that says show/hide when you hover over it, and the dialog box says display paragraph markings and other hidden formatting symbols when you click it.

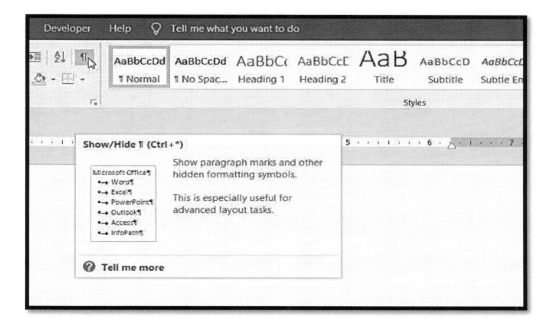

If you enable this, you will see that the little paragraph mark appears everywhere there is an Enter, as well as the little arrows that indicate the tab.

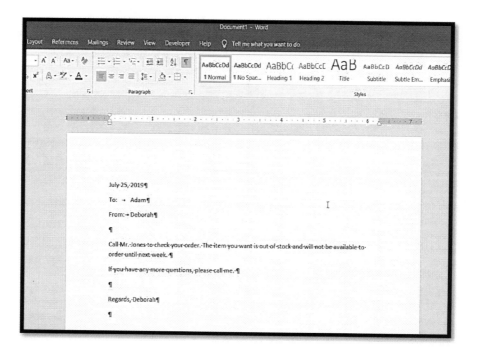

Have you ever printed a document and received a blank sheet of paper at the end, which you couldn't figure out why because you didn't have anything on that piece of paper? If you turn on your paragraph marks, you'll usually find that you have a rogue or a few rogue paragraph markers or extra Enter keys on the next page, which is why that page is printing. All you have to do now is go in and delete those extra lines, which you wouldn't be able to see if you didn't turn on that show/hide feature. So having these non-printing characters visible is beneficial, and you can turn it off by clicking the same icon again.

Spacing between lines

When you press the Enter key in Word, you'll notice that there's a large space between the lines that don't appear to be single line spacing; its double line spacing by default. If you want to clean this up a little bit, you can select your entire document or all of the text in your document using the shortcut key **Ctrl + A**, which highlights everything. Then go to the Paragraph group in your home ribbon and pick the little dropdown for line and paragraph spacing. You may browse through the options and as you hover over them, more or less space will appear between the lines in your text, so it's really up to you which one you choose.

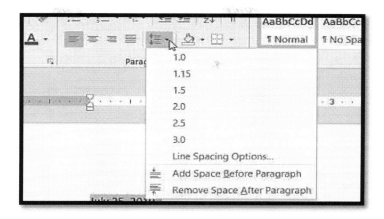

If you select your entire document, it will adjust the line spacing based on what was already there. So, if you only wanted to adjust the line spacing in one area, you could simply highlight that area, go up and make it smaller or bigger, or you can go into **line spacing options** and play around with how much spacing you want, and if you don't like the space in between, you can reduce it to zero, click **OK**, and you'll have no space in between.

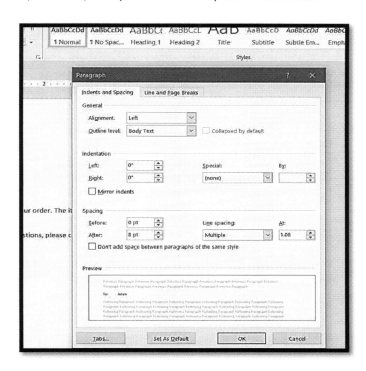

It's certainly worthwhile to experiment with some of the line spacing possibilities. You also have a couple at the bottom where you may **add space before or after paragraphs**,

46

depending on what you want to do, but everything in this area is quite configurable. So far, we've learned how to turn off and on paragraph markers, as well as how to show and hide non-printing characters and change line spacing. Let's move on to paragraphs now.

Paragraphs

With the paragraphs, you can easily manage the text distribution. Every time you make a new line with the Enter key you create a text paragraph, such as a collection of sentences that share the same topic and properties. You can show all of these by clicking on Show-Hide under the Home tab. Each paragraph has its alignment and distribution options. Click within the paragraph and go to **Home**, then **Paragraph** to set its alignment, choosing Justify to spread the words to cover the whole page width. With Line Spacing adjust the distance between the paragraph lines as you need.

Use shading to apply a custom background color to the whole paragraph and Borders to add borders around it. Switch to the Layout tab to manage the paragraph indentation and spacing, concerning the previous or the following paragraph. Before we move on to the next section, you'll see how to make some basic modifications to a document. These are just some fundamental editing functions that you should be familiar with. We've already spoken about how to edit a document in a few different ways, and now I just want to show you how to **delete**, **backspace**, **undo**, and **redo** items in your documents.

Getting Rid of Unwanted Text

When it comes to deleting, the Delete key on your keyboard always deletes everything to the right of it, so if you start pressing it, you'll notice that it deletes the word on the right. Backspace, on the other hand, deletes everything to the left of it, so if you start typing, you'll see it deletes the word to the left. Just keep in mind that they function in slightly different ways.

Undoing and Redoing

Another thing to remember is that the **Undo** and **Redo** buttons are really useful.

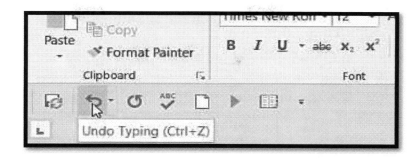

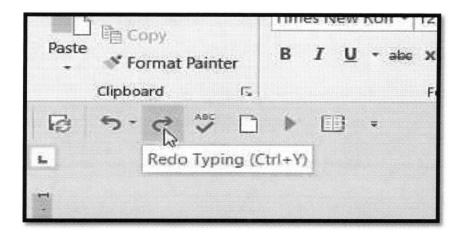

It's amusing how many people can't function without their undo button. These two buttons will always be there by default on the quick access toolbar to make them incredibly easy to find. If you look up there, you'll notice the Undo button, which allows you to undo what you've just done. If you've just backspaced the word "Property," for example, clicking undo will give you the P back, the R back, and so on, and you may keep undoing to reverse your last action.

The same thing happens when you redo something. If you decide you don't want that word there, you can redo and the deletion will be undone. It's also worth mentioning that beneath or adjacent to your undo icon is a small drop-down menu that allows you to go back and select how far you want to undo; it also allows you to undo many times in one go, so keep that in mind. These have a shortcut key as well. The shortcut key for Undo is Ctrl + Z, so if you accidentally do anything and then think, "Oops, I want to backtrack out of that," a simple Ctrl + Z is your greatest buddy. The shortcut key for Redo is Ctrl + Y.

CHAPTER FOUR

SAVING YOUR DOCUMENT

Updating and Saving a Document

If you had previously saved this document and then made modifications, you could just click **Save** and nothing would happen; it would simply save your changes to the file name.

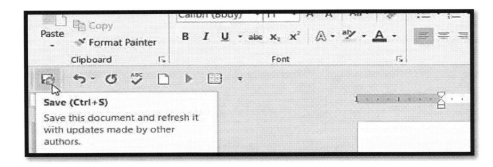

The First Time You Save

If you have a document that you've just generated, it's tough to know if it's been saved or not at first glance, but there are a few indications. The greatest clue is that if you look up the title bar at the top of the document, it only says Document 1 at the moment. You haven't saved this document since it doesn't have a name; recall that Document 1, 2, 3 is the default name you get when you create a new blank document. So now you know that this document hasn't been saved, and the first thing you should do is save it to a location of your choice. There are several different ways to save a document in Microsoft, as there always are. You can go to your **Quick Access toolbar** and find the **Save** icon.

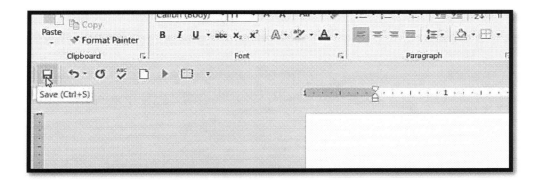

49

Because you haven't saved this document yet, clicking **Save** will take you to the **"Save as"** area.

So that's the first option; if you have the symbol on your **Quick Access toolbar**, you may click on it. The second option, which essentially takes you to the same location as we just left, is to enter the backstage area. You navigate to **File** and then to **"Save as."** If you're not used to it, this **"Save as"** page may appear strange; nonetheless, it's the same in all Microsoft products. On the left-hand side, you'll see a list of recent folders, which will show you all of the folders that you've lately saved.

Putting files on OneDrive

Alternatively, you have other options for saving your document; for example, you could save it to OneDrive, a cloud storage service, which would be a wonderful option if you wanted to collaborate on it.

So, if you wanted to share it with others and also make sure that you could access it from anywhere, you would save it to OneDrive; to the Cloud.

Any Other Location for Saving

You can save it to any other area; for example, you can save it to your PC's local disks. You can also opt to browse to a certain location, and if you click on browse, you can now select a destination from your local files.

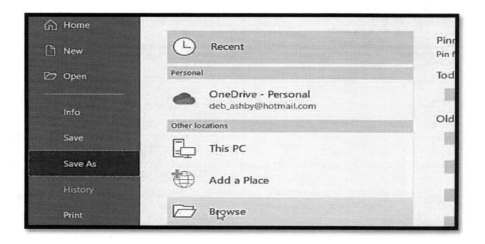

So, you choose a folder and drop your file into it, after which you can give it a name.

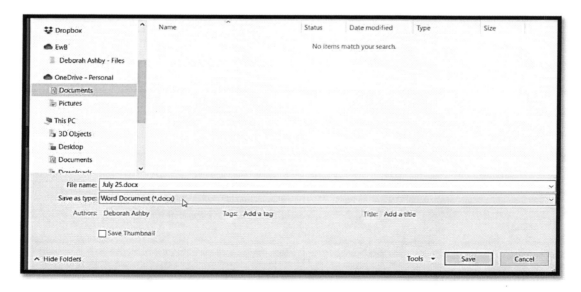

As you can see in the File name field, it took the first line of the document and used that as the default file name; it will always use the first line of your document as the default file name, which is usually not what you want to call your files. So, you're going to swoop in and make a shift. Also, if you click the dropdown under Document type, you can save your document as a variety of alternative file kinds.

You might want to use some of these, and that will store them in that format. You can also save your work in the old Word format; but, why would you want to save your document in an older version? Well, as mentioned briefly in one of the earlier sections, if you plan to send this to someone who you know doesn't have the same version of Word as you or has a much older version, you can help them out a little by saving your document as a docx file. This ensures that when they open it, it will open in compatibility mode and they will be able to read it, so just be careful who you're sending it to. You can also save it as a template, save it as a PDF if you want to reuse it, and we'll go over some of these options as we go through this book, but for now, keep it as a docx file extension, then click Save, and that's all there is to it. If you look up to the top of your document, you should notice that it now has a name.

What this means in terms of saving is that if you make a change to this and want to save it, you can go to your quick access toolbar and click on **Save**; you don't need to go back into **"Save as,"** and if your Save button has those little arrows over the top, it's because you've saved it into a cloud location, so when you save it, it's essentially doing a refresh with the cloud version, so if you click Save, it just saves. Another option is to use **Ctrl + S** on your keyboard, which is a shortcut for saving as well.

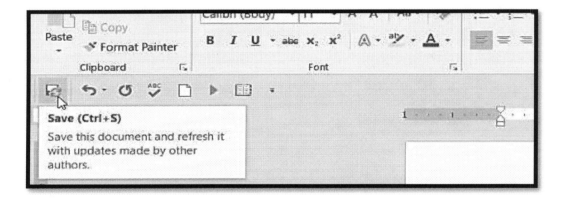

When working on a document, if you've saved it and know the filename, it's a good idea to press **Ctrl + S** now and then to ensure that your changes are saved. Now, if you make one more change and don't save it, but instead choose to dismiss your file by clicking the cross at the top, you'll notice that it prompts you to save your changes. As you exit Word, it will detect any unsaved changes and prompt you to save them, allowing you to choose whether or not to save them.

CHAPTER FIVE

DOCUMENT NAVIGATION

We've arrived at the chapter where we will talk more about Documents. **In this chapter,** we will focus on opening a document, we'll have a look at a couple of different methods to examine your document once it's been opened.

Opening a Document

It's quite straightforward because it's essentially the inverse of saving. If you've already closed a document and wish to reopen it, head to the File tab, which, as you may recall, takes us to the backstage area. If you have nothing open, it may take you to the open area automatically; Word is expecting that you will want to open a file. That could be the case, or it could be that you wish to start over. The **"Open"** page appears to be identical to the **"Save as"** screen we were in earlier; you'll notice that **"Recent"** is highlighted, and you also have documents underlined, indicating that it's showing you underneath all of your recent documents, which you should be able to see right at the top. Now, if you want to open a document, all you have to do is select it from the list and it will open.

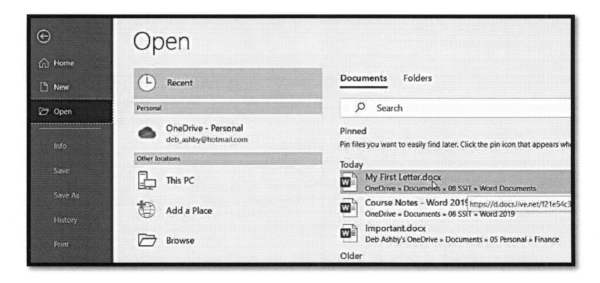

You can also open a Word document by browsing your computer and selecting the file you wish to open, then clicking open.

54

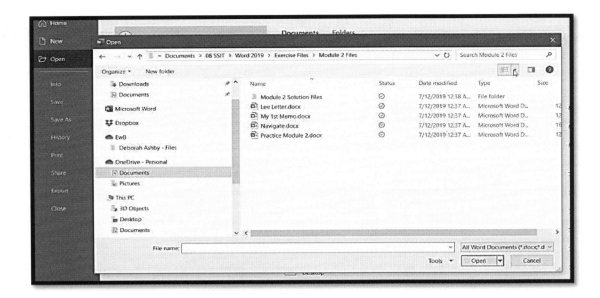

If you also want to open another file, say a recent one that you just saved, go back to "**File**" and select it from your "**Recent**" list, then click and it will open that document over the top of the other one, and remember that you can switch between them by going up to View, selecting "**Switch windows**," and then switching between the two. You may also use your mouse to hover over your word icon at the bottom and navigate between the two of them.

Using File Explorer to View Your Document

Also, concerning the Explorer window, let's take a look at something a little different but very significant. There are several ways to view files before you open them if you go to browse and then move up to a location where you have several different word files. You might know what you're looking for most of the time, but sometimes you won't, and you might need to see a little bit more detail about a file. There are several different ways to view the file list in Explorer, and you can do so by clicking on the little option at the top right-hand side. It will give you several different ways to view the file list in the Explorer window. You may currently have the "**Details**" option selected, but if you switch to Extra Large icons, they will appear in this format. Large icons are little small, medium icons are a little smaller, and small icons are the smallest. We have a popular feature called Lists. Most people prefer the Details option because it not only provides you the list, but also offers you a little bit more information about each file, and you can see in the status column that they're all saved to the cloud and synchronized. You can also view when these files were last edited, as well as their kind (whether they're Word documents, PDFs, or Excel files) and size. It's useful to be able to view the file size sometimes, especially when working with very huge files.

There are a couple of others in here, such as Tiles and Contents, which provide a little bit more information such as the author, date modified, and other details; just be aware that you have different ways to view your files so you can see a little bit more information and decide which one you want to open.

Side-by-Side Document Viewing

Another feature that comes in handy from time to time is the ability to compare two papers side by side. If you're comparing two papers or cutting something from one and putting it into another, this is useful because you don't want to continually switch between them. You can put them side by side and compare them. You'll see a "**View Side by Side**" option on the View ribbon; click it and voilà, both of your papers are now taking up exactly half of the screen.

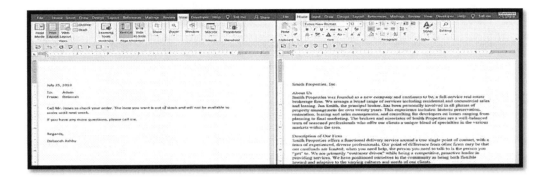

If you simply want to restore one of the documents to its original size, simply click on the "**Maximize**" button in the corner.

Creating a Document Split

On that same View ribbon, you can also use the "**Split**" option, which is quite fascinating. Let's see how that works out. When you click "**Split**," it will split the same document into two parts of the screen, allowing you to scroll each document independently.

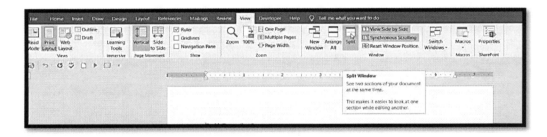

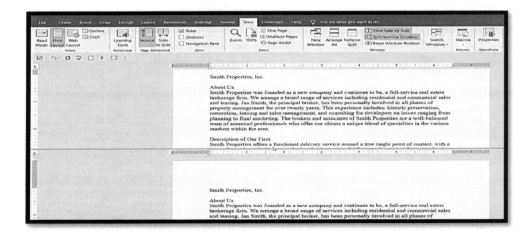

This is useful if you're doing some comparisons or copying and pasting; you can perform a variety of things with the Split option if you want to see two separate portions of the same page at the same time. If you wish to return to it being just one document, select "**Remove Split**" and you're done.

Arranging your documents

The "**Arrange All**" button is a final option that you might choose to use. This is found on the View tab, and when you click it, it tiles the documents over each other. If you have a lot of documents open, definitely more than two, being able to see them all arranged next to each other can be beneficial.

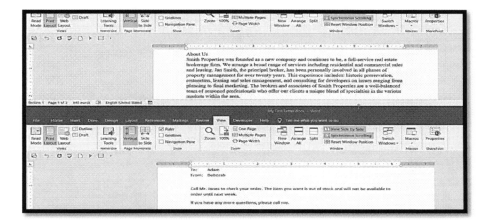

Simply click the "**Maximize**" button on one of the papers to exit.

Getting Around in Documents

In this part, we'll look at how to navigate your document. Let's imagine you have a document that has been created; the first thing you should do is look down to the bottom left hand of the screen and look at Section 1, Page 1 of 3, 845 words, as shown in the document below. We're obtaining a little bit of information about this document, and you can see from our status bar that it has three pages, the number of words and that we're presently in section 1. We'll touch on how to section up documents a little bit later, so doesn't worry about that for now. What we want to talk about today is how you can rapidly navigate your document using some of the capabilities in Word, which is especially beneficial if you have a big document.

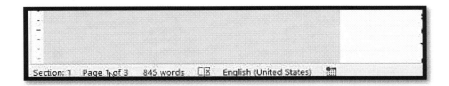

Although the document above is only three pages long, many of the documents you write will be hundreds of pages long, so being able to hop around fast to get what you need is critical and will improve your efficiency. Let's start with the most obvious point.

Scrolling through Your Document

The right or left-hand Scroll bar is a simple method to navigate through your page. If your document only has a few pages, you can simply utilize it to scroll up and down.

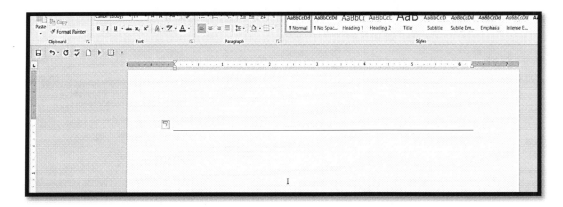

Other Alternatives

Let's look at how you can use various utilities to make a lengthier document. If you had a manuscript with hundreds of pages and wanted to jump to the bottom of it, using the scroll bar and scrolling down would take a long time; by the time you finished, you'd probably be taking a risk. A quick way to do it is to use your keyboard to hop straight down to the bottom; in Word, use **Ctrl + End** to leap down to the bottom. You may confirm this by going down on the left-hand side of your screen and checking your status bar to see if you're on the last line of that document's last page. If you want to go back to the top, use **Ctrl + Home**, which will do the opposite.

A couple of other shortcuts: holding down **Ctrl** and **pressing your arrow keys,** such as the **right arrow key**, jumps you around that document per word, and **using the left arrow key**, you may go the other way. **Arrow keys + Ctrl** Up and Down will jump you up one paragraph at a time, and if you want to select everything in your document, press **Ctrl + A**, which will select all of the text in your document. We'll be using **Ctrl + A** a lot as we go through this book because it's a really useful feature when you want to make mass changes to your document. This chapter covered a lot of ground on documents, and hopefully, it gave you a better understanding of how to open one or more files and the many methods to view them while working on them. You also saw a few simple techniques to navigate about your page using your keyboard, and you can use these to make Word more efficient.

CHAPTER SIX

GO TO, FIND, AND REPLACE FUNCTION

We started looking at some of the basic ways to use your keyboard to navigate around your document in the previous chapters, and in this chapter, you'll be introduced to a few more utilities that you can use in Word to navigate around your document and increase your efficiency when working with your documents. In this chapter, we'll concentrate on the Go to, Find, and Replace options.

Looking for a Word

When working with enormous files, you may require a quick way to get to a certain page or to replace a word in a document. To access your "**Find**" and "**Replace**" options, first click at the top of your document, then go to the **home** ribbon. Across on the right-hand side is an editing group, which is where you'll find them. You can see that "**Find**" has a little drop-down arrow next to it, indicating that it offers three options: **Find**, **Advanced Find**, and "**Go to.**"

In this example, we'll start on "**Find**", which opens up a little navigation window on the left-hand side where you can put in exactly what you're looking for. It brings up results once you type in the term you're looking for, and you can see them listed underneath in the results section, as well as highlighted in your document, making it incredibly easy to find them. By clicking on the cross, you can close this navigation panel. That's one approach to searching your document for a specific word.

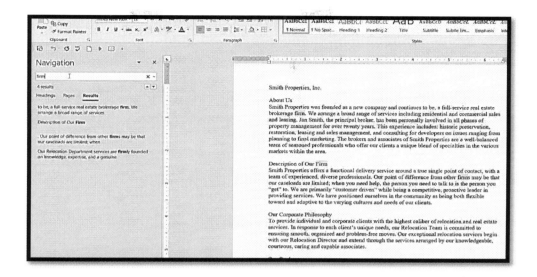

Using advanced Find to Search Your Document

If you select Advanced Find, you'll be sent to a little dialog box that asks you what you're looking for and displays the last item you looked for. If you want to skip this one by one, you can say "**Find Next**," and it will highlight the word in the document the first time it finds it. You can then say "**Find Next**" again to step through each one in your document one at a time, and when you get to the end, it will tell you its finished searching, and you can click OK.

Getting specify with Find

The "**More**" option in this Find and Replace box is also something to be mindful of. When you click it, you'll see that you have a lot of options. For example, you can tell it to **match the case**, which means that it will only find the word "firm" if it matches that case. If the word "firm" is in this document with an uppercase F, it won't find it because you told it to match the case.

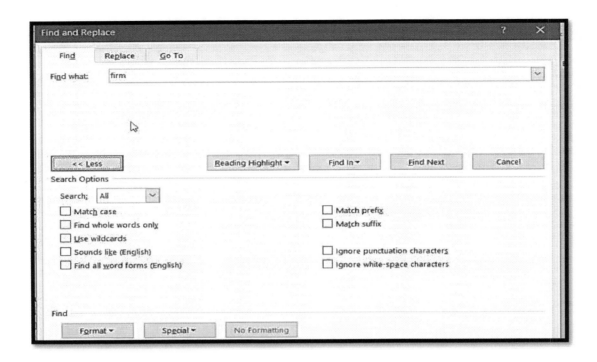

You can choose to "**Find whole words only**," which means that if what you're looking for is a part of another word, it won't be found. You can also say "**Use Wildcards**" and place a wildcard in front of the word, midway in the middle, or at the end. If you type in A*, for example, it will discover everything in that document that begins with an A, regardless of what comes after it. You can also include a wildcard at the start, such as *S, which implies it will look for anything that ends in S, regardless of what follows before it. It's worth noting that wildcards come in handy when looking for certain items. Another thing you can do up here is to type "A" and then two question marks (A??) to indicate that the word must begin with an A and contain no more than three characters in total. It doesn't matter what those three characters are, but they must be three. You can also use the "**Sounds Like**" option, which will find any words that sound similar to the one you're looking for. It might pick up words like turn, burn, study, or anything along those lines for a word like "firm", for example. "**Find all word forms**" will find any form of that word, and you can then choose between "**Match prefix**," "**Match suffix**," "**Ignore punctuation**," and "Ignore whitespace characters," among other possibilities. Just keep in mind that beneath the "More" drop-down, you have a variety of different options for customizing what you're looking for in your document, and it can become very detailed.

Replace One Word with Another

Make sure you're at the top of my document and select the "**Replace**" option this time. We have "**Replace**" under "**Find**" in the editing group, which allows you to **replace one word with another**. For instance, if you want to replace the name "Smith" in your document with "Ashby," you may say find "Smith" and replace it with "Ashby," and you'll have all of the prior possibilities to choose from. If you merely want to replace Smith with Ashby, pick "**Replace all**." You'll get a little window telling you that the replacements have been made, and if you look at the document behind you, Smith has been replaced. This is a quick and easy technique to replace several words in a document.

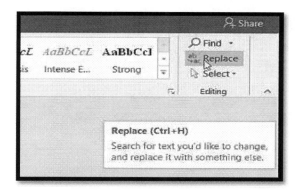

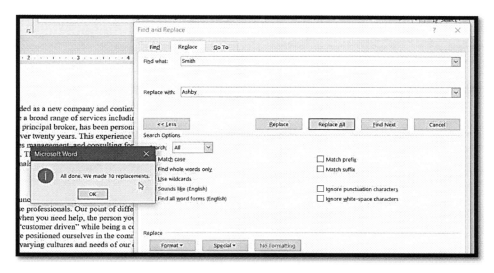

Go to any point in your document

The "**Go to**" option, which lets you perform different things in your document, is the last item you should know in this chapter. When you go to Find and select the "**Go To**" option, you'll be able to browse around your document. You can accomplish this by entering a page number and saying "**Go To**"; for example, if you input page 2 and say "Go To," it will take you to page 2.

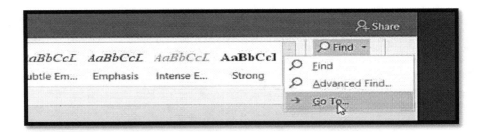

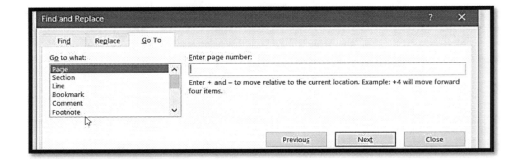

- You can go by **Section**; you'll learn how to break your text into sections in later chapters, and then you can go to any area you want.
- By going to a specific line number, you can navigate by **Line**.
- You can navigate via **Bookmark**; bookmarks are something we'll talk about later, but they're a way of placing a small bookmark in a certain spot on a page so you can jump to it fast.
- You can also use any **Comments** you have in the text to browse.
- We also have **Footnotes**, **Endnotes**, **Fields**, **Tables**, and a variety of other features. Which one you use depends on what you have in your document at the time. But keep in mind that those Go to choices are still available.

Let's move on to the next chapter now that we've covered the basics of Find, Replace, and Go to.

CHAPTER SEVEN
SPELLING CHECK ON WORD

In this chapter, we are going to discuss how to check your work for typing and spelling mistakes. We will go further to discuss AutoCorrect settings, how to adjust, add and undo AutoCorrect correction. Also, we will look at how to get rid of grammatical mistakes to make sure that everything is correct and finally on document proofing.

Introduction

It is said that one of the most important parts of writing well is spelling, which is the art of putting words together correctly from their letters and helps people read better. Hence, it is very important in Microsoft Word.

Checking Your Spelling

To start a check of your document spelling and grammar, use the shortcut F7, or follow these steps:

- Click on the **Review tab** is on the ribbon.
- Then Click on S**pelling or Spelling and Grammar** as shown in figure 1 below.
- The program finds spelling mistakes and a dialogue box shows all the words that are wrongly spelt.
- You can use Word's Spell Check right away. The red zigzag line on any word indicates wrongly spelt words and mistakes as shown in figure 2. In figure 2, the word 'Content' was wrongly spelt as 'contrent' hence a red zigzag line is displayed on the word. The spell-check feature also tells you if you've used the same words over and over again by underlining them with a red zigzag. You can either delete the word that is repeated or you can choose not to pay attention to it.

Note: You can choose to correct the word, delete the word, leave it if it's correct and add it to the dictionary if it doesn't recognize that word.

Figure 1: The Spelling and Grammar icon on Microsoft Word

Figure 2: Microsoft Word showing a Red Zigzag line

Turning On or Off Spell Check on Microsoft Word

- Click on **File**
- Click on **Options**
- Next, click on **Proofing**
- Clear the Check spelling as you type box, and then click **OK.**

To Turn Spell Check Back on, all you have to do is repeat the same process and select the Check spelling as you type box.

Fixing Words That Aren't Spelled Right

- Choose Check Spelling from the Edit menu to make sure your words are correct.
- Select the misspelt words that you want to find, then press the Enter key
- The spelling submenu is displayed
- From the submenu, type the correct and click Ok

Words That Have Been Mistakenly Flagged.

You might have typed a name that Microsoft Word doesn't know. To correct a word that has been falsely accused, you can do any of the following:

- Right-click it and choose the correct word from the list.
- **Add to the Dictionary:** click on add the word to the dictionary. The word will no longer be marked as spelled incorrectly in this or any other document because it is now correct.
- **Ignore** This command tells Word to ignore the word and accept it as spelt correctly through the whole document.

AutoCorrect in Microsoft Word 2024

AutoCorrect is a useful feature in Microsoft Word that checks your spelling and corrects it for you automatically. Word quickly fixes a lot of common typos and spelling mistakes on the spot, so you may not even notice the red zigzag when the AutoCorrect feature is on. AutoCorrect fixes that typo as soon as you hit the spacebar or punctuation marks at the end of a word. It also turns common text shortcuts into the single characters they should be. It corrects common punctuation mistakes, when you start a sentence; it capitalizes the first letter of it. When you forget to capitalize your name, AutoCorrect corrects it; it fixes the inverse caps lock problem and other common typos, as well as a lot of other mistakes that can be made when typing.

How to Turn On and Off AutoCorrect on Microsoft Word

- Go to **File** and click on **Options**
- Click on **Proofing** and choose AutoCorrect Options from the drop-down menu on the right.
- Click on the **AutoCorrect button.** This is shown in figure 3
- On the AutoCorrect tab, you can choose or choose not to replace text as you type.

For AutoCorrect to work, make sure that the Replace text as you type box is checked or unchecked.

Figure 3: The AutoCorrect Feature on Microsoft Word

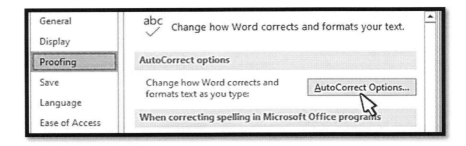

Undoing a Correction Made by AutoCorrect

You can easily undo a correction made by AutoCorrect. To do this, click on Ctrl+Z (the Undo command).

Note: You need to press it right after AutoCorrect makes its correction.

Adding a New AutoCorrect Entry

To do this follows the steps below:

- Right-click a word that you want to add to your AutoCorrect list.
- Type a word or phrase that you often misspell in the Replace column, and then click Replace.
- In that column, type the correct word.
- Then, click **Add**.

Note: If you want more information about the AutoCorrect tab, check out the AutoCorrect options page and you can add as many entries as you want. Add a new entry for each new thing that you do and click adds.

Adjusting AutoCorrect Settings

To change how AutoCorrect works and the words it corrects, follow these steps:

- Click on the **File** tab.
- Then, choose Options and the Word Options dialogue box appears
- Choose the **Proofing** category on the left side of the window.
- Then click on the **AutoCorrect** Options button on the right. When you open the AutoCorrect tab, you can see all of the things that AutoCorrect can do, like capitalize

69

the first letter of a sentence, change words that don't follow the rules, click the Exceptions button and so on

To remove an entry from the AutoCorrect list, scroll down until you find the item you want to remove, click on it, and then click the **Delete** button on the right.

Grammar Check

Microsoft word grammar checker works the same way as to spell check. The main difference is that offenses are marked with a frigid blue zigzag. When you right-click the blue-underlined text the pop-up menu shows to find out what's wrong. You can also choose to ignore it if you wish. The grammar proofing tool looks at the text and thinks about how the actions and the people or things that are doing them are linked together. When the subject and verb don't match, this is the most common cause of grammatical mishaps in the English language. The grammar checker is very good at spotting when there are two spaces between words when there should only be one space between the words.

Turning on Grammar Check

- First, put on Microsoft Word
- Click on the Tools menu, and then click on **Options**.
- When you're on the Spelling and Grammar tab, change the Writing style box to Grammar and Style.
- Then click **OK**.

An All-in-One Document Proofing

There is an all in one process for spelling and grammar checker if you don't want to look at the red zigzag underline or if you don't have that feature turned on; you can just simply do a final document proof with these steps:

- Click the **"Review"** button.
- The **"Spelling & Grammar button"** is on the Proofing group. To get to it, click it.
- The **Editor** pane shows up. Errors are shown one at a time as they happen in your text. You must check each of them one after the other.
- And then correct each of them.

Note: The Spelling pane or the Grammar pane shows up depending on what the person did. You can choose to ignore, ignore all, however, If you make the same spelling mistake or similar grammatical mistakes again, you'll be reminded of them. You can choose to delete repeated words, add to dictionary etc. You can choose to select the correct answer from the list that's shown and then click the Change button to change the text. You can also click the correct word, and then click Change All to change all of the places where you made that spelling mistake.

- Afterwards, click the **OK** button.

Note: Another way to go through spelling and grammar mistakes one by one is to use the Spelling and Grammar Check button on the status bar. You can use that button to jump from one spelling or grammar mistake to the next.

Checking a Document Again

The Ignore or Ignore All button has consequences. If you've used the ignore all options too many times, you can tell Word to recheck your document, which brings forgotten misspellings and grammatical mistakes back into the word document proofing, so you can fix them again, too.

Follow these steps:

- Click the **File** button.
- Choose **Options** to open the Word Options window.
- Then choose the Proofing option on the list.
- To check the document again, click the Recheck Document button on the toolbar. It's under the title "**When Correcting Spelling and Grammar,**" and it says "When."
- Click the Yes button to say that you want to UN-ignore things you've chosen to ignore in the past.
- Click the OK button to close the Word Options window.
- Then the document shows itself again, highlighting all the words and things you've chosen to not read before.

Note: Rechecking a document doesn't erase any changes you made to Word's dictionary. If spelling and grammar errors don't show up when you recheck them, it might be because the option to hide them has been turned on that is "Hiding all proofing errors in a document" is turned on.

Settings for Document Proofing

There are a lot of settings and options you can use to control Word's document-proofing tools.

i. Making Changes to the Custom Dictionary

You build the custom dictionary by adding words that are correctly spelt but have been marked as misspelled to the list of words. If you want, you can also manually add words, remove words, or just look at the dictionary to see if you're making any mistakes.

Take these steps:

- Click the **File** button.
- Choose Options to open the Word Options window.
- Then, choose **proofing.**
- Click the button that says "**Custom Dictionaries**" to make your own.
- The Custom Dictionaries dialogue box comes so you can add words to it.
- Make sure you put the words you want in a custom dictionary in the text box that says Word(s). When you're done, click "**Add**."

To remove a word from the custom dictionary: click on the word in the scrolling list and then click Remove from the custom dictionary. To delete, click the Delete button. **Note**: Click OK when you're done with your dictionary. Then, click the OK buttons on the open dialogue boxes to close them and go back to your text.

ii. Putting an end to automatic proofing

To get rid of the red zigzag underlines and blue underlines from your document, while typing follow these steps:

- Click on the File tab and then choose Options. The Word Options dialogue box comes up
- On the left side of the dialogue box, click on Proofing and then click on the button.
- You can uncheck the box that says, "Check Spelling as You Type."
- Remove the checkmark from the item while you're at it. Mark Grammar Errors as You Type, then Check Your Work.
- Choose "OK."

iii. Cutting back on grammar-checking

To change grammar settings, do the following:

- Click the **File** button.
- Choose **Options** to open the Word Options window.
- Then, choose proofing.

People who use Word to correct their spelling and grammar should look for the Writing Style item below the title. Here you can choose what kind of grammar to use, and how you want things to look. To the right, there is a button that says "Setting."

- Click the Settings button to go to the next step.
- The Grammar Settings dialogue box comes up.
- In Word, you can uncheck the boxes for things that you no longer want to be marked as offensive.

iv. All proofing mistakes in a document can be hidden.

The **red zigzag** and the chilling **blue underlines** can be hidden if you tell Word to keep checking your spelling, but you can also tell it to hide them. Words are still marked as misspelled, but they don't show up in the text. Make sure you follow these steps:

- When you open the Word Options dialogue box, look for the Proofing area.
- There are options in Word called "**Options**" that let you hide spelling and grammar mistakes only in the document you're working on.
- To turn them off, check the boxes next to them and uncheck them.
- The proofing flags disappear all over your document.

This is how to hide spelling and grammar mistakes in a paper.

How to Hide a Word Document That Has No Spelling or Grammar Errors.

If you only want to hide spelling and grammar mistakes in one Word document and not all of your other documents, follow these steps:

- Click on the "**File**" tab.

73

- When you get to the bottom of the left-hand pane, click on "**Options**"
- The "**Word Options**" window will show up, so you can make changes.
- Click on the **"Proofing" tab. T**he proofing tab is where you go to make sure everything is
- Make sure the "Hide spelling errors in this document only" and "Hide grammar errors in this document only" boxes are checked at the bottom of the window. Click "Yes." This is shown in figure 4 below.

Figure 4: The 'Hide All Error in a Document only' icon

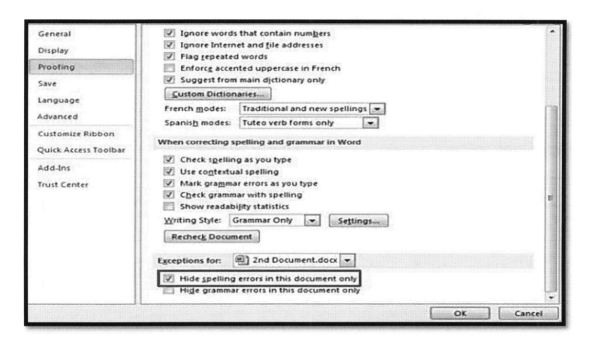

Finally, In Word, when you check your document for spelling and grammar, it keeps track of which mistakes you choose not to fix. And with all mistakes corrected, the document is ready.

CHAPTER EIGHT

WORKING WITH TEXT BLOCKS

You'll learn how to use Microsoft Word's Blocks in this chapter. We'll begin by discussing what text blocks are, and then we'll go over the many options for picking text blocks, which may seem simple at first, but you must grasp the numerous alternatives available. If you master the fundamentals first, you will be more efficient.

It's Time to Get Acquainted

What is Microsoft Word blocks and how do you use them? A block is nothing more than a grouping of text. It could be a single word, a group of words, a sentence, a line, or an entire paragraph. You can move, copy, and edit text blocks once they've been selected in your project.

Selecting a Block

There are numerous methods for selecting a text, and we will go over all of them.

Using the Mouse and Keyboard

As a general rule, the **text** is **highlighted** or **selected** when you **drag your mouse** across it, so if you want to change the color, size, font, or anything else related to it, make sure it's selected first. Otherwise, Word won't know which text to apply the changes to. As you would already know, the most frequent method is to **click** and **drag**. When you click and drag, a tiny **toolbar** appears which you can see off to the right. This is just a brief toolbar that appears with some formatting options. Word has presumptively assumed that you'll want to do something with the formatting of this text, so instead of having to go all the way up to the ribbon, it's just popped up this little mini toolbar, so you don't have to go too far to make your text bold, italic, or whatever you want to do with it; Just keep in mind that it will appear.

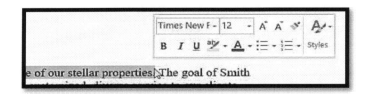

If that bothers you, you can turn it off in the backstage area, which I'll demonstrate later. Simply **click anywhere else on the screen** to **deselect** the text. If you want to pick just one word, double-click on it; if you want to select the complete sentence, **hold** down the **Ctrl key** and **click anywhere** in it; it will select the text or highlight only that sentence up until the first full stop. If you hover your mouse over the white space along any line and click, it will choose the entire line, regardless of whether it's a sentence or not. If you stay clicked in the margin with that arrow and drag down, you will select all of the sentences or all of the lines. If you wish to select from one point to another, you can do so in another way. If you **click** your mouse just before the text, **hold** down your **Shift key**, then **click** after the word you want to end, and it will pick that section. If you want to **add** to that section, **hold** down your **Shift key** again and use your **arrow keys** to make additional additions to that selection.

If you want to **choose multiple sections** that aren't next to each other, **click** the first area and then **drag** and **select** that sentence while holding down the **Ctrl key**. To make numerous selections, remember to hold down the Ctrl key. The final option, as we've suggested a few times before, is to use **Ctrl + A** to select everything in your document, and then use the formatting choices in the toolbar to make whatever adjustments you need.

Using Ribbon

Ribbons are another item on your list. We've mostly used the keyboard and mouse, but if you go back to the **home ribbon**, all the way over on the right-hand side, there's a select option that lets you choose everything, similar to **Ctrl + A**.

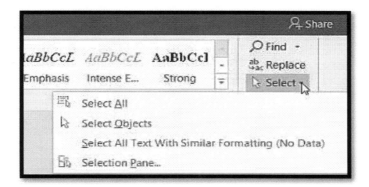

You also have the option to "**Choose Objects**," which is useful if you have things like shapes on your screen and want to select them all; it will allow you to create a spotlight around them and it will select all of those objects, which we will use later in this book. Always keep in mind that such selections are also available on the home ribbon.

76

A Unique Selection

Remember that if you **click the left mouse button** and **drag it down** to choose a block of text, it will select all of the lines you cover, but what if you don't want that? What if you simply want to pick a portion of a text block? To do so, hit the **left mouse button** and **drag** it down while **holding the Alt key** on the keyboard. It will now just choose the region you want to format.

The Good Old Cut, Copy and Paste

Cut, **Copy**, and **Paste** are the backbone of Microsoft applications, and we'll start exploring them in this section. These are probably instructions you've used before, and they're the same in all Microsoft apps; whether you're working in Word, Excel, or PowerPoint, the functionality is identical, including the keyboard shortcuts. What we want to accomplish in this section is to make sure you understand what Cut, Copy, and Paste can do, and if you already know how to use them, you might pick up a couple of new tricks. Each of them has four steps, the first of which is making a selection. You might wish to choose a sentence and cut it. It's crucial to understand the difference between Cut and Copy. When you **cut** something in your document, you're effectively **deleting** or **removing** it and pasting it somewhere else; it's similar to moving in many respects, thus cutting the sentence and inserting it somewhere else will move it. You can highlight the same line, copy it, and paste it elsewhere on the page using "**Copy**," and it will **generate an exact copy** without moving it. Let's take a look at the "**Cut**" option first. There are a few different ways to cut a line of text in Microsoft, as there are always. If you right-click on your selection, you'll notice a "**Cut**" option in the right-click menu.

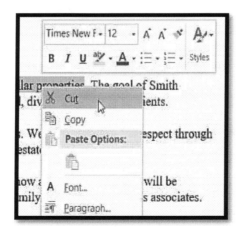

Alternatively, you can navigate to the home ribbon and find a "**Cut**" option in the first group under the Clipboard group.

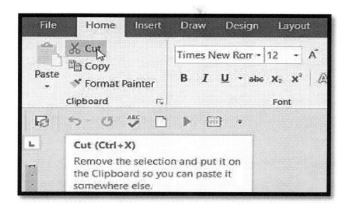

A third option is to utilize the **Ctrl + X** keyboard shortcut, which you can see when you hover your mouse over the cut icon on the home ribbon. After clicking "**Cut**," go to the area where you wish to move the text and paste the sentence you just cut. You can paste text in a few different ways. You can select one of the pasting choices by **right-clicking your mouse**. You can also use the keyboard shortcut **Ctrl + V or jump up to the home ribbon and click the paste button there.**

The Paste button is separated into two pieces; the top half is marked in gray, and if you click the lower half, it will give you a couple of different options to paste that line.

- You can opt to paste and keep the source formatting, which means that the formatting will be carried over to wherever you've cut the sentence from.

- You can select to merge formatting as you paste, so if you're pasting this line into a document with completely different typefaces, you can choose to merge the formatting to match the font style or color of the page you're pasting into.
- You could paste it as a photo, which turns it into a picture object rather than text.
- You can choose to keep text only if you just want simple text without any styling; you have a few alternatives there.
- If you just want to perform a direct paste, click the top half of the paste button, your cut-out sentence will be pasted, and you'll notice that it's no longer in its original spot.

There are many more possibilities under "**Paste special**," but we'll go over those in greater detail later. Let's go on to "**Copy.**" **Ctrl + C** is the keyboard shortcut to remember. You can alternatively utilize the "**Copy**" button on the home ribbon, browse to the location where you want this line or word to appear, and then paste by clicking your Paste button. This time, it will appear as a copy rather than a move.

Also, when you paste something, you'll see this little pop-up appear, and if you click it, it'll bring you the paste options we discussed before in a fast drop-down menu in case you wish to use them.

Viewing the Clipboard

You should also be aware of the Clipboard. It's not immediately obvious how to bring up the clipboard, but if you go up to the **home** ribbon, in the first group where we have **Clipboard** written at the bottom, click on the little drop-down arrow, you'll get this little pane open up on the side that says "**Clipboard**," and you can see it has the last item that you copied or cut on it.

Every time you cut or copy something, it is temporarily saved to your clipboard, and as you continue to copy, a list of all of them appears on your clipboard. "Why is that useful?" you may ask. It's great if you want to go through and cut and copy a lot of things, then paste them in different orders that aren't necessarily the same as the ones you copied. You may now go to your Clipboard and select to paste this bit of text into the document by selecting "**Paste**" from the drop-down menu. This Clipboard can hold up to **24 items**, allowing you to copy a large number of items and paste them wherever you like on the page.

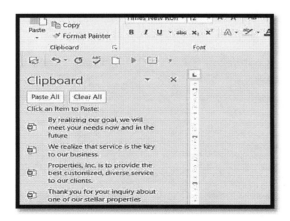

If you wish to **empty your clipboard**, simply click "**Clear All**," and everything on that clipboard will be removed. You can also dismiss your clipboard by clicking the cross icon. If you want to use it, just be aware that it's lurking in the background.

Changing the Position of Your Text Block

There are a few additional options for moving items about in your text. You can use your keyboard and mouse to execute a Cut or a move if you highlight a word, sentence, or paragraph. You can drop it wherever you want and move it that way if you hold down the **Ctrl** key and then click and drag with your mouse. Hopefully, you now have a better knowledge of the Text block, the **Cut**, **Copy** and **Paste** commands, how to move things around with your mouse and keyboard, and how to copy and paste items from the clipboard into your project.

CHAPTER NINE
CHARACTER FORMATTING

In this chapter, we'll go deeper into character formatting possibilities. After you've finished working on your documents, you might notice that nothing sticks out; all of the text is very uniform, it's all the same size, it's all the same font, there are no real headings, and nothing shines out. You can use some formatting at this point to emphasize particular points and make it more interesting and simpler to read. When you create a new document in Word, you'll notice that everything stays the same until you change it, thus whatever font size you choose will stay the same until you change it, and the font color will always be black unless you go in and change it. The term "**formatting**" refers to the process of altering the appearance of text.

Text in a Basic Style

You can use some formatting to spice up your document and make it more interesting than it is now. If it relates to your document, the most apparent place to start would be the Title. You can highlight your title here, and the first thing you might want to do is modify the font to make it stand out from the rest of the text.

Choosing a Font

Your current font may be set to **Times New Roman** on the **home** ribbon's Font group, but if you click that drop-down, you can choose from a variety of fonts to apply to your selected text.

It's worth noting that the default font in later versions of Word is Calibri, which is a lovely font to use, but you can change it to something else if you want to make it stand out.

Text Size Selection

You can make your text a little bigger than the rest of the text after choosing your font. Moving up to the **Font** group, you'll notice that next to the font style is the font size, and if you hover over any of these, a live sample of what it will look like appears.

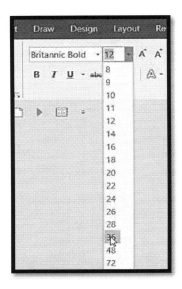

It's also worth mentioning that these font sizes are listed in increments, so if you want font size 15, for example, you won't find it in that list, but you can manually type it into the box above to acquire that font size. Next to your font size, you'll see two buttons: **Increase font size** and **Reduce font size**.

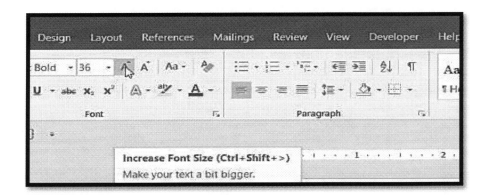

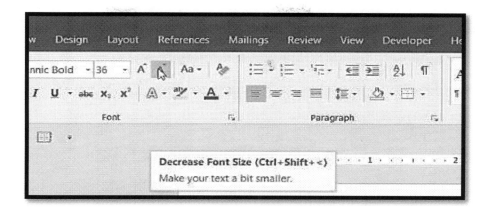

These are useful if you only want to modify the size of your font in increments without having to go inside the drop-down menu. You may either go in or increase the font size by one each time, or you can select to lower it back down.

Changing Text Case

Change the case with the option next to "**Reduce font size**." You can choose uppercase, sentence case, lower case, capitalize each word, or toggle case.

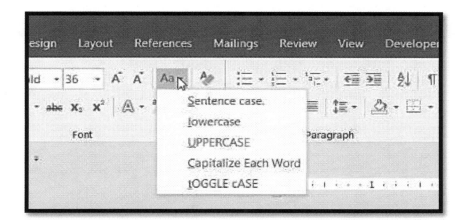

Clear Formatting

The "**Clear All Formatting**" option is next in this small group. If you decide you don't want all of the formatting you've applied, simply click the "**Clear All Formatting**" option to remove it all.

Other Formatting Options

In the bottom row of this small group, we have "**Bold**," which will make your text bold, "**Italics**," which will make your text italic if you like, and "**Underline**," which will underline your text.

You'll note that the underlining has a small drop-down menu that allows you to select an underline style, such as **solid line**, double line, dash line, and so on; so, you do have some more options down there.

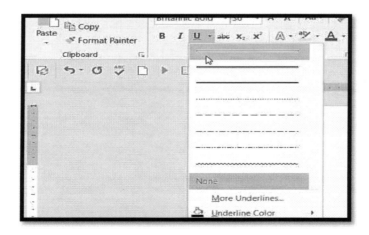

You also have a "**Strikethrough**" option, which you could find useful if you deal with a lot of contracts; it allows you to strikethrough a section of selected text.

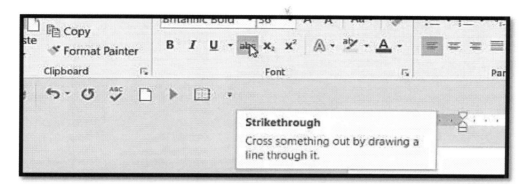

Then there are **Subscript** and **Superscript** options, which are useful for words like H20 and other related terms.

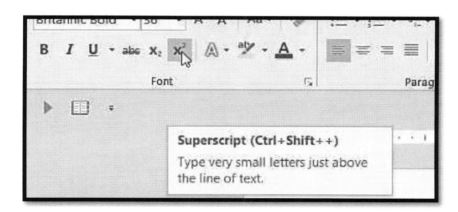

Aside from that, there are some text effects. This changes the color and appearance of the selected text, and there are several alternatives available, some of which are much nicer than others, but depending on the sort of document you have, some of these can seem very effective. Always keep in mind who your audience is when applying effects, colors, and other elements to your documents; you don't want to design anything that looks too jokey, too humorous, or too unprofessional if it's for work purposes, so keep that in mind. If you're making a flyer, a newsletter, or something similar, go ahead and fill in the blanks, but keep in mind who your target audience will be if you choose this option. You have more options in there for changing things like the **Outline color**, applying a **Shadow**, **Reflection**, or **Glow**, and so on. There are a few alternatives for you to experiment with.

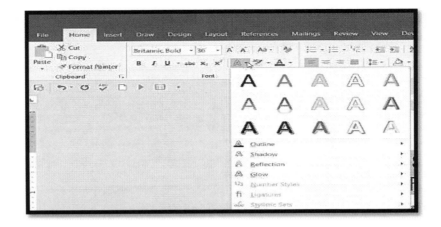

The next button is a **Highlight color**, which is perhaps best found farther down on this page and allows you to highlight a section of text.

This is equivalent to simply striking through a piece of paper with a highlighter pen. We also have **Font Color** options, so if you want to alter the font color, simply choose it and then choose from the color palette.

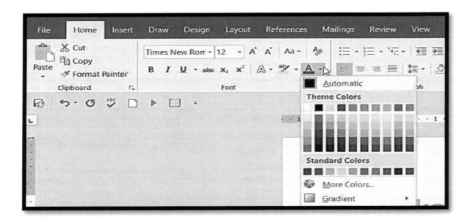

The Dialogue Box for Fonts

There are several possibilities in that font group, and if you click that little drop-down, you'll see a few more options down here as well; many of them are repeated, so you've got Font style, size, font color, Underline style, and all of those on the ribbon. We don't have an option for **"Underline color"** on the ribbon; therefore if you choose an Underline style, you can choose a color from the color palette for that particular Underline. Strikethrough, Double strikethrough, Superscript, Subscript, Small caps, all caps, plus a few other things that aren't on the ribbon are all present.

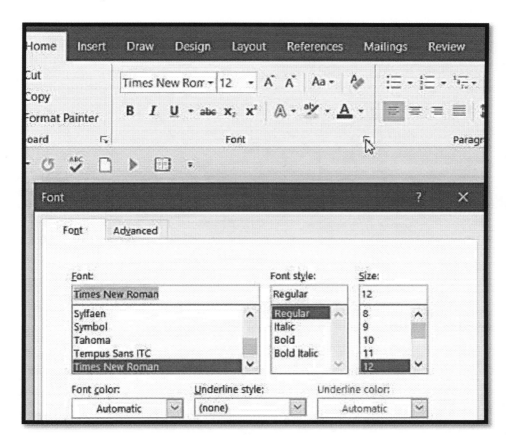

You also have an **Advanced** tab, which allows you to change things like Character spacing, which is the amount of space between each letter. If you want to broaden it out, this will assist, and there are many additional options here as well in the Advanced section.

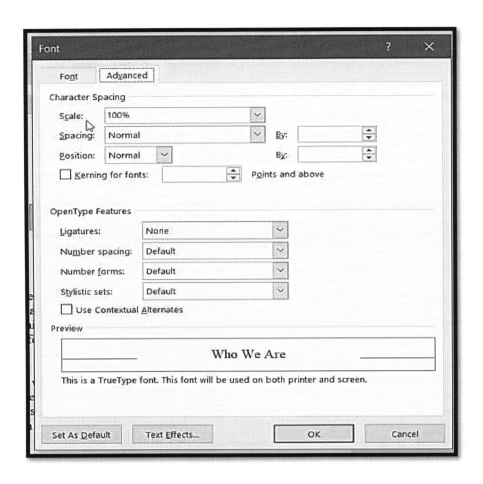

Using a Formatting Copy and Paste

We'll use the Format Painter here, which is a very effective means of copying formatting from one piece of text and putting it into another. We looked at some of the formatting options for the text in your document in the previous section of this chapter. If you have some formatting applied to a text or sentence and want to apply it to another sentence or paragraph further down in the document, you could do so by highlighting the text, going into your font group and applying those different attributes, selecting the text effects, changing the font size, font color, and so on, but that's not a practical solution. A much better approach to do it is to use the **Format Painter** to **copy the formatting** from the text and paste it over the top of the other text. Let's look at how you might go about doing that. The first step is to pick the text with the formatting you wish to copy, then go to the **home** ribbon and select **Format Painter** from the first group, which is the **Clipboard** group.

89

You'll click it once, and when you return your mouse to your text, you'll notice that your cursor has changed to a miniature paintbrush, indicating that your Format Painter is now active.

All you have to do now is click and drag it over the text where you want to paste the formatting, and there you have it; it's applied that same formatting. What if you wanted to accomplish the same thing with a different text? Once you've copied it once, the Format Painter will be off, and your cursor will return to its normal appearance. The trick is to double-click on the format painter if you want to do a lot of Format Painting in a document. After selecting your text, double-click on Format Painter and swipe it over your text. You will see that the Format Painter is still active because you double-clicked, and you can keep swiping throughout your page. You can exit Format Painter by pressing the **ESC** key on your keyboard or just clicking on format painter again to return to a standard cursor. Instead of manually applying those individual font properties, this is a much more efficient approach to copying formatting over. **In this chapter,** you studied the fundamentals of applying Character Formatting to selected text and you also learned how to copy formatting to other areas of your document.

CHAPTER TEN
STYLE FORMATTING

Styles are a very nice way to format your document if you've never used them before. It's simple to update, and you can even include an automatically updated table of contents. They provide numerous advantages, and if you've never used them before, this chapter will completely transform the way you work with Word documents. Hopefully, this has piqued your interest; why don't you fire up your computer; it's time to show you how to use Styles.

A Quick Overview

"**What is the advantage of using a Style**?" you might be wondering. Let's take a look at an example of how Styles can help. You may already have a Microsoft Word document open that you've created or are working on, and you'll need to refer to this sheet from time to time. Let's say you're working on a document and have a lot of varied text on this page, as well as a lot of headers in your sheet or pages. Simply put, it's a basic Word document that hasn't been formatted in any way. In this situation, you might want to make the headers stand out a little more; simply highlight and bold them, increase the font size or even alter the font color, and you'll have a new header. The only issue is that if you go down to other headers, you'll see that they're still in your original design. You could redo all of the formatting by using the format painter to copy the format, paste it there, apply it, and then go through your entire sheet and do that, but there are a lot of different headers in a sheet, so that will be a lot of work. This is where Styles come into play, and they can help you save a lot of time.

Finding and Applying a Style

You can identify your current style by highlighting all of the different headings in your document and looking under the **home** tab for a section named "**Styles.**"

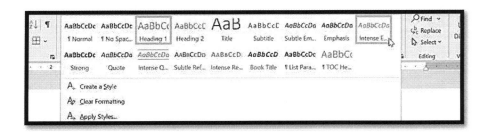

You can check the current style of the headers here, and you can also **apply a style** to a specific header by clicking on it. You can also scroll through them or see them all at once if you click the small drop-down next to it. This way, you'll be able to see all of the Styles you have.

Modifying a Style

After you've applied a Style, the cool thing is that any changes you make to it now will affect all of the other locations where it's applied. This implies that if you **right-click** on "**Heading 1**" for example, you can choose "**Modify**" from the drop-down menu. You can change the fonts, size, bolding, and color, as well as the paragraph spacing and borders around it, when you click Modify. There are a lot of different things you can tweak for the style of this header when you click Modify.

After you've made your changes, click "**OK**," and you'll notice that all of the headers in your document have been automatically modified, and any place that references that style will automatically update as you work on it. As you can see, the benefit is that as you make changes to a style, it will rapidly apply those changes to all areas where that style is used, providing you a lot of flexibility and making it very easy to update a document's appearance and feel. In Microsoft Word, there's a **design** pivot up top, and if you click there, you'll see all of the available numerous themes, all of which take advantage of the styles that you've set.

If you select a theme, it will now search for all of the headers that have a specific style that you are using and apply that theme. You can choose from a variety of themes here, and it takes advantage of the fact that you can define multiple styles for different elements inside your document, making it incredibly simple to change the appearance and feel of your document. You can even use different colors and font types, which will swiftly scan and update throughout your text. One of the advantages of styles is the ability to update them fast.

Adding a Table of Contents

Another reason to use Styles is that you can not only adjust the document's appearance and feel, but you can also add some functionality. If you want to provide a table of contents for all of your content, you'll usually have to fill in headings first, and then add each of them as a part to your table of contents. It's difficult to maintain that up to date manually, so you'll go to the "**References**" page and select the option to **insert a table of contents**.

You can either **insert the contents of the automatic table of contents** here or **create a custom table of contents**. When you use the automatic table of contents, you'll notice that all of the page numbers correspond to the page where the headings appear, indicating that the table of contents is taking advantage of the fact that you've included all of these headings in your document. You can delete the table of contents if you want to get rid of it.

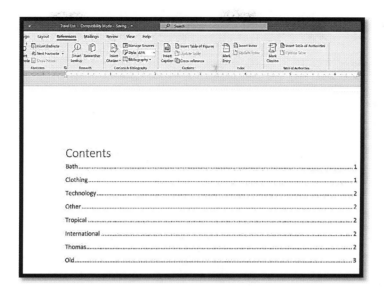

If you wish to create a custom table of contents instead, one thing you'll notice is that you can have the table of contents take advantage of the styles (Heading 1, Heading 2), so as you define additional styles in your document and more heading Styles, the table of contents will benefit.

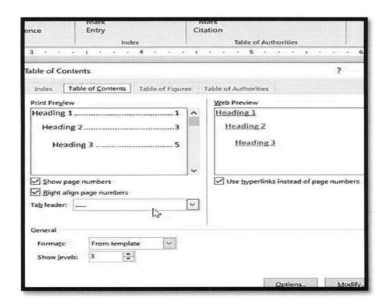

This is a useful feature if you wish to use a table of contents, and it's also important to employ styles in your document when doing so.

Getting Around in Style

Also, if you click on the "**View**" tab, you'll find the **Navigation Pane**, which, if you click on it, will offer you a quick view of your document headings. If you want to jump down to a specific heading, simply click on it, and it will take you to that location in the document.

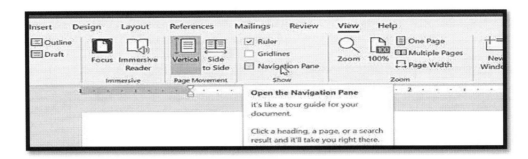

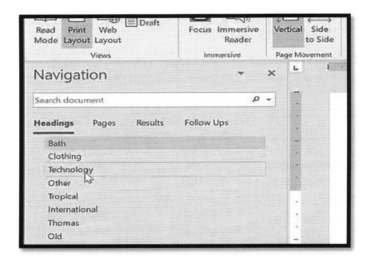

This is a great way to quickly navigate your page using headings you've set, and you may do it by using multiple Styles. This is just another advantage of using Styles.

In this chapter, you learned why you should use Styles in your document and what benefits you should expect. One of them is that you can quickly update the look and feel of your document without much effort; you can also use styles if you want to insert a table of contents and have it automatically generated; you want to keep the page numbers current, and you can also use styles to navigate throughout your document and jump to different sections within your document.

CHAPTER ELEVEN
PARAGRAPH FORMATTING

We're down to alignment alternatives in this chapter. We looked at how to change the formatting of individual characters in the last chapter, and now we're going to look at how to format full paragraphs. If you have a document with no formatting and everything is left-aligned, you'll notice that the text on your page that is left-aligned wraps around, so there is never a broken word at the end of the line. It will just put it on the following line, and there will be no hyphenations or anything like that.

The Formatting Commands for Paragraphs

These are a set of commands that can be used to format a paragraph. The most obvious component of formatting is to center the title on the page. To do so, first, choose your title by hovering your mouse over the margin and clicking once, and then go to your **Paragraph** group on the **home** ribbon, where you'll see your alignment options right here.

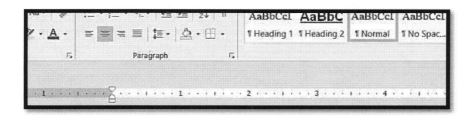

You may have **left alignment** enabled; you may also have **Center** or **Right alignment** enabled. There's also one here called "**Justify**," which will center everything equally on the page, ensuring that the text goes up to the end of the left and right margins, respectively. This is common in newspaper printing and books, and it implies that if Word needs to space out a word a little bit more, it will do so to align your text on both borders. The paragraph group on the home ribbon contains only those four buttons.

Justification and alignment
Everything in the middle

Click the "**Center**" align button (there's also a keyboard shortcut of **Ctrl + E**) to move a title in your document to the center of the page.

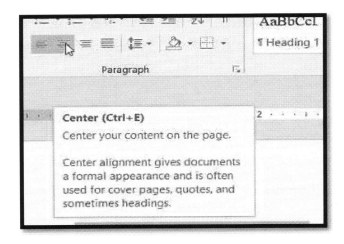

Left or Right

You can use the left align button to simply realign that back to the left.

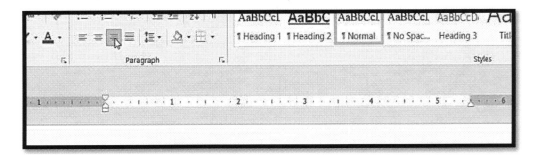

Let's see what occurs if you Right-align your text. To do this, use the **Ctrl + A** keyboard shortcut to select all of the text in the document, then click "**Right-align**", and as you will now see, everything is aligned on the right side, but not on the left.

A document that entices

Now select all of our text once more, and look at the "Justify" option that was stated earlier. If you click "**Justify**" and look at your sentences and paragraphs, especially where the text wraps around, you'll notice that they're aligned both on the right and left sides, so Words goes ahead and adds some extra spacing to make that work.

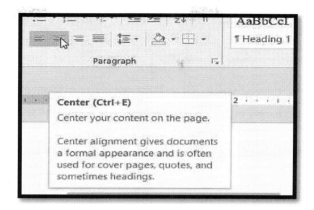

Paragraphs and line spacing

Let's look at how line spacing works in paragraphs now. It's self-evident that when we talk about line spacing, we're referring to the amount of space between each line of text. If you input a word and tap **Enter**, you'll notice that the cursor doesn't appear right beneath the text you typed, but rather a bit further down, leaving a small gap. This was created mostly because many users did not want to type right beneath the text above them. You generally want a little bit of space after a title, so you'll find that the default in Word nowadays is to have a little bit of a gap in there, and of course, you can alter it, which is what we'll discuss in this section. How can you identify what line spacing you're using right now?

Finding out what your current line spacing is

If you go back to that Paragraph group, you'll notice that there's a button right in the middle labeled "**Line and Paragraph Spacing**" with a drop-down arrow that, when clicked, will show you where you have your line spacing set to, as indicated by the tick next to it.

However, if you don't use any, it won't display any line spacing to you. If you're not happy with the amount of line spacing, you can modify it to anything you like, and you can see how the line spacing changes as you hover over them. As you descend, it becomes wider.

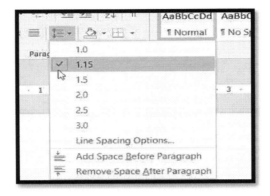

In general, 1.15 is easier to read than 1.0, which is a touch too close together; hence, if your document is pretty long and others will be reading it, 1.15 is a good line spacing, but you can raise it if you like; it's entirely up to you. You have the option to "**Remove Space after Paragraph**" at the bottom, which is another sign that line spacing is there.

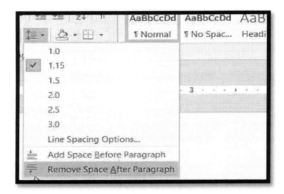

If you have your entire document chosen, everything will change as you hover over these options; however, if you only want to modify the line spacing on a single paragraph, simply make the appropriate selection before going in and changing the line spacing.

Choosing a Line Spacing

Another thing to keep in mind is that if you go to Line spacing options from the Line spacing drop-down menu, a small dialog box will appear. The spacing group is the third small group here, and this is where you can get quite specific about how much space you want before or after the text. You may already have these parameters set, but you can modify them to **single line spacing**, **1.5 lines**, and see what it looks like in the preview at the bottom. You can pick "**At least**" and then adjust how much space you want in there with double line spacing. As a result, you can make it seem any way you like.

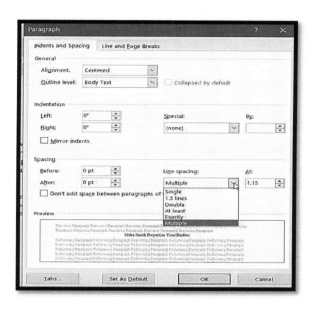

You can also opt to "**Set as Default**" if you've already set your spacing and how you want it to be for all of your documents.

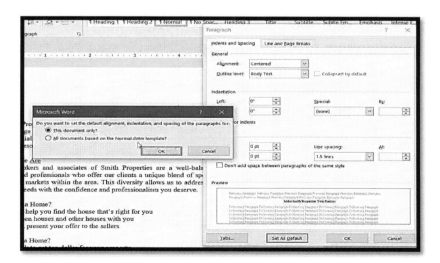

It will then ask you if you want it to be the default spacing for "**This document only**" or "**All documents based on the normal.dotm template.**" It's all up to you. Just keep in mind that if you set it for all papers, you'll get whatever line spacing you specify in this box every time you create a new document. That's all there is to line spacing, so have fun with it. If you want to use the same line spacing throughout all of your documents, come in here and set it as default.

Working with Indents

We'll now discuss how to use indents in your documents. We've talked a lot about formatting options for paragraphs in the previous sections, and you may want to indent the left side of a paragraph when you have a document. You could indent the first line with the tab key, but it will only do so for the first line. Indenting the entire paragraph is what we're talking about here, and you can do it with the small indent marks that we have on the ruler. You might notice that a line has been changed half an inch while trying to alter things with your indent marker, as shown below.

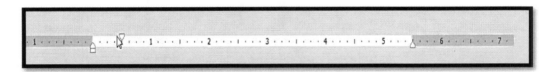

How would you indent the entire paragraph if you didn't want it this way or if you couldn't use the tab key? You can use the small markers on the ruler at the top to establish the spacing between your paragraphs or indents exactly how you want it.

Indenting the First Line of a Paragraph

Let's have a look at the functions of these tiny buttons. When you hover your mouse over them, starting with the **downward-facing triangle** at the top, you'll notice that it says "**First Line Indent**," which means that this small button only controls the first line of your paragraph.

You can see that because it's the First Line Indent, it only moves the first line if you **highlight a paragraph**, **go up to your ruler**, then **click on your First Line Indent button** and **drag** it to roughly three-quarters of an inch and let go. It works in the same way as the tab, but this time you can specify the size of the indent; keep in mind that the tab will only allow you to advance half an inch by default.

The hanging Indent

Let's look at the little **upwards-pointing triangle** below that on the ruler. This is the "**Hanging Indent**," and dragging it across the page will show you that it moves everything but the first line, almost like the First Line Indent.

Can you think of any examples of a hanging indent at this point? Let's say you have a list that you've numbered. You can see what's going on here if you glance at your ruler. The First Line Indent, as well as the Hanging Indent, has both moved out.

Using Indents to Adjust a List

You can use them to change the appearance of your numbered list. If the items in the list appear to be too near to the numbers, click and drag the Hanging Indent out to move them further away.

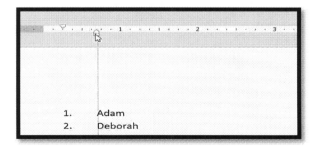

The numbers, which are set to the First Line Indent, are the same way. You can change those by dragging that in or out.

That's an example of indents in your document, which Word does for you when you apply Numbering.

Indenting a Paragraph

The **Left Indent**, which is positioned beneath the Hanging Indent, is the other object we have here.

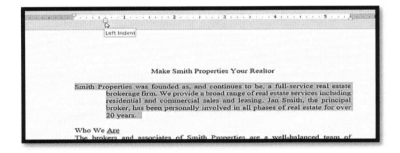

If you drag that, it will drag the entire text across. The **Right Indent** is a corresponding one on the right-hand side of the document.

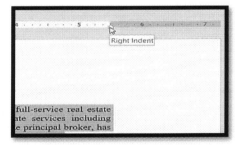

You can grab it and drag it in, but keep in mind that these modifications only apply to the paragraph you've chosen; if you want to do it for the entire text, hit **Ctrl + A** and then drag your indents in and out. That's a quick rundown on how to use your ruler's indents.

CHAPTER TWELVE
TAB FORMATTING

Welcome to the Tabs section of the book. This is where we'll discuss how to use tabs in your documents, which is a valuable feature in Microsoft Word. This means that pressing the Tab key will allow you to override the half-inch tab spacing that is set by default. As we've seen before, clicking your mouse on the top of a document and pressing the Tab key will move you half an inch each time. You can modify the space between tabs to anything you wish, and you can even change the type of tab you're using in your project. If you look at the document below, you'll see that everything is neatly organized in columns and everything is in order.

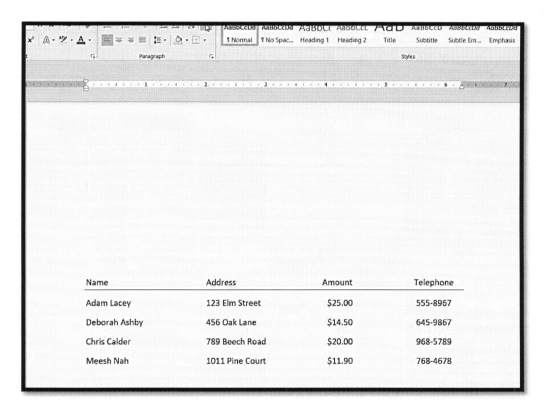

Name	Address	Amount	Telephone
Adam Lacey	123 Elm Street	$25.00	555-8967
Deborah Ashby	456 Oak Lane	$14.50	645-9867
Chris Calder	789 Beech Road	$20.00	968-5789
Meesh Nah	1011 Pine Court	$11.90	768-4678

This may appear to be a table, but it is not. It was made with tabs, and if we turn on our **Show/ Hide paragraph markers** (which we looked at in a previous chapter), you can see all of the tabs in there, so everywhere there's a tiny arrow, there are tabs.

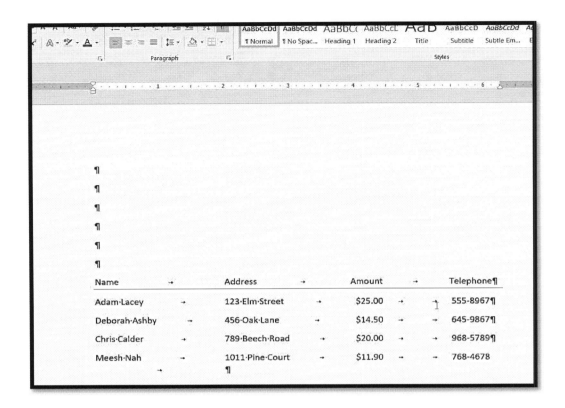

Identifying Your Tab Stops

Let's have a look at how to create tabs in a document now. If you're wondering where your tabs are, they're fairly difficult to find if you don't know where they are. If you glance up at the ruler and cast your gaze to the left, you'll notice a very small **back-facing "L" sign** just there, and if you hover your mouse over it, you'll see the "**Right tab**."

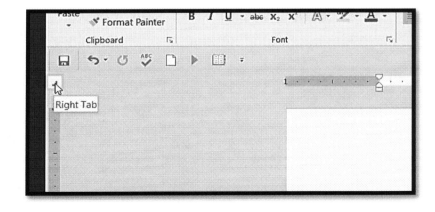

If you click it, you'll be taken to the "**Decimal tab**," which is the following tab.

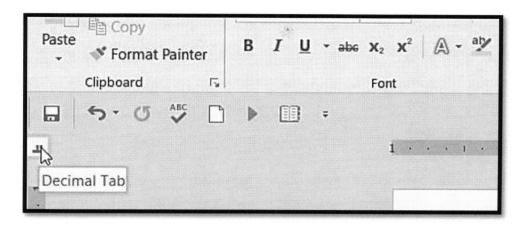

Let's have a look at what they are.

The Left and Right Tab Stops

The Left and Right tabs allow you to align your text to the left or right, respectively.

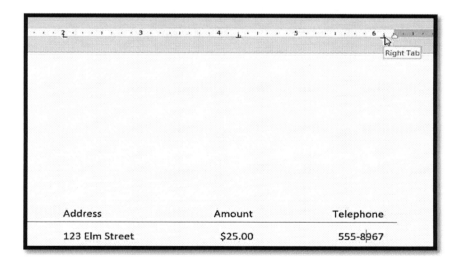

The Decimal Tab

The Decimal tab allows you to align your text using decimal points, so if you have numbers in your document, you can use that option to align all of the decimal points.

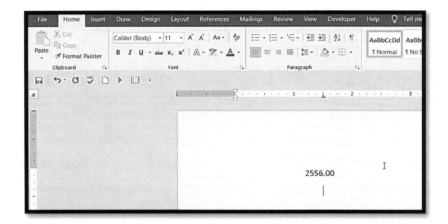

The Bar Tab

Then there's the Bar tab, which you'll occasionally see in resumes, and if you've ever seen a resume with a line going down the middle with information on both sides, you've seen a resume with a Bar tab.

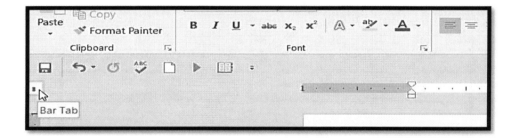

Working with Tabs

Then there are indents like the **First Line indent**, which is the same as the one on the ruler.

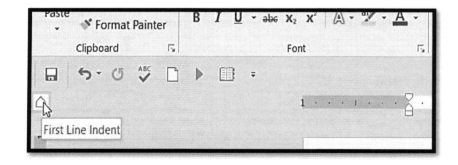

If you click again, you'll see the **Hanging Indent**, and then you'll be back on the left tab.

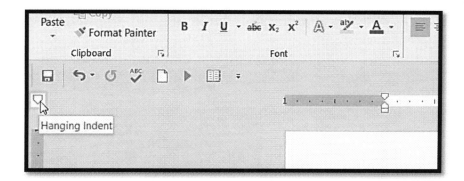

You may just click on them to rotate between them and then select the tab you want to use in your project. Let's have a look at how they function. You can see the small "**L**" if you select the Left tab and then go over to the ruler and click where you want to drop it. When you press the tab key, you'll be taken exactly underneath the tab you've set, where you may input your text. The same thing happens if you press Enter, then tab to the following line, and you'll be immediately underneath the line above.

To remove a tab, simply click and drag it off the ruler.

- Let's have a look at some of the other tabs and see what they can achieve. Returning to your small tab indication, if you select the **Decimal tab**, go to your ruler and, by clicking on the ruler, drop this at roughly one-and-a-half inches. When you type a number with a decimal point, you'll notice that the decimal point shows just beneath the decimal tab.

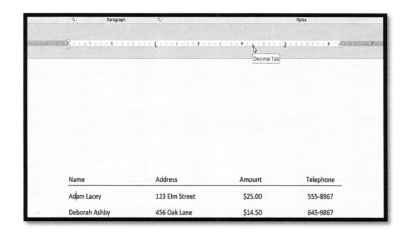

- Moving on to the **Bar tab**, if you place it anywhere on your ruler, it creates a small line in there where you can input some text, hit the tab, and go to the other side, as seen on resumes where your personal information is on one side and you're schooling or prior career is on the other.

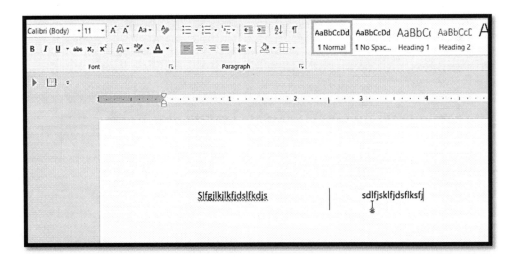

- Moving on to the following tab, **Indents**, we've already looked at those in the last chapter, so we'll skip over them and concentrate on the **Center tab**. You can see that it's exactly centered underneath that tab if you set it to roughly 2.5 inches, click on the ruler, then type your words.

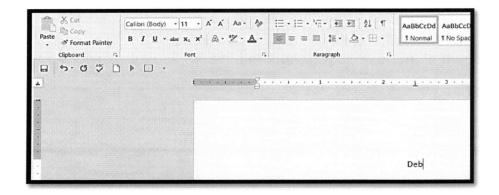

- The **Right-align tab** is the last one we'll have a look at. If you click on the end of the ruler, your cursor will jump to the right-hand side, and as you type, your characters will print to the left, ensuring that everything is lined up beautifully on the right-hand side.

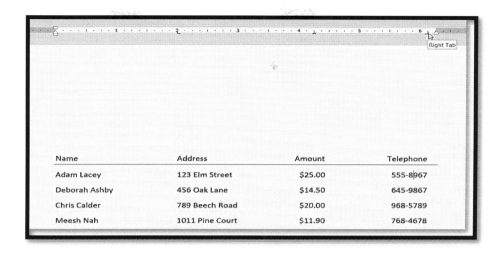

These are the many tabs available in your document, and which ones you select will depend on what you're trying to align.

Creating a Tabbed Table

If you look at this table, you can see the tabs that have been set up for these columns down here if you click within it.

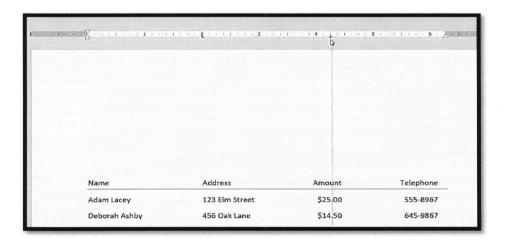

If you look at the ruler, you can see that we have a left tab set up there, which aligns all of the addresses to the left, a decimal tab set up for the "Amount" column, which aligns everything to the decimal points, and finally, a right tab set up for the last column, which aligns everything to the right.

You can reproduce this tiny table that we have above in your document for mastering, and let's do it together for further assistance.

- First and foremost, you'll set up your tabs. All you have to do is grab the Left tab and drag it to the desired location.
- After that, you'll take your Decimal tab and place it where you want it.
- Finally, you'll take your Right tab and place it at the very end of the document.

After you've set up your tab on your ruler, you can begin recreating the information from the previous section. Remember to press your tab key to go across to the tabs as you text, then hit Enter to continue to the next line.

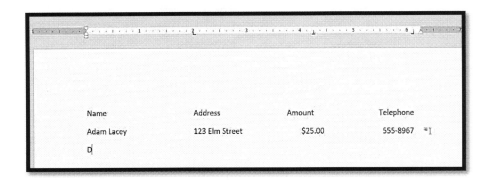

You can see how we made that table above, and if you don't like where the tabs are now or how the document looks, simply drag and drop these tabs left or right.

Leaders of Tabs

The last point we'll talk about is something called **Tab Leaders**. This may not be a term you're familiar with, but if you've ever looked at a table of contents in a book, document, or manual, you'll notice the page number, a few dots, and the title of the chapter or topic are frequently included. A tab leader is essentially that (those dots).

You'll see how to add those on when you set up your tabs in a few seconds.

- The first step is to highlight all of the text where you want tab leaders, and there are a couple of different ways to get to tabs: you can **double-click** on any tab stop on the ruler to go to your tab box, or you can click the little drop-down arrow at the bottom of this box to go to the same place.

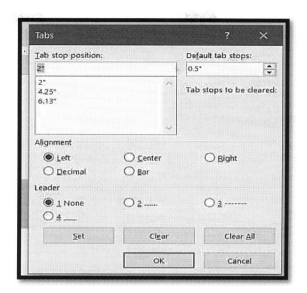

- All of the tabs you've set up for the selected region are displayed here. We have tabs at 2 inches, 4.25 inches, and 6.13 inches, as you can see above. We have "**Leader**" at the bottom here, which is now set to none. We'll now set a leader, and all you have to do is choose your initial tab stop and a leader style (dots, dashes, or a solid horizontal line), then click "**Set**" (very important and very easy to forget).

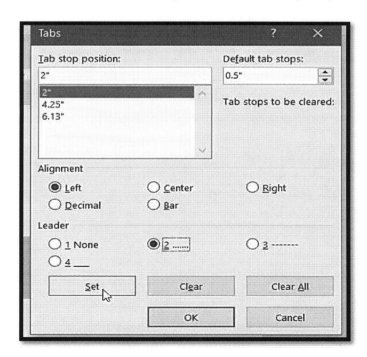

- You must repeat this process for each of the tabs, so go to the next tab (which is 4.25 in this example), select the **Leader style**, click "**Set**," and then go to the last tab (6.13 in this case), click "**Set**," and then click "**OK**."

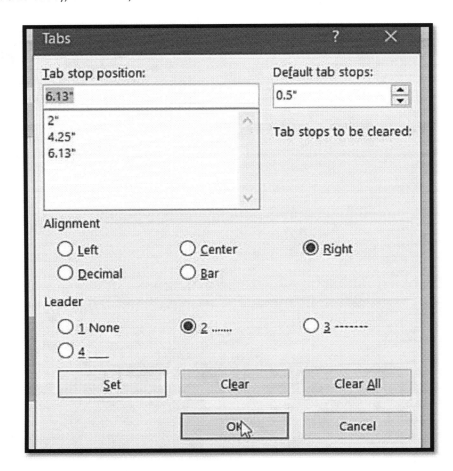

In between your columns, you'll see your leaders. If you're doing anything like a table of contents, that's great; it just adds a professional touch. Hopefully, it gives you a better sense of how to build up different sorts of tab stops on your ruler, as well as how to incorporate those leaders.

CHAPTER THIRTEEN
PAGE FORMATTING

Welcome to this chapter. Here, you'll learn how to set up your website so that you can start working on a simple document right away.

Page Setup

When you initially start a document, it comes with only the default pages, which are all portraits. The first thing you should look at is your **margins**. You may be okay with them by default, but some individuals like to adjust them just to vary the look of their work or to fit more content on their page. You'll be able to fit more content on the page if the margins are smaller.

Setting Up your Margins

You have two rulers in your document: one at the top and the other on the side. If you can't see your rulers, click up to **View** and check **Ruler**. You'll be able to view your margin line after that.

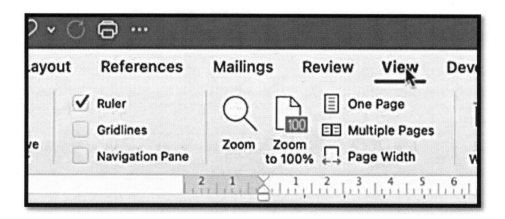

Remember that **your margin is the gray area**, while **your document is the white area** where your words will appear. If you want to adjust them, go up to your ruler, place your mouse between the gray and white sections until it changes into a **double-headed arrow**, click, and you'll see a faint line come up a vertical line, and all you have to do now is pull your margin to the right.

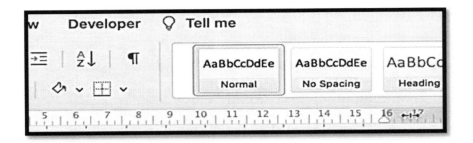

As you can see, this has reduced your margin and increased the amount of text on your page. You can repeat the process on the left. These arrows can get in the way, so sometimes you just have to move them out of the way; this will shift part of your text, but don't worry, just grab the margin, in the same manner, we did the other side, make sure your cursor is a double-headed arrow, and drag it over to the left once more. Because your arrows up here have moved, you may notice that some paragraphs have been indented. All you have to do now is move those back into place, and everything will fall into place. The left-hand half of this method is a little tricky. Moving your margins up and down to the top and bottom of your page, on the other hand, is significantly easier; you simply click and drag to shift those margins up or down, and you can do the same with the bottom. By decreasing your margins, you can fit a lot more text on your website. If none of it appeals to you, click the Layout tab and then "**Margins**." When you click the drop-down menu, you'll find a variety of options.

If you merely want to decrease the size of your margins, "**Narrow**" is an excellent option, and if you click on it, it will automatically modify your margins.

Creating Your Margins

If you wish to choose your margins, navigate to "**Custom Margins**."

When you click that, a dialog box will emerge, allowing you to modify the top, bottom, left, and right margins. So, you can either use the up or down arrows and as you does, a tiny little preview will appear here, showing you precisely what you're doing.

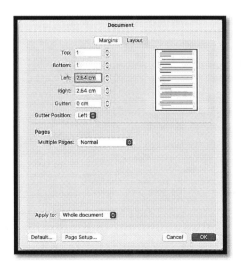

Alternatively, you can just insert a figure for each of these and click "**OK**" to see how the margins have changed. Once you're satisfied with all of your margins, you can go on to your headers and footers.

Headers and Footers

Page numbers, document titles, report titles, and other data will appear in the headers and footers at the top and bottom of your page. They'll be in the margin all through your document.

Accessing Your Headers and Footers

You can get to your headers and footers in two ways. The first option is to go to the "**Insert**" ribbon and then to "**Header and Footer.**"

Simply click on "**Header**" and choose from a variety of options and graphics; similarly, you can do the same with the Footers.

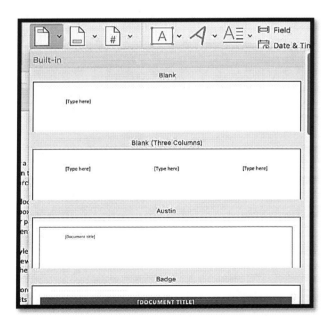

If you don't want any of these graphics, simply move your cursor to the top of your page and double-click. You can go to your headers and footers from here. Your header will appear on each page as you type.

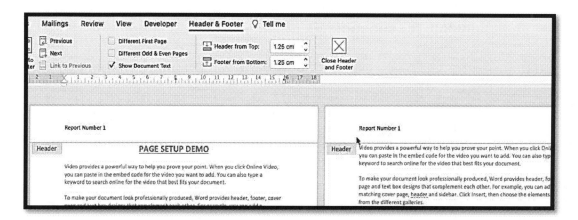

If you don't want this header on your first page, go to the header and footer menu and choose "**Different First Page**." If you do so and then double-click on your main document, you'll see that a header appears only on the second page.

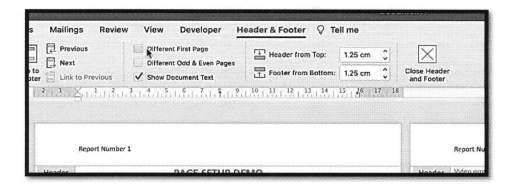

Return to "**Headers and Footers**," uncheck it, and it should display again.

Removing Headers and Footers

To exit your Headers and Footers, simply **place your curso**r within your main document and **double-click**. The Headers and Footers are grayed out, which means you can't alter them by clicking on them unless you double-click back into the Headers and Footers.

Page Numbering

You can insert a page number while you're on Headers and Footers. You can go up to "**Page Number**," click on the drop-down, and select "**Page Number**" if you go down to your footer and click with your pointer in your footer.

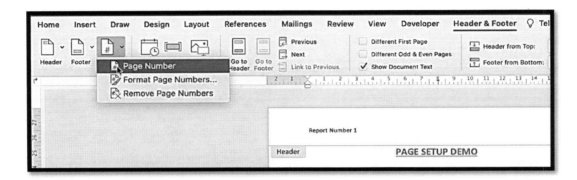

You'll get a dialog box once more, this time with the choice to position your page number on the left, middle, or right of your page.

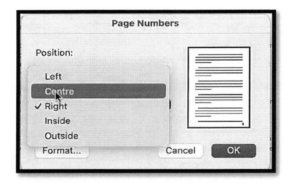

Choose your preferred option, and you'll be given the option of whether or not that page number displays on the first page. If you check or uncheck the box, then click "**OK**," your page number will appear on your pages. You can also add text here if you want.

Changing the Orientation of Your Page

If you wish to change the orientation of your page, for example, if you've completed your work and believe it should be in landscape format, go to the "**Layout**" tab, go to "**Orientation**," click on the drop-down menu and select "**Landscape**."

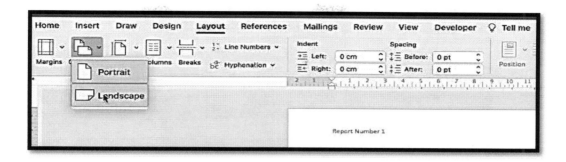

All of your margins will remain the same once you select "**Landscape**," but if they don't meet your needs, return to "**Margins**," select a different margin and your document will adjust accordingly.

A Fresh Start

You're working on a document and you've reached the end of one page; how do you insert a new page inside or between some previous pages? This section explains how to add a new page to any document.

Text on a New Page

If you're typing and you reach the end of the page, the obvious solution is to place your cursor there and press Enter. A new page will be automatically created and added.

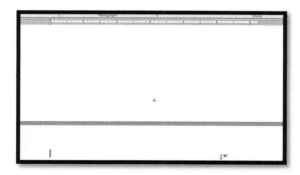

Inserting a Blank Page

What happens if you need to insert an empty page inside the one, you're working on now? Simply move your cursor to the end of the current page. To create a new blank page, go to the **Insert** tab and select "**Blank Page**."

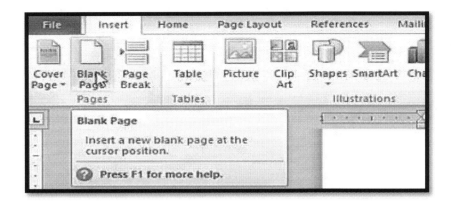

Please keep in mind that if you position your cursor at the start of a page before inserting a blank page, the blank page will appear first.

A unique Page Background

In this section, you'll learn how to change your word document's background color, add textures to the background if desired, and insert images. We'll also go through how to print coloring pages in a Microsoft Word document, as well as how to add a watermark.

Changing the Color of Your Pages

The word document's background color is set to white by default, but you can alter it to any other color you choose. You can do it in an already-created document or a blank document before you begins typing. To do so, go to the **Design** tab, select "**Design**," and then pick the second-to-last option, "**Page Color**," on the right-hand side.

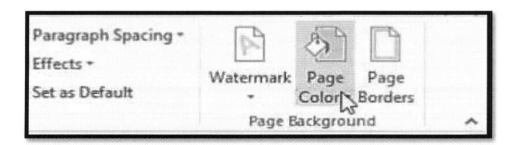

Hover your mouse over these several colors and select one by clicking on the small drop-down arrow. The default is restored if you click where it reads "**No Color**." You can see a preview by hovering your mouse over the color.

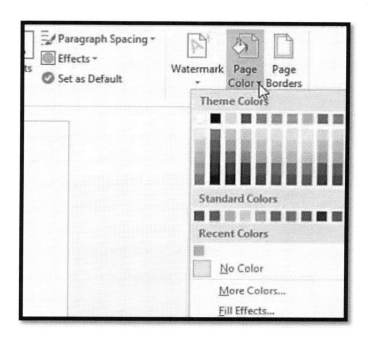

If you'd want to make a custom color, go to "**More Colors**" and make one.

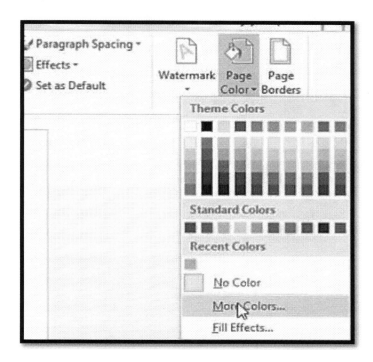

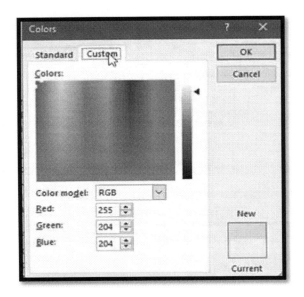

When you're satisfied with the color you've chosen, click "**OK**," and the color will appear throughout the page.

Adding Texture, Patterns, and Images to Your Page

- To apply texture, go back to the page color option and select "**Fill Effects**."

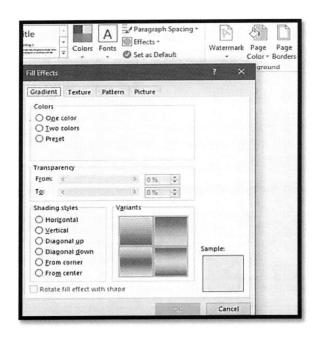

123

This opens a window with four tabs: **Gradient**, **Texture**, **Pattern**, and **Picture**. Let's begin with the **Gradient**. You can have two colors with Gradient; one will be darker, while the other will be lighter. A preview of how an option will appear in your document appears while you are selecting it.

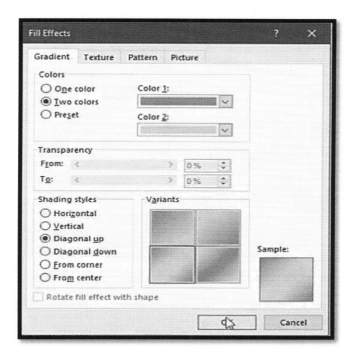

If you go to the Color area and choose "**Two colors**," you can then choose your first color and your second color. The Shading Styles allow you to customize the appearance of the gradient. After you've made your selections, click "**OK**," and the document's entire background will be transformed into the gradient you chose.

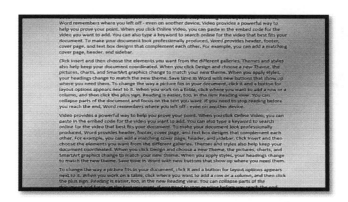

Under "**Colors**," there's also a "**Preset**" option that, when clicked, pulls up a selection with a variety of options including Early Sunset, Late Sunset, and others. Moving on to **Texture**, a large number of textures are available in Microsoft Word if you click on it. By **selecting a texture** and pressing "**OK**," it is added to the background.

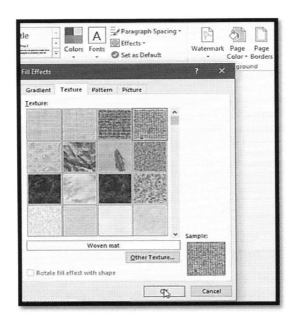

You can alter the color of your text if you don't like how the texture looks with it. Simply pick the text, navigate to the **home** tab, and then to the Font color option to alter the font color.

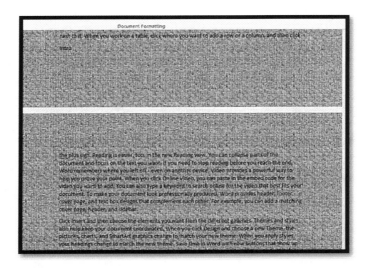

Let's have a look at the next effect, **Patterns**. A large number of patterns (in black and white) are displayed when you click on "**Pattern**". It's worth noting that if you've previously chosen a gradient, the pattern in the gradient colors will be displayed.

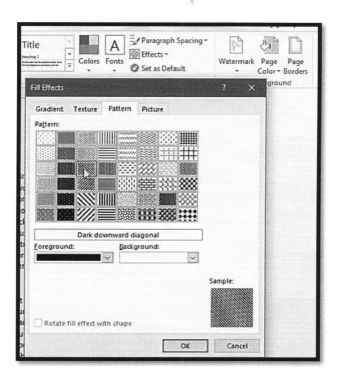

After you've chosen a pattern, click "**OK**," and the pattern will be applied to the entire document.

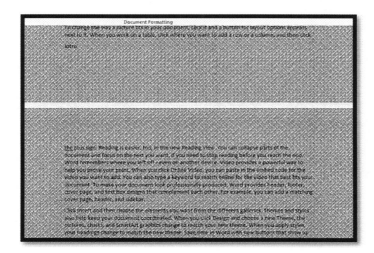

Finally, let's take a look at the last option in this window: uploading a background image. Go to "**Picture**" and click the "**Select Picture**" button.

Then go to the folder with the background image you wish to insert, click on it, and then click "**Insert**."

As you can see, it will display a sample before allowing you to click "**OK**."

The image has now been added to the document in Word.

This is how you can make your page look more interesting by changing the background color and adding textures, patterns, and photos.

Inserting a Watermark

Here, you will see how you can insert a Watermark into a Word document. Let's say you have a secret recipe or a logo and you want to make sure that no one shares; you can add a watermark to keep your document a lot safer. First, we will look at how you can insert a preset watermark and we will also look at how you can customize it. To insert a watermark, on the top ribbon, click on the **Design** tab. Within this tab, over on the right-hand side and you will see an option that says "**Watermark**".

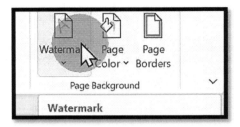

Clicking on the drop-down menu brings up a lot of the preset categories. There is a set of confidential watermarks, Disclaimers, and also Urgent.

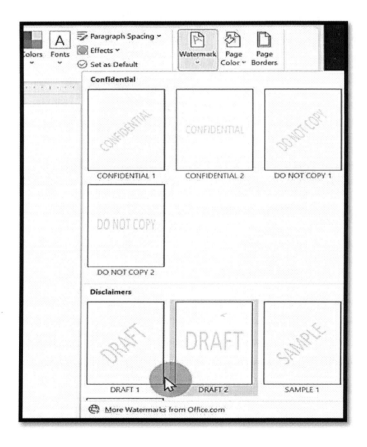

If you select any under the confidential category, that inserts a confidential watermark into your document.

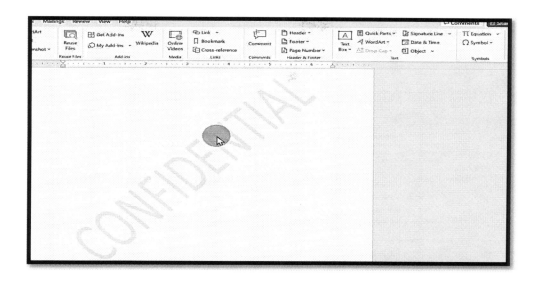

If you insert another page into your document, you can see that the watermark carries over to the new page; that's one thing to keep in mind when you are working on a document.

Customizing a Watermark

Now if you want to customize your watermark to make it more personal, go back to the **Design** tab and once again, click on "**Watermark**", and at the bottom, there is the option to customize the Watermark by simply clicking on "**Custom Watermark**".

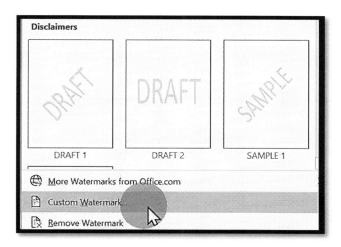

This opens up a dialogue where you can now customize your watermark.

Text-based

If you want to do a text-based watermark, go over to "**Text Watermark**" and start by choosing a language.

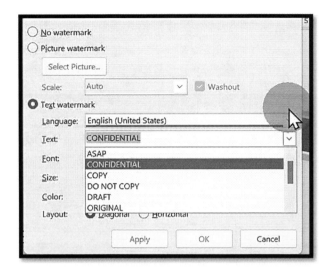

You can view all the preset watermark options but you can also type in a text. You can also set the font, size, and color, and right next to that, there is an option called **"Semitransparent"**. This would wash out the watermark just a little bit more. So, if your watermark is a little too dark and interferes with your text, you can set it to Semitransparent.

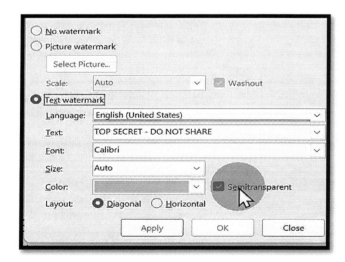

Down at the bottom, you can also choose the layout. You can have the text go diagonally across your document, or you can have it go across horizontally.

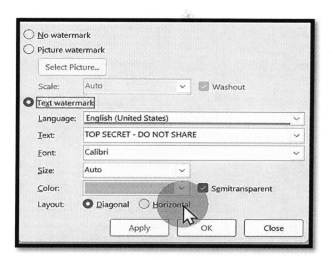

Picture-based

The text watermark works fine, but if you need something more serious, you can try inserting a **Picture Watermark**. Right here, you select a Picture Watermark and select a file on your PC.

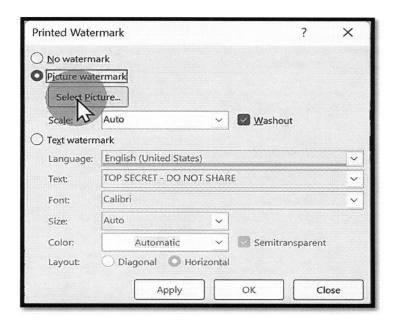

Below that, you can adjust the scale but by default, it is set to Auto and that will ensure the best fit.

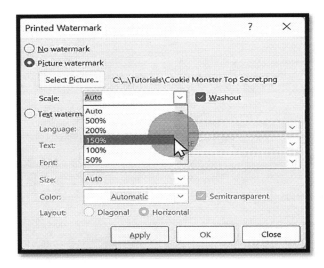

To the right of that, there is a check-box called "**Washout**" and this is similar to the semitransparent option we talked about earlier. When you click on it, it washes out the image a little bit more and when you uncheck it; you can see the image a little bit better.

Removing A watermark

To remove a watermark, within the dialogue we talked about, at the very top, you can simply click on "**No Watermark**".

Back on the main screen, you can also remove the watermark by going back up to the **Design** Tab, the "**Watermark**" **drop-down**, and down towards the bottom there is the option to "**Remove Watermark**".

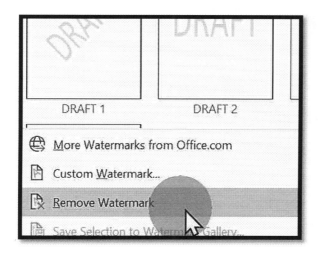

That is how easy it is to insert a watermark and keep your document safe.

Printing Colored pages

To print this document with the entire background color after applying a background color to your page, simply select "**File**" and then "**Print**."

Please note that if you try to print a document with a colored background, you will notice that there is no color applied and instead, you have a white background.

To print the page with the background color you choose, go to "**Options**".

Then select "**Display**" from the menu. Here, there is an option called "**Print background color and images**", simply check the box to enable printing with background color and click "**OK**".

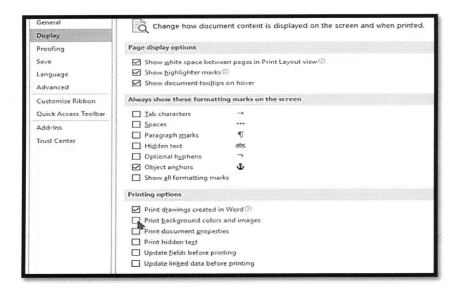

When you return to print, the background color is now visible in the Print Preview, indicating that you can print your Word documents with the full background color.

CHAPTER FOURTEEN
SECTION FORMATTING

This chapter will demonstrate how to format and create chapters, sections, and subsections. You'll learn how to create multi-level lists and format your styles to match the different styles, headings, and levels in your document, allowing you to easily format all of your headings and sections and organize your document. You'll also learn about section breaks and how to use them as we go. Finally, you'll discover how to manually insert a cover page into your document or use templates.

Sectioning a document

While your document is open in Word, go to the **home** tab, under the **Styles** section, click the small button right here, and then scroll down to the third button over, which is labeled "**Manage Styles**."

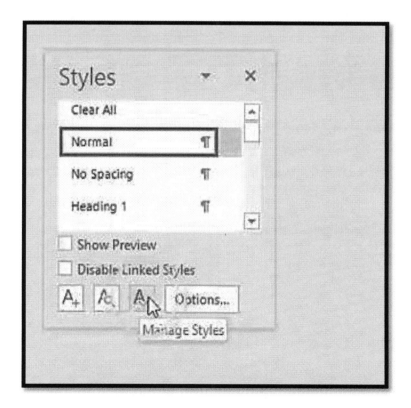

After that, go to the "**Recommend**" tab.

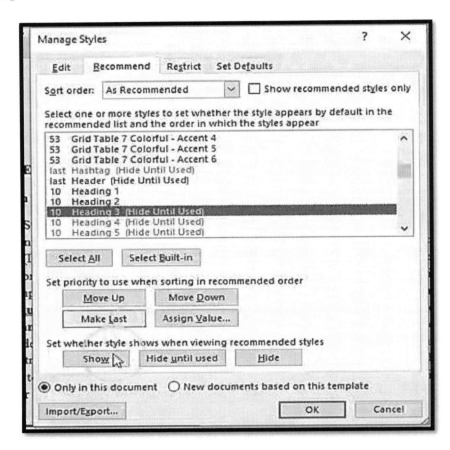

You're turning on the various headings because you want three levels: Chapters, Sections, and Subsections, and you want each of them to correspond to a distinct heading in your Styles section. **Heading 1** may already be visible, while the other headings are grayed out. To make them visible, click on a heading like Heading 2 and select "**Show**," do the same for Heading 3 then select "**OK**." That way, all three of those headings will be shown. You can now close the Styles box because you don't need it any longer, and you can start creating and formatting your levels.

Creating Chapters, Sections, and Subsections

While staying in the home tab, go to the Paragraph section and look for the multi-level list. Select "**Define New Multilevel List**" at the bottom of the page.

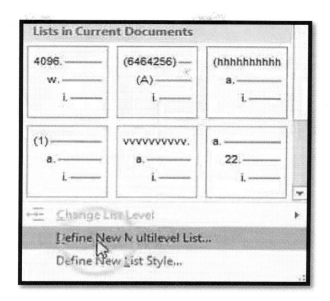

From here, you'll create three levels: Level 1 for chapters, Level 2 for sections, and Level 3 for subsections, with a variety of tasks to complete for each. To begin, go to Level 1 and remove the "**Enter formatting for number**" box and type in "Chapter," then select the "**Number style**," and last, go to the bottom right corner and "**Follow number with**" a space. That will prevent the first chapter's title from colliding with the chapter's real title; you must include that space.

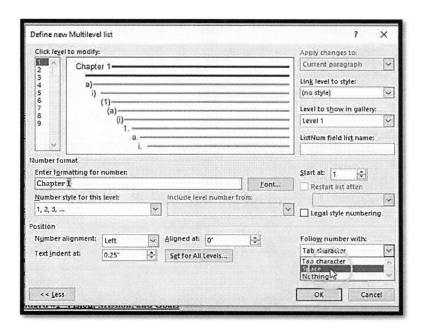

You may also make it so there are no indents by clicking the **"Set for all levels"** button, adjusting the numbers to zero, and then clicking "**OK**."

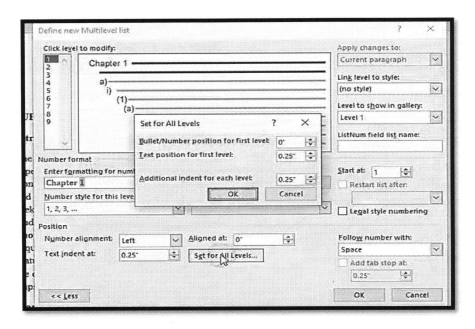

The next step is to format the font, which you can accomplish by selecting "**Font**" and making the desired changes.

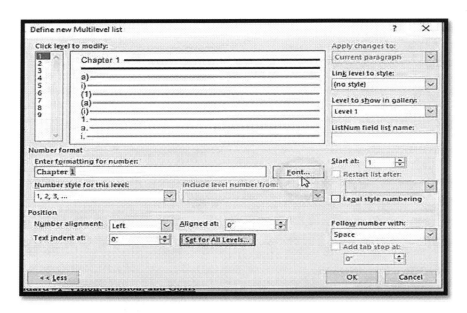

Before moving on to Level 2, you must attach this level to the style you desire, in this case, heading 1 because that is the style you will use for your chapters.

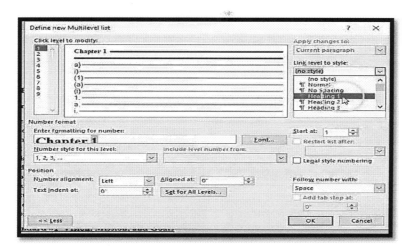

Once you've completed that, you're ready to move on to Level 2, which is your section. You'll start with "**Enter formatting for number**," then continue to "**Include level number from**" and choose level 1, which will insert the chapter number.

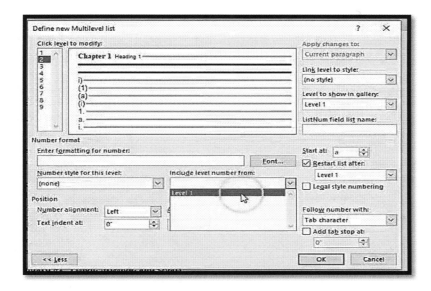

You can start with a period or a stop, then choose a number style, and finally finish with a space. Because you already set your indent for all levels, you don't need to do it again. You can also proceed to format the font and size before clicking "**OK**."

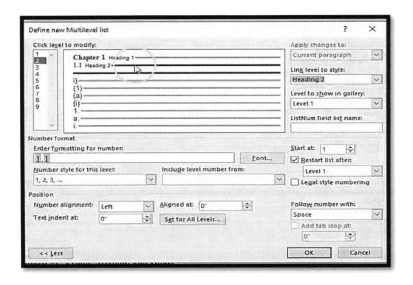

Before moving on, you must link level 2 to the desired style, which will be heading 2. You will see an example of it here once you've done that. The next step is to go to Level 3, which is where your subsections are located. You'll start with your **chapter number from Level 1** and the full stop, then your **section number from Level 2** and the full stop, and finally, you'll **select a Numbers style for this level** and place a space after the number. You won't need to set your indent; simply pick a **Font**, select a **size**, and click "**OK**." The next step is to **attach this level to your Heading 3** style, and once you've done so, you've specified all of your multi-level lists; simply click "**OK**."

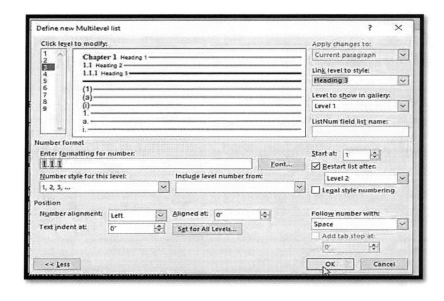

You can now see that chapter 1 for your heading 1 is right there.

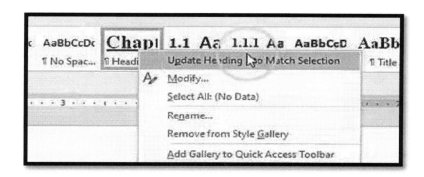

Before continuing, go up to Styles, heading 1, right-click, and select "**Update Heading 1 to Match Selection**." This will ensure that everything is properly formatted, including the chapter, number, and title.

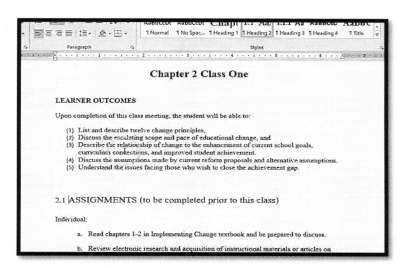

Now that you've done that, go down the page and look for another title. When you've done that, click there and then on Heading 1, which will add that to Chapter 2. It'll put in your chapter, the number, and then the real title of the chapter once you've got everything set up and they've matched your levels and heading styles.

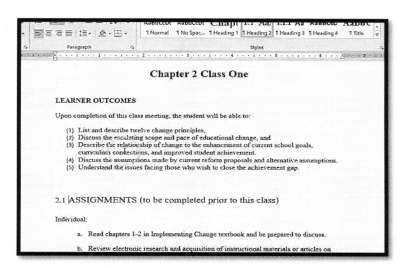

Now you can look at your level 2 or sections by scrolling down. Simply click a phrase or sentence to make it your first section, then go to heading 2 and do the same thing as before (match to your actual level formatting), then go to Heading 2, right-click, and update Heading 2 to reflect your selection.

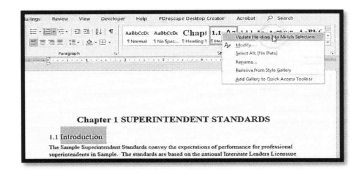

As you do this for your sections, you'll see that it puts in 2.1 for a certain chapter, such as chapter 2, because you're presently in section 1 of chapter 2.

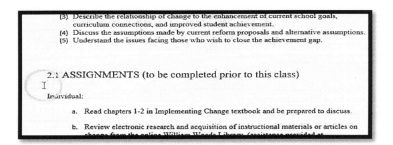

You can now add your subsections by picking your text and going to Heading 3, updating heading 3 to reflect the selection, and you're done.

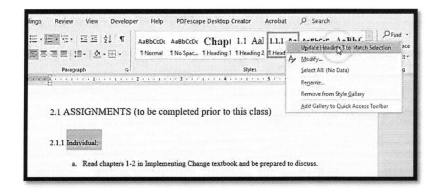

Section Breaks

Let's imagine you want your new chapters to always start on a new page, regardless of what content you add to the prior chapter because the heading just goes down the entire time when you add information. That's what we're going to talk about here, so let's get started.

Adding a Section Break to a Document

To do so, go to the page just before a new chapter, select the **Layout** tab, and then "**Breaks**." Go to "**Section Breaks**" and select "**Next Page**."

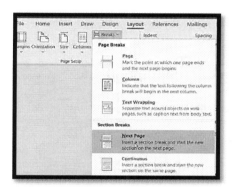

This creates a section break and moves on to the next page to begin the next section. If your page numbers aren't aligning, for example, if you have a page 2 and instead of seeing a page 3 (which is the following page), it goes back to page 1, that's not what you want and it's simple to change. Simply select a particular page number, **right-click**, and select "**Format Page Numbers**."

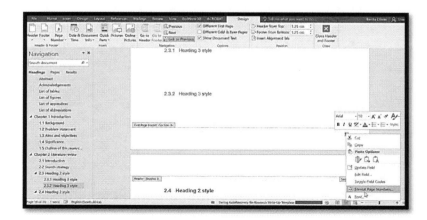

Click the "**Continue from the previous section**" button, and it will remember to continue from the previous section on the next page. That is something you can do for each of your chapters.

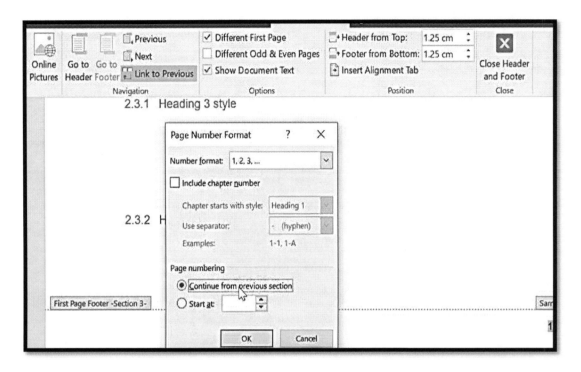

The Very First Page

There are instances when you'll want to include a cover page in an assignment, presentation, or any other document you make; for example, let's say you've written an excellent paper for your project or work and want to include a good cover page. This is a straightforward process. There are some really attractive templates that you can use for this, and we'll show you how to add a cover page or insert a cover page in a Microsoft Word document step by step.

Adding a Cover Page

The first step is to learn how to include a cover page in a document. Place your mouse at the start of the document, then go to the Layout tab, select "**Breaks,**" and then "**Next Page**" under **Section Breaks**.

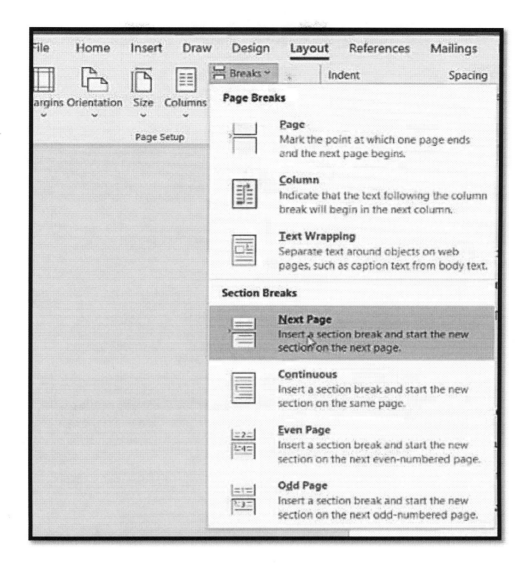

You'll have a distinct cover page for your document once you've done this. You can fill in details for the cover page here, such as your name, the date, and any other information you like.

Inserting a Cover Page Using template

The "**Cover Page**" button can be found under the **Insert** tab. By selecting the drop-down menu, you will be presented with all of the available options. If you don't find one that you like here, scroll down to see a variety of other options.

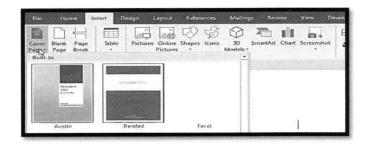

You can go to the section that says "**More Cover Pages**" and click on there to see a few more alternatives.

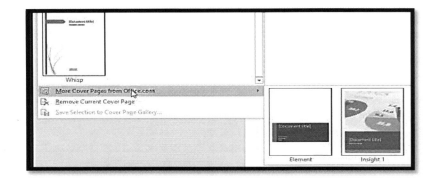

Because there are only a few, go to the **File** tab, select "**New**," then type "**cover page**" into the search bar. This opens up lots of new alternatives you weren't aware of previously. When you click "create" after selecting a template, the template is downloaded and inserted into your document. You can now type in your title, subtitle, and other relevant information.

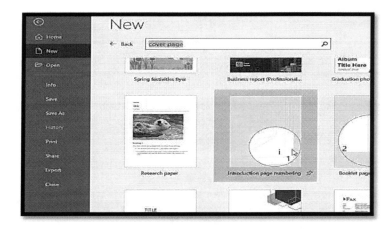

If you decide you no longer want the cover page, simply select "**Remove the cover page**" and the cover pages will be removed.

In this chapter, we demonstrated how to format and create chapters, sections, and subsections. You learned how to create multi-level lists and format your styles to match the different styles, headings, and levels in your document, which is helpful and allows you to easily format all of your headings and sections and organize your document. You also learned about section breaks and how to use them. Finally, you saw how to manually insert a cover page into your document and with templates.

CHAPTER FIFTEEN

TEMPLATE AND THEMES FORMATTING

We've arrived at the chapter where we'll delve into the amazing world of Word templates and themes. You've seen how to get access to Microsoft's templates and how to load them up in the previous chapters. In this chapter, we'll look at how to create custom templates from scratch or an existing document, as well as how to save a document as a template to reuse it later. We'll also go through how to make themes in Word, how to use them, and how to save a current theme as the default.

Making your templates

The great thing about templates is that you can put whatever you want on them, whether it's text, images, styling, or formatting, and then it'll be ready to go the way you want it every time you open it. The nice thing is that when you open it and click "**Save**," it'll want to save it as a new document. This is handy because the majority of users will open an existing document (such as an invoice), enter in the data, and then "**Save as**." As you surely know, it's easy to hit save by accident, and autosave has the potential to overwrite an existing document, which you don't want to happen. This is a fail-safe function, as it will produce a new document each time you open one. You can have as many templates as you need to complete your assignment. If you go to "**File**," then "**New**," then "**Blank Document**," it will appear at the top of the page as a new document. We'll use an invoice template as an example, but this process of building a template can be used for any document you want to make. When you click on your document template (in this case, an invoice), it opens as a new document, preventing you from losing it. You can now type in some information, and when you hit the save button at the top or go to File and save; it will save it to the location you specify.

Using an Existing Document to Create a Template

Now we'll look at how to make one from an existing document. You can notice in the example invoice sheet below that the date and invoice number have been cleaned away, as well as the address and some other information. The good news is that we're going to save this as a template, and when you save something as a template, it always goes into a specific folder for templates. You'll go into File, choose "**Save as**," and over here, where it says **Word**

document, you'll click the drop-down and select **"Word Template"**; this is the one with **"*.dotx"** at the end of it.

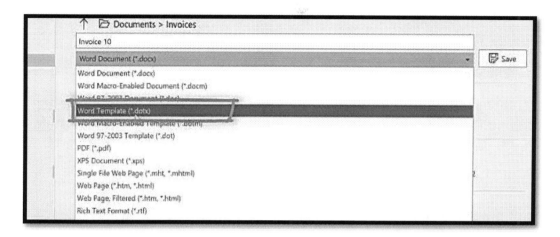

There's also a **"*.dotm"** if you've put macros in there, which is something different entirely, but you'd have to save it that way. As you can see, there is an earlier format; this should not be a concern. You simply go to the current version of the Word template here, click **"Save,"** and it will save it to the appropriate folder.

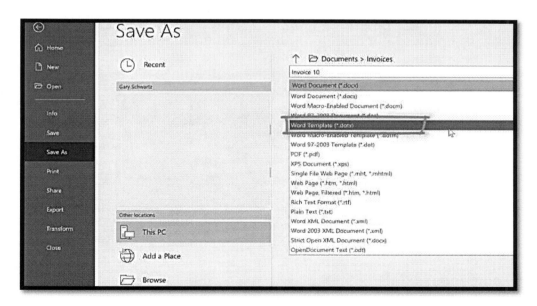

If you go to **File**, then **"New,"** your newly created template will be found under the **"Personal"** menu.

It's as simple as clicking on it to open it, and it's ready to use. The good news is that if you hit "**Save**," it will prompt you to save it in, so you won't mistakenly overwrite it.

Making Modifications to a Template

So, you've got a template and want to be able to customize it. It is suggested that you make any necessary modifications here, then "**Save as**" and rename the file. The beautiful part is that you can go into "**File**," then "**New**," and it will be under the "**Personal**" tab, with the other one intact, exactly like before.

Using the Mac

When using a Mac, this is in a slightly different location. You'll notice that it looks a little bit different on your Mac; all you have to do is go to "**File**," select "**New from templates**," and you'll find a variety of templates to choose from.

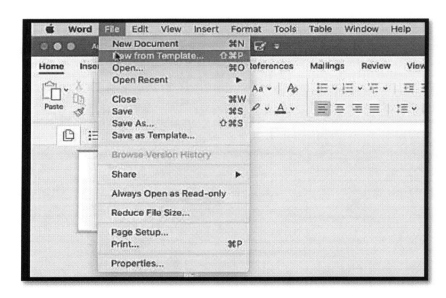

These are all Microsoft-provided, and if you looked at the ones on Windows, you would have seen ones that were similar, if not identical. The difference is up to where it says "**Featured**," and next to it is "**Personal**," which is where your templates are located. Simply double-click on it, and it will open as a document.

If you've just finished creating a new template and want to save it, go to "**File**" and then "**Save as Template**."

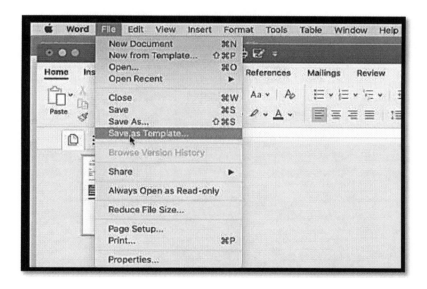

It will automatically place it in the same location as all the other templates, so you don't have to bother about choosing a template space for it. If you go back to **File** and select "**New from templates**," your new template will appear under the "**Personal**" option. One intriguing feature is that if you have a template on a Mac or Windows machine, you can copy it to another machine's template folder and it will operate just as well.

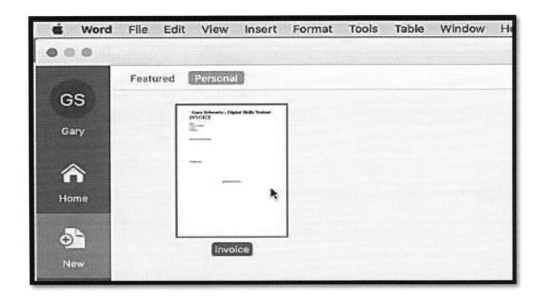

Creating a Template from Scratch

We'll take a look at the stages involved in building a template from scratch in Word. The first step would be to **open a basic Word document**, then **format** it and type any content you want to add each time you utilize the template. Finish any formatting modifications, such as bolding the title and headings, then **save your work as a template** with the extension "***.dotx**." Word will save the template to your custom templates folder by default, but you can specify another place.

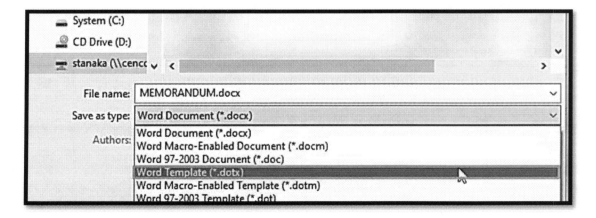

When you return to the usual interface, where it previously said Document 1 as a placeholder, you'll see the name of your template at the top of the screen.

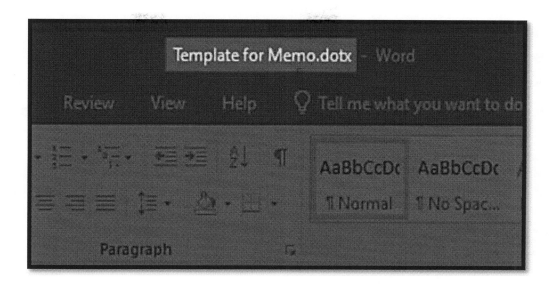

Double-click on the template file's icon, which looks like a notepad, to open a new Word document based on the template you just made. This is a new file that you can modify just like any other Word document; the only difference is that you've given yourself a good start.

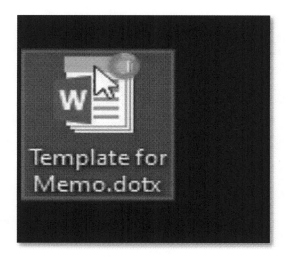

Applying a Theme to a Document

In Word, a theme is a set of styles, colors, fonts, effects, and paragraph spacing that you can use to customize your document. To apply a theme, go to the **Design** tab, then to the **Document Formatting group**, and select "**Themes**" from the drop-down menu.

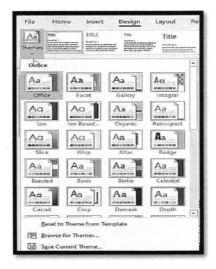

Hold your mouse over a theme in the drop-down menu to preview it in your document, and then click it to **apply** it to your work. To delete an applied theme from your document, go to the **Design** tab in the ribbon and select the "**Reset to theme from template**" option from the themes drop-down button in the document formatting button group.

Saving and Customizing a Theme

Individual aspects of a theme can be customized by changing the style, color, font, and paragraph spacing, and after making changes to a theme, you can save it as a new theme to use in subsequent Word documents.

- To do so, simply **change a theme** to your liking.
- Then, under the ribbon, select the **Design** tab, then the themes drop-down button in the document formatting button group, after which "**Save current theme**."

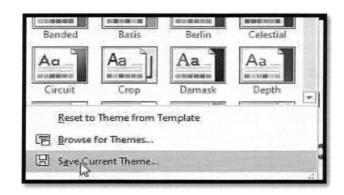

155

This opens the theme dialog box, which saves the theme to the document themes folder by default. To make it easier to apply custom themes in the future, leave the folder location unchanged, then type the name of your custom theme in the file name field, and click the Save button in the dialog box to save it as a theme file with a "*.thmx" file extension in the selected directory.

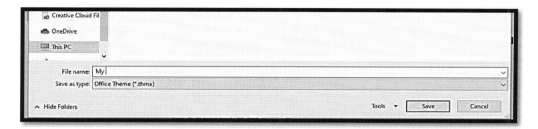

Your custom theme will now display as a theme option in the theme buttons drop-down menu of options, which you can select from the list. Click the **Design** tab in the ribbon, then click the "**Set as Default**" button in the document formatting button group to make the currently applied theme the default theme for any new blank documents you create.

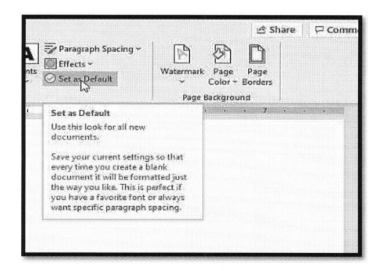

We talked about templates a lot in this chapter, and you learned how they can save you time and prevent you from accidentally overwriting existing files if you open up a file that appears similar to the one you already have. You learned how to make a template from scratch as well as how to apply a template created from an existing document. Finally, we discussed themes and how to create and use them in Word documents.

CHAPTER SIXTEEN
LISTS AND NUMBERINGS

You may have a list in your Word document that you'd like to number, and by numbering, we mean using numbers, letters, Roman numerals, or something similar. You can also number paragraphs, which is what this chapter will go over. We'll also look at using bullets and outlines as an alternative to making lists stand out.

Making Numbered Lists for Your Document

We'll start by making a list. You have the option of working with an existing document or starting from scratch. Now you'll make a simple list and number each item. The next step, as with most things in Word, is to choose what you want to number: thus, you'll use your mouse to highlight all of those names, and then go to the **home** ribbon, where you'll find your **Numbering** drop-down in the **Paragraph group**.

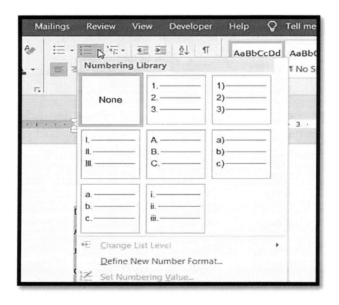

You will notice the tour advice their states "**Create a numbered list**" as you hover over it. You can also click the arrow for more numbering formats, and you can see if you have any selected, but if you don't, you'll notice it has the gray box around the outside and also gives you several options for your list, so it depends on whether you want it numbered (1, 2, 3), with Roman numerals, or with letters instead (A, B, C). You can also see that we have capital and lowercase letters, as well as many variations on those. You can start with a simple list by selecting one of these options, and your list will be numbered. The advantage of utilizing numbering in this manner is that if you add a name to the bottom of the list and tap **Enter**, the following number is immediately entered. If you decide at this time that you don't want that number there, you can either hit backspace or opt to turn off numbering by clicking the numbering button again, which will return you to the margin where you may continue putting paragraphs or anything you want into this page. Also, if you want to change the way this is numbered, all you have to do is highlight it, go back up to your numbering options, and choose the option you want. When you go to the numbering drop-down, you'll notice that the formats you've recently used are placed at the top, making them much easier to find.

Making Your List More Personal

If you go down to the bottom, you'll see "**Change List Level**," which we'll look at when we look at outline numbering. Our focus here is on the "**Define New Number Format**" option, which allows you to change the style of your numbering.

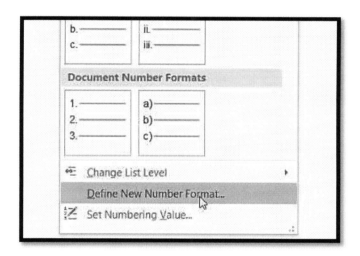

If your number style is set to A, B, C, you can change it to something else if you want, and you can also change the font of your numbering; so, if you want it to look slightly different, you can change the font style, color, and size, and you can see what that looks like in the preview at the bottom. You have the option of selecting your alignment as well. If yours is set to left alignment, you can select to center it or move it to the right, which will change the positioning of the numbering.

Set Numbering Value

We'll also take a look at another numbering option called "**Set Numbering Value**." If you want to make a list underneath, this is beneficial. If you start a new list and add some numbering, you'll notice that it follows the numbering from the previous list. This is where you would define the new number if this is a distinct list and you wish to restart it.

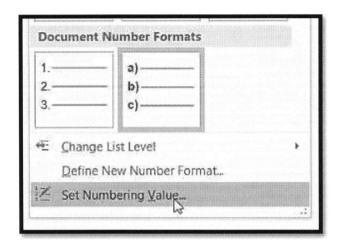

Return to Numbering, select "**Set numbering value**," select "**Start New List**," and set your value to the first letter (a) or number one, then click "**OK**" to create your distinct list. If you don't specify that, it will continue from the previous list, so keep that in mind while you work with your numbering.

Numbering in Paragraphs

Let's have a look at how Numbering works in paragraphs. If you click at the beginning of the first paragraph in your document and then on the Numbering button, you'll see that it's numbered the entire paragraph, and if you do the same for the second, it continues.

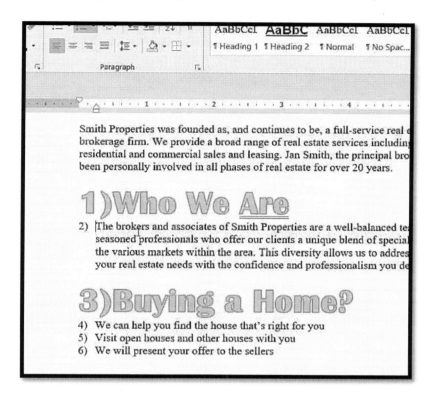

When you click at the beginning of a paragraph and apply the numbering, you'll see that only the first line is numbered at first. The reason for this is that this paragraph has a line break in it, so if you hit Enter and move to the second line, Word considers those to be whole new paragraphs, whereas the other paragraphs, which do not have line breaks, are continuous sentences that just keep going. This is to demonstrate that numbering is not limited to the lists you build; it can also be applied to paragraphs. It's also worth mentioning that you don't have to have a list ready to use Numbering. If you wish to use Numbering before you start creating your list, you can do so by simply clicking the numbering button. Keep in mind that it will always continue from the previous list unless you instruct it to restart. You can go ahead and click on the drop-down menu, where you'll notice a useful "**Restart numbering**" button, and then construct your next list.

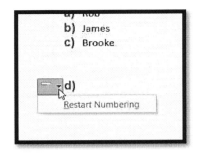

That is how you work with fundamental numbering in a document, both in terms of lists and paragraphs.

Making Use of Bullets

We've just finished working with numbered lists in a document, and now we'd like to focus on working with bullets, which is significantly different from numbering but similar in concept. Let's suppose you have a basic list in your document that is currently numbered, and you want to replace the numbers with **bullets**. If you're not sure what a bullet is, it's just a symbol, and there are many various symbols that you can use as bullets; most of the time, you'll see some Round solid black bullets in documents, but as we'll see as we go through this part, you can use a variety of different things as bullets.

- The first thing you'll do is do your selection, which will **highlight your list**.
- Next, head back up to the **paragraph group**, and next to numbering, there's a small button that says "**Bullets**." "**Create a bulleted list**," the tooltip says, and "**Click the arrow to customize the look of the bullets**."

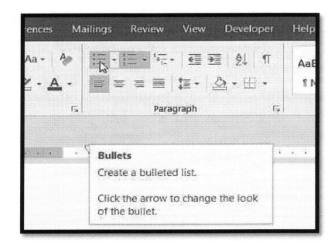

When you click the arrow, you'll be provided with a bullet library, which will show you some of the most popular bullets that people might use, as well as a handful of ones that have been used previously. Still, you can select any of these and see what they look like by hovering over them.

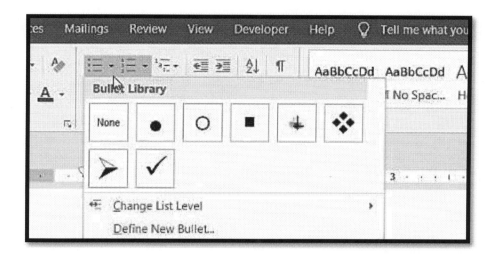

The trick is ideal for to-do lists, and you can select the type of bullet that best suits the document you're working on.

Defining New Bullets

Alternatively, you can go to the "**Define New Bullet**" option and pick a symbol that will work for your document.

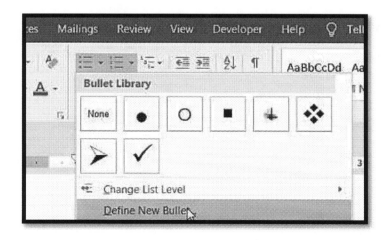

As you can see, bullet characters are available, as well as the options of Symbol, Picture, or Font.

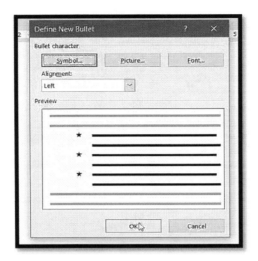

Let's use Symbols

First, we'll take a look at "**Symbol**." This will open your symbol dialog box, and symbols are essentially just fonts divided into fonts, so there are a lot of different symbols. Because there are so many, it would take a long time to go through them all looking for something appropriate, but a lot of the best ones that you'll use or some of the most popular you'll find under "**Webdings**," where we have lots of interesting things that you can add into a document.

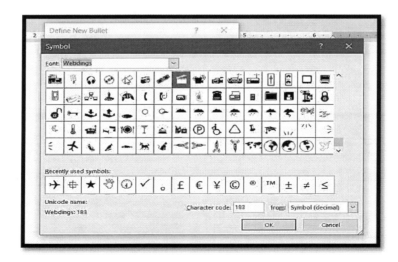

You can **scroll through this selection of symbols** until you find one you like, and then click **OK**. You'll receive a preview of what that symbol will look like in your document, and then click **OK** again, and your numbering will be changed to that symbol.

How about some pictures?

Pictures that are saved or that you can obtain on the internet. Keep your list highlighted and move back up to the bullets drop-down, then back down into "**Define New Bullets**" and select the **picture** option in the middle. You have a few options here: you may choose a picture from a **file**, so if you have one saved to your desktop in "**My Documents**" or a **local Drive**, you can select it from there; you can also choose to search the **internet** for an image, or you can select one from your **OneDrive cloud storage**.

Always check the copyright on photos if you're merely downloading anything off the internet to make sure it has a **Creative Commons License** so you can use it in your work if you're searching for a Bing image.

After selecting an image, click "**Insert**" and "**OK**," and you're done; your document now has a cute little image that adds a little more interest.

An Example in Action

Another example of when you might want to include bullets, graphics, or even symbols is if you're typing something about a phone number and want to include the phone symbol in your phrase. To begin, place your cursor where you want it, then select the "**Insert**" ribbon and scroll across to the "**Symbols**" group on the right-hand side.

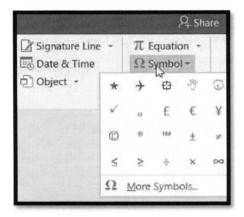

Click on "**Symbol**" and it will show you a list of all the ones that have been used recently, but you'll go to "**Add additional symbols**" and select the telephone icon under the "**Wingdings**" font, then click on "**Insert**" and **close**.

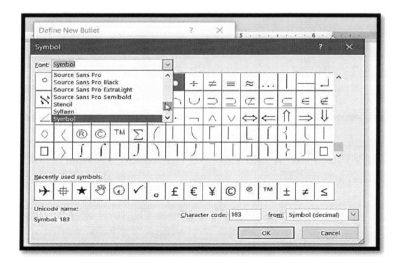

165

You can see how you've used those symbols not only in your bullets but also within a single line of text. That's another nice thing you can do with symbols in your documents, and it's worth remembering that they're regarded like fonts, so you can do things like alter their color by highlighting them, and use your font settings because they're essentially fonts, not photos. Hopefully, that provides you an idea of how to use basic bullets, as well as some more complicated bullets, in your documents utilizing symbols and images you've stored.

Creating an Outline

We're going to look at how to outline from scratch in this section. If you click your cursor after the first item on your numbered list and hit the Enter key now, it will just resume the numbering. What if you wish to add a second level to this number? You can simply use the tab key on your keyboard to add a second level of numbering to your list. You must be familiar with this terminology; for example, using the **tab key** to **demote a level** and the **Shift + tab** to **advance a level**. If you enter something in here and press **Enter**, the numbers will continue at that level. You can exit by using the **Shift + tab**, which will return you to the previous screen. If you want to get rid of it completely, you can **backspace**.

A More Organized Paragraph

Now let's look at how you can number paragraphs at the outline level. To begin, you must first identify and choose the paragraphs to which you want to apply this.

- To get started, go to the home ribbon and then to the "**Multilevel List**" button.

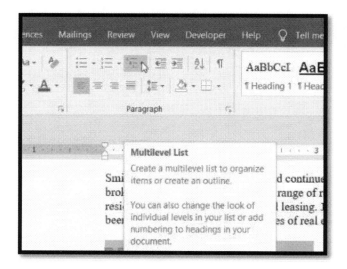

- Then click the **drop-down** menu, which will give you a few options to choose from. It all depends on the style you want for your outline-level numbering.

After selecting an option, you'll see that it has been applied to the paragraphs you've chosen, but you'll notice that it hasn't recognized what should be on the second level.

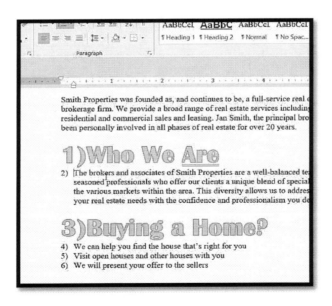

- Simply click in front of the first sentence in the first selected paragraph and hit the tab key to demote it to the second level, and you'll see that everything follows through. You can do the same for the ones down here: just hit the tab and keep going until you get everything looking just right.

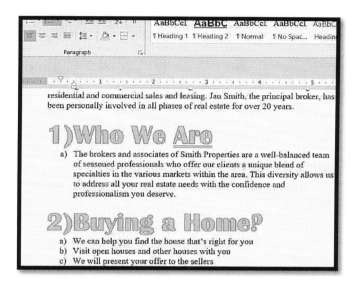

It's fairly simple to outline, and you can even add a third level if you wish. If you press the tab key again after completing the second level, you'll be taken to the third level, where you can make those little tweaks.

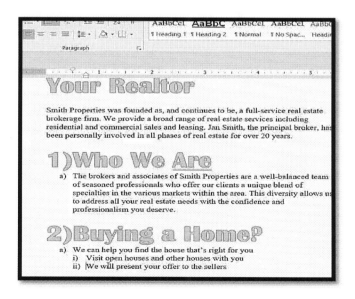

A Simple Modification

What if you wanted to redo the entire outline? Make another selection, and then move up to the outline level numbering and "**Define New Multilevel List**."

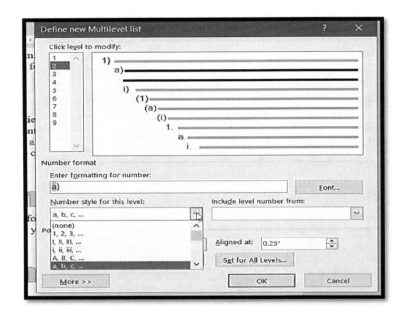

You'll be able to go more specific and personalize the appearance of your Multilevel List as a result of this. There are nine levels listed here, as well as those that are listed elsewhere. Number one will be the first level, followed by "a," "I," and so on. You can go in, choose a level, and tweak the formatting to your heart's content. You can alter the font for your level 1s by going into the options and changing it to something completely different. You can modify the number styles for this level, the number alignment, the text-indent, and a lot of other things on level two, so its worth getting in there and customizing so you can quickly apply your newly customized Multilevel numbers to your document.

Just keep in mind that you can define that new multilevel list in this section. If you already have a document written out, you can go in, highlight everything, select your multi-level list, and then promote and demote as needed, or even get detailed and edit each level of your list. **In this chapter,** we looked at how you can use bullets, lists, and an outline to add numberings to your documents to make them stand out and be more exciting to read.

CHAPTER SEVENTEEN

TABLES

This chapter covers a lot of ground in Microsoft Word when it comes to tables. When it comes to document structure, tables are extremely important. They enable you to present data in columns and rows, making data more ordered and easier to understand. Tables have their contextual ribbon, which includes a variety of choices for restructuring, modifying, and formatting the table to match the overall appearance and feel of any page. We'll walk over the process of adding a table into a document in this chapter, as well as some formatting tips and tricks.

Adding a Table in Your Document

There are a few different approaches you can take, and we'll go over a number of them. The first method is to go to the **Insert** ribbon and look for the **Tables group**.

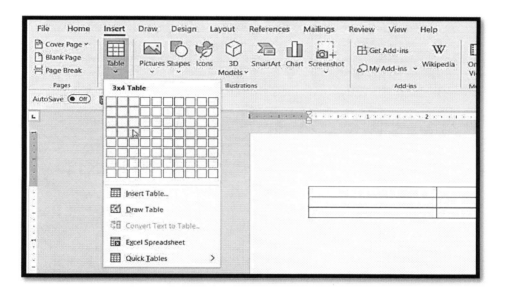

There's only one option in there, which is "**Table**", and when you click on it, you're taken to a small grid where you can choose how many rows and columns you want in your table. When you move your cursor over this grid, it creates the table instantaneously in your document; for example, if you want a table with three columns and four rows, all you have to do is select that many squares in the small grid and click, and your table is ready.

Inserting a table

When it comes to inserting tables, you can go back to the **Insert** tab, select the **Table drop-down**, and choose "**Insert Table**" instead of utilizing the grid.

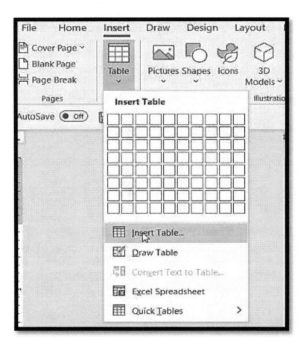

This is where you can choose the number of columns and rows you would like in your table.

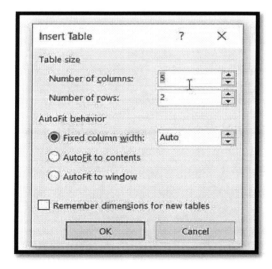

You also have the option of selecting "**AutoFit behavior**." "**Fixed column width**" in this case indicates that each column in the table will be the same width as determined by Word, and you have this set to automatic so it will do the best fit. "**AutoFit to contents**" implies that each column will extend to be consistent with the table's left and right margins, and "**AutoFit to window**" means that the columns will expand to be even with the table's contents. Most of the time, the **Fixed column width** is just great because you can resize or change the width of the columns once you've created the table. After you've made your selections, click "**OK**," and your table will appear.

Make a table for yourself

You can also draw your table when it comes to inserting tables. This can also be useful since it gives you greater control over the appearance of your table, such as setting the row, height, column, width, and overall table size. Return to the **Insert** ribbon and select the table drop-down menu; there is a "**Draw Table**" option there.

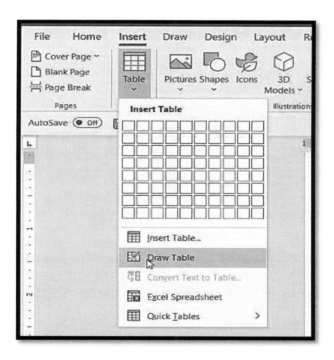

When you click on it, your mouse pointer will change to a pencil icon. This will allow you to draw your table; you'll begin with the outside border and then draw rows and columns using your pencil.

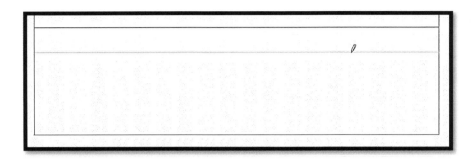

This option is much more flexible and allows you a little more control than the others. If you see that you still have the pencil icon after you've completed designing your table, simply go to your ribbon and deselect the "**Draw Table**" option. After you've drawn or inserted your table, you'll see the table tools' contextual ribbon. You must first choose the complete table. If you look up at your ribbons, you will notice that because you have a table selected, you have access to the **Table Design** ribbon and the **Table Layout** ribbon, and you can pretty much manage every part of your table with these two ribbons.

Deleting a table

You can also delete tables. You'll notice a small cross in the top left-hand corner, which when clicked will instantly select the entire table.

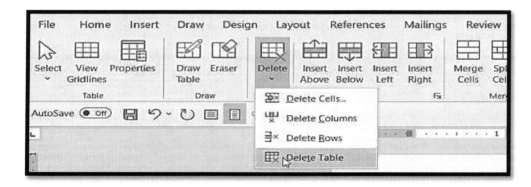

You can delete this by right-clicking and selecting "**Delete Table**" from the right-click menu. You can also use the "**Delete Table**" option on the **Layout** ribbon.

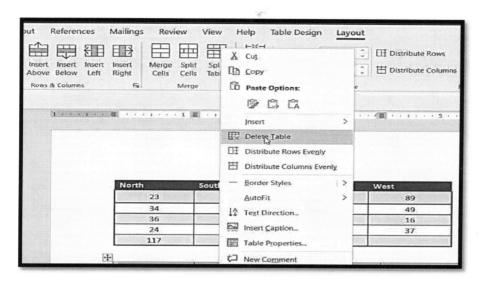

Designing your table

Let's start with the design of the table. This is where you may make changes to your table's formatting. You have different table styles in the middle here that you can apply, and as you mouse over them, you get a live preview so you can see which one you want to use before you apply it; it's a nice simple method to add formatting.

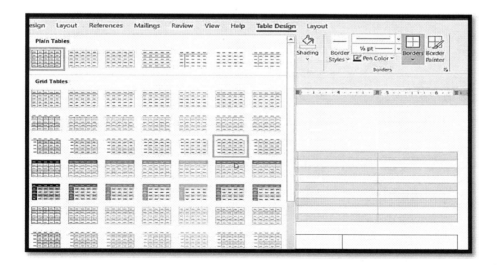

You can apply a table style and then change various formatting elements, so you're not limited to your current color scheme. If you like the table design you've chosen but want to change the background shading of the header row, simply click it, go to "**Shading**," and choose a different color.

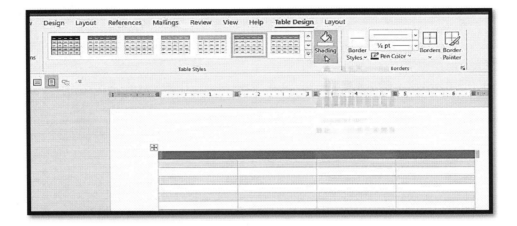

Tables with text

You can add text to your table by clicking in the first cell, typing the word, and then pressing the tab key to proceed to the next cell. It's worth noting that hitting the tab key will allow you to travel between your various cells and enter data.

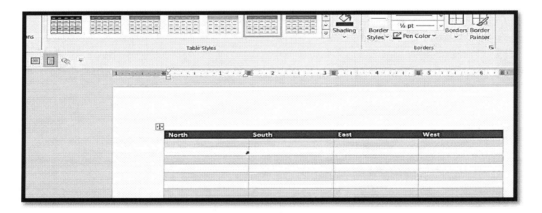

It's also worth mentioning that clicking Enter while clicked in a cell will just make that cell taller, rather than moving you down to the next row. You can either click on the cell below with your mouse or use your down arrow to move to the next row.

Aligning text in a cell

Another thing you might do to improve the appearance of your table is to align all of your text. You'll first highlight everything in this table, and then under the alignment group, you'll find a variety of options for aligning your items within the cell. If you choose "**Align Center**," all of those will be aligned in the center.

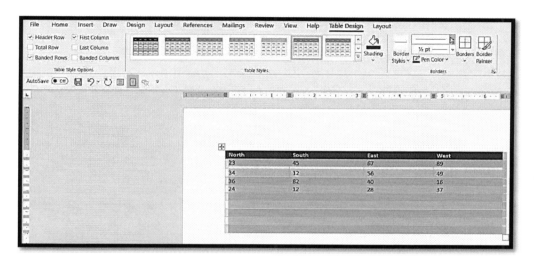

Converting tables to text

Converting tables to ordinary text is something else you might wish to do. If you wish to delete the table's borders and headings and just have them as plain text on your page, Word has a convenient little button for you. Select your table first, and then click the "**Convert to Text**" button on the **Layout** ribbon's Data group at the bottom.

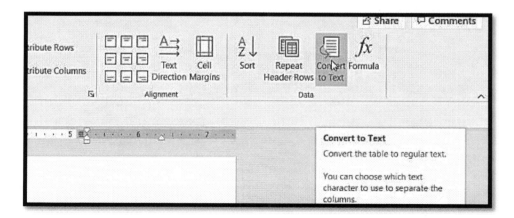

When you click that, you'll be asked how you'd like these fields separated. Because there will be no columns or rows to separate these values once it is removed from the table, Word will ask you how you want to divide the text: with paragraph marks, tabs, commas, or anything else.

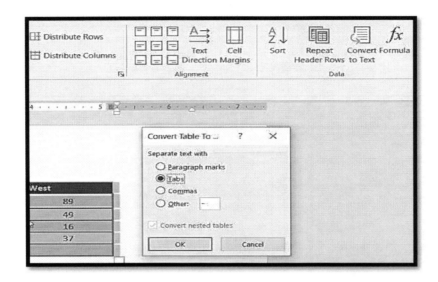

If you opt to use tabs, for example, click "**OK**," and the data will be removed from the table and separated by a tab. You can put this data back in a table by selecting it, going to the Insert ribbon, navigating to Tables, and selecting "**Convert Text to Table**."

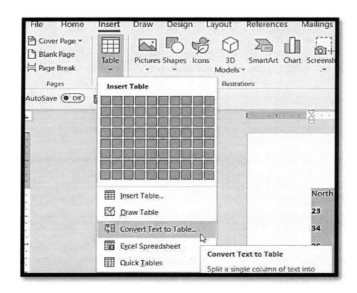

When you click "**OK**," Word will recognize the number of columns and rows in your table.

Modifying a Table

On the Table Design ribbon, you can choose from a variety of styling options. The Layout ribbon is the other ribbon we have here, and it allows you to do things like insert rows, and columns, merge cells, split cells, change the text direction, and align your text within your cells. Let's take a look at a few of these fundamentals.

Adjusting rows and columns

You can also change the width of these columns by hovering your mouse over the column border and dragging it in or out. You can do the same thing with the rows by dragging them up and down.

After you've entered some data into the top part of your table, there are a few formatting options available. You have several table designs options, so if your table has some alternate colors, it's because you've enabled the "**Banded Rows**" option. If you turn them off, they will be gone.

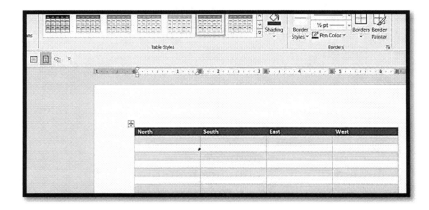

Instead, you can use "**Banded Columns**."

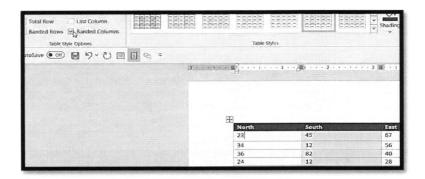

You can format the "**Last Column**," and you can see how it has bolded all of the numbers.

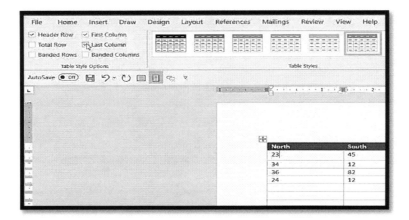

A **Total Row**, a **Header Row**, or a **First Column** could all be added.

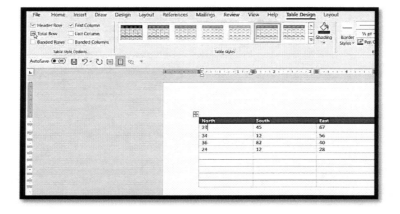

Adding Borders

You may also use borders to add some spice to your table. You may currently have extremely faint borders going through your table; however, if you want to change this, choose your table and look up the borders group. By picking a solid line, you can give it a pretty thick boundary. You can even change the color of the border entirely. Then, using the "**Borders**" drop-down, you can select the type of border you desire.

You can see how these different options apply if you hover over them; for example, the "**Left Border**" option will give you a left border. You can create a border around everything by doing "**All Borders**," or you can only do an "**Outside Border**" or an "**Inside Border**."

Adding and removing rows and columns

To insert a new row between cells, simply highlight the row and select "**Rows & Columns**" from the **Layout** ribbon's "**Rows & Columns**" **group**. From there, you can choose to create a new row above or below where you've clicked.

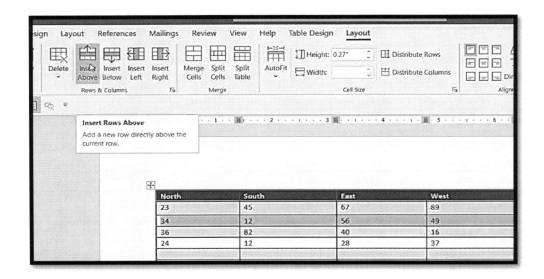

Columns work the same way, so you can highlight one and choose whether to put a blank column to the left or right. Another easy way to add a row is to click slightly outside the table and then press the enter key. This will add a new row to the table. Similarly, if you want to remove a row or column that you've added, you can select it and then click the "**Delete**" option in the Rows and Columns group, where you can say "**Delete rows**" or "**Delete columns**."

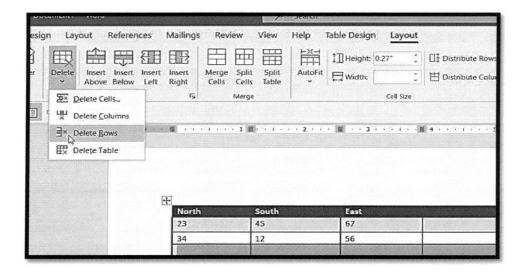

You can also delete rows or columns by right-clicking your mouse and selecting Delete Rows or Columns from the right-click menu.

Merging and Splitting Cells

Another important aspect of tables is the ability to split and merge cells. If you want to split a cell into two, you can do it by clicking within the cell, going to the Layout ribbon, and selecting "**Split Cells**" from the **Merge group**.

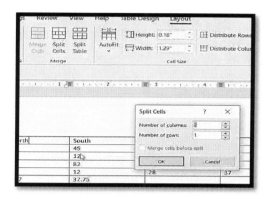

It will ask you how many columns and rows you want this cell to be divided into. You can split it into two, three, or four cells as long as there is enough room; click "**OK**," and you'll notice that the cell has been split. Merging columns is the inverse of that. If you want to merge these two cells back into one, click both cells, go to Layout, and pick "**Merge Cells**" from the drop-down menu.

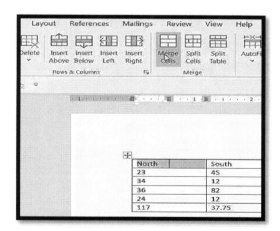

As you can see, there are a lot of options when it comes to table formatting, and there's a lot more than what you've seen in this chapter, which should pique your interest. You can add a table to a document and play about with it to see what you can do with it.

CHAPTER EIGHTEEN

BORDERS

In this chapter, we will discuss the borders and shading of a page in Windows Word. Let's say you have a fairly simple document, such as a certificate, a notice, a poster, or something similar, to which you'd like to add a border.

Accessing Borders

To access and insert borders, go to the Design tab and then to the icon here that reads "**Page Borders**" along with the ribbon.

When you click on that, a dialog window will pop up. You can choose from several options on the left-hand side, including **No Borders**, a **Box border** (which is just a basic box), a **Shadowbox**, a **3D box**, or a **Custom box**.

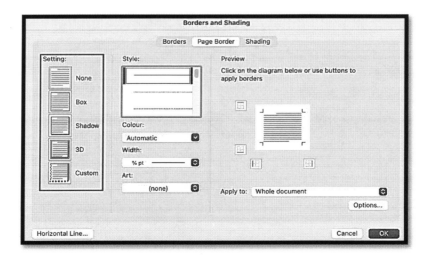

Applying a Page Border

While they are all fairly self-explanatory, let's have a look at the options to the right of the Box border. If you want to place a Box border around your page, you have a variety of styles to choose from, and if you grab the slider and drag it down, you'll see all of the different lines that you can use for your Box border.

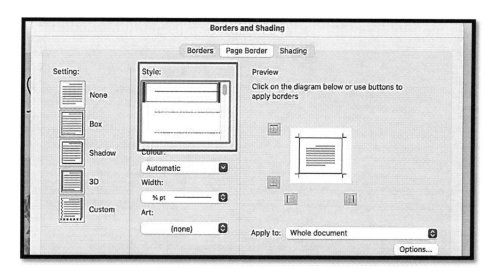

You can get that border by selecting one of those lines and clicking "**OK**." In addition to choosing a style, you can also choose a **color**. You can select any color from this drop-down menu by clicking on it.

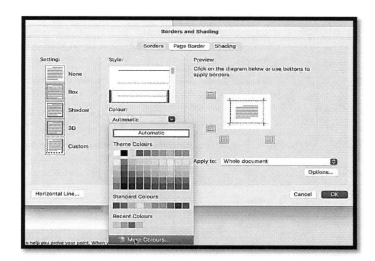

184

You can also go down to "**More colors**" and look at your color wheel, place your cursor anywhere on the color wheel, and move this slider to the left or right. The color of your choice will appear in this box; simply select "**OK**."

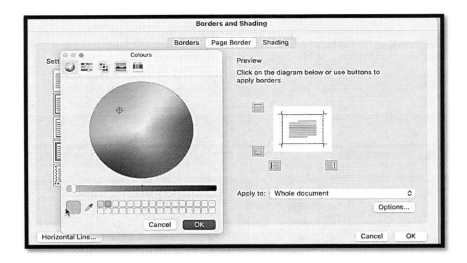

If you choose a color, let's say red, you'll notice that all of your preview boxes have turned red as well.

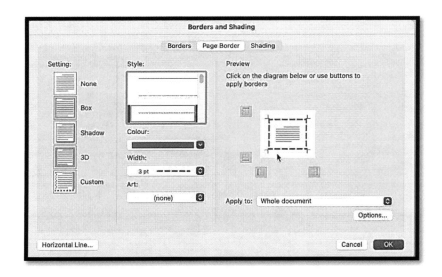

You can also customize the border's weight and width. If you click on the drop-down menu, you can choose a heavier weighted line if you wish, and you can see how it will look in the preview. Simply click "**OK**," and your thicker border will appear.

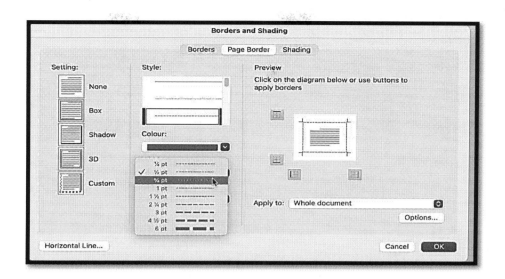

You can choose some more creative options right here at the bottom. You can scroll down the drop-down menu, and there's an arrow at the bottom that allows you to browse down and look at all the numerous options available.

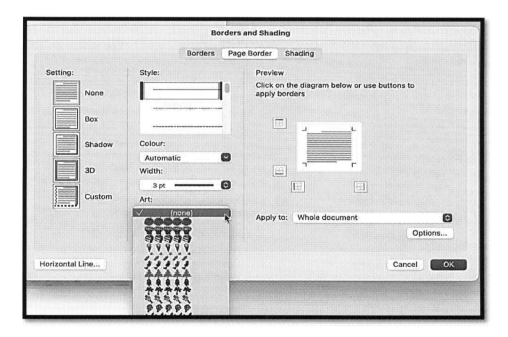

When you have colored options, such as globes, these colors are set, and the color option is grayed out, indicating that you can't change the color of this option but can modify the size.

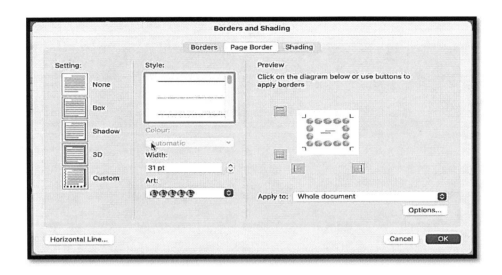

You can see from the preview that the globes change the size and become smaller if you make them smaller by clicking on the Width drop-down, and if you click "**OK**," you can see that you now have slightly smaller globes for this particular border. You'll find some black and white options if you return to the art area and scroll down. These options are a little more flexible, and you can see that the color option is no longer grayed out when you select a design. You can now select any color by clicking and selecting it, so let's select red once more and click "**OK**." You can see that you now have the same design as before but in red.

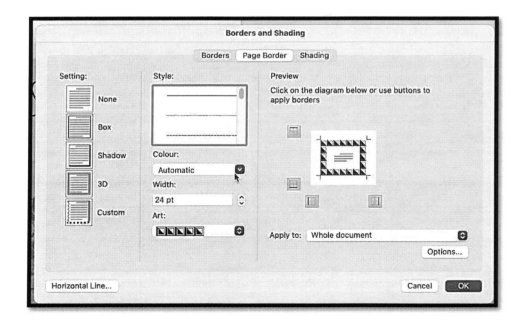

You may want your border to match a color in your text or an image. When you click on Page Border, you'll notice that the overlay is slightly grayed out or blue, so if you choose a color from your image, it won't be the same. To demonstrate, go to the color options and click on the eyedropper tool here.

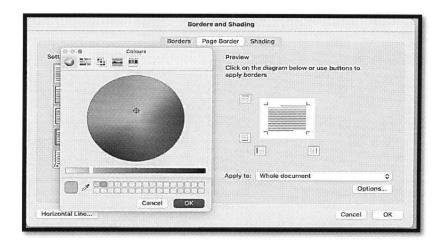

It allows you to navigate through your document and identify whatever color you want by magnifying it, and then using the middle square, you can just click on it and it will match the color in your color wheel.

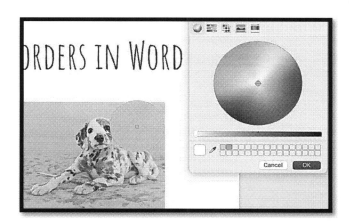

Because of the overlay shading visible here, it will be difficult to match the color of the image's backdrop. The solution to getting around this is to leave this dialogue box and go to a new color option, which you can do with page colors or other color options like text in Word. You will notice that your image is no longer grayed out or shaded if you go to "**Page Color**" and then down to "**More Colors**." You can now use the eyedropper tool to select, then go to the backdrop and select that color.

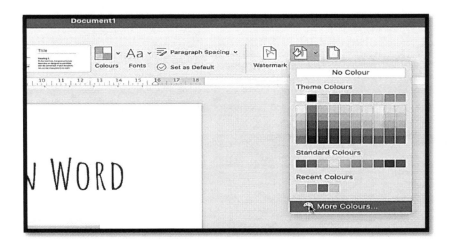

You can see that it's been identified in this window, and then simply click "**OK**." Although the page background has changed, you can simply return to "**Page Color**" and choose "**No color**." When you go to Page Borders and then to "**Color**," you'll notice that your color has shown in recent colors. All you have to do now is select the desired option, and then scroll down to the artwork you've chosen; you can see how it appears in the preview. You can now apply it to the "**Whole document**," but if you don't want borders around your page, for example, if you only want to remove the right-hand border, you can use the icon shown below.

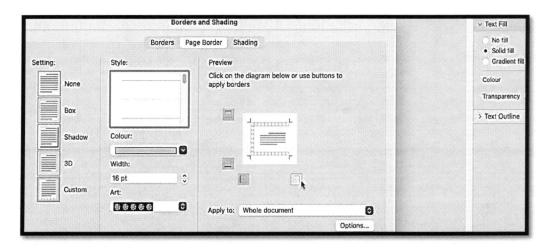

It will send the border across your page, not just to where it would connect up with the next border, and if you click "**OK**," you can see how it goes all the way to the page's edge, not just to where it would link up with the vertical border there.

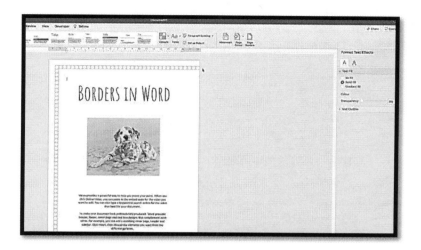

If you don't want that, return to Page Borders, select the option you want, and then click "OK," and your page borders will appear.

An Advanced Technique

Also, if you want to improve or extend the borders in some way and have a few more options, there is a more complex procedure. Go to the "**Shapes**" on the **Insert** tab, and then to the square here.

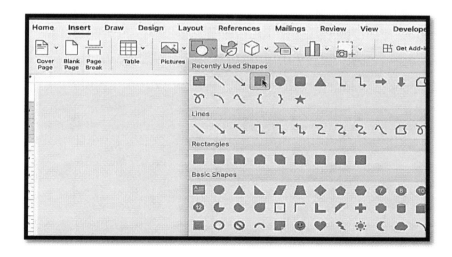

Click and drag it after you've clicked on it. Attempt to make this form slightly larger than your borders. You can do this with your cursor, but if it gets a little awkward and doesn't quite fit, say the bottom bits are a little too broad in comparison to the top, you can select it, go to "**Shape Format**," and then to the **Height and Width section**.

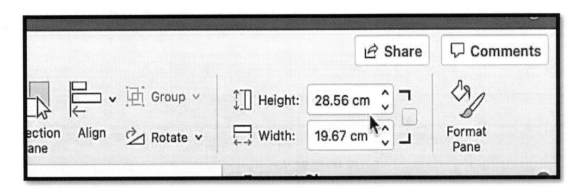

Because you want to reduce the height of it slightly, you can move over and use the arrow keys to select the down arrow to reduce it, and you can see how it will be equal to the top with one click. Once you've done that, you'll notice that all of your text and everything is hidden, and all you have to do now is make sure it's selected, go to Shape Format, and select the "**Send Backwards**" option.

You can click once to see your picture, then again to see the text, which is gradually moving this shape backward while bringing all of the other information forward. You can double-click on the shape or move up to **Shape Format** and along to the Format Pane button here if you merely want to apply it as a border. This will open the Format Shape menu, where you can choose from a variety of alternatives under "**Fill**": You can either fill the existing color or remove it and just fill it with a transparent fill.

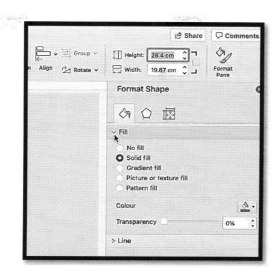

You may then make the line thicker or alter the color by going down to "**Line**" and clicking on "**Solid line**." If you wish to change the color, go to the drop-down menu and select Recent Colors, then select the desired color. As you can see, you now have an additional border. You can also use this to extend your border by filling it with a gradient. Select the shape again, and then go to "**Fill**," then "**Gradient fill**," where you can modify the gradient using these stops.

192

Once you've completed that, you'll notice that it looks wonderful on the outside, but the border patterns here are fairly close to the border's edge. If you copy and paste this current shape that you've placed in, you can see it's copied across to make it a little thicker like it is on the right-hand side. You must send it backward, and then you must reduce the size of it so that it fits within the border arts, and if it's a little clunky, you can go up and to the right to the height and just increase it one stop. To make sure everything is precisely aligned, go to **Shape Format**, make sure the shape is selected, then go to "**Align**," click on the drop-down, and select "**Align to Center**," then "**Align to Middle**."

This will place this shape in the center of your document, and you can do the same thing with the outside border: click on the outside border, go up to "**Align**," **align to the center**, and **align to the middle**. That means all of your borders are now precisely aligned, and you can modify the gradients if you wish. So, if you don't want the gradient, go across and select "**No fill**," and you'll just have a thicker line on the side of the border arts, or you can go back and select "**Gradient fill**," and then adjust the sliders accordingly. Remember, in your Gradient fill, you can modify all of these colors. You don't have to use white for your Gradient fill; you can use whatever color you like, and you can add markers if you want. Simply select a different hue by clicking on the plus symbol. You can also experiment with all of these colors to achieve the precise effect you want. Also keep in mind that the Border can be applied to a paragraph or a text, while the Page Border can be applied to the whole document, a section, the first page only, or all except the first page. If you are writing any documentation and you want the page border to be there from the second page onwards, or after the contents page, you can go with the last option.

CHAPTER NINETEEN
COLUMN OF TEXTS

Welcome to this chapter, where we'll look at word processors in Microsoft Word and discuss Columns and how you may make your text look like columns.

What you should know

When you think of a newspaper, the text doesn't appear like what you'd see on a standard Word page; instead, it's divided into little columns that run across the page. Let's have a look at how to make your content appear in columns.

Creating a Two- or Three-Column Text

The first step is to choose the text you want to transform. **Columns** can be found under the **Layout** tab. Then you can click on the columns drop-down menu, specifying whether you want one, two, three, or more columns.

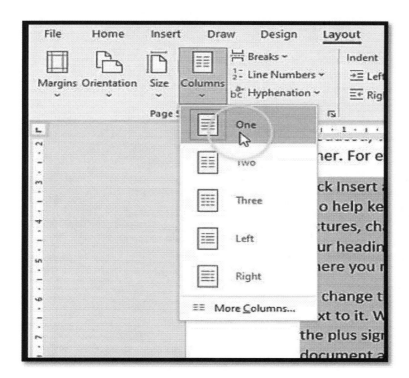

Let's use the three-column option for this illustration, and when you click on it, it will appear in your document.

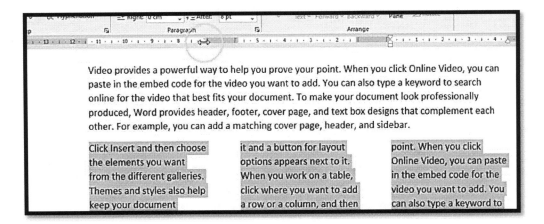

You'll note on the ruler that you can change the width of each one or the margins between them all if you wish. That is one method to go about it. The other option is to go to "**More Columns**" and see what else is there.

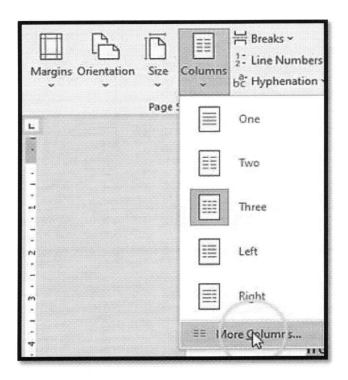

195

You can specify the number of columns you want and even draw a line between them, so if you only want to draw a line between them to separate them, you can do so by selecting that option. If you like, you can do it with just the selected text or the entire document.

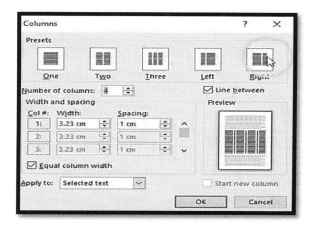

You may also make changes to these columns from here. Let's say you want the first column to be a little broader than the rest. You can increase the width of that column while decreasing the width of the others. So, the first column is exceptionally wide, followed by two smaller columns. You will see the line in the middle of the two columns if you click "**OK**," and you will also see that the first one is broader than the other two.

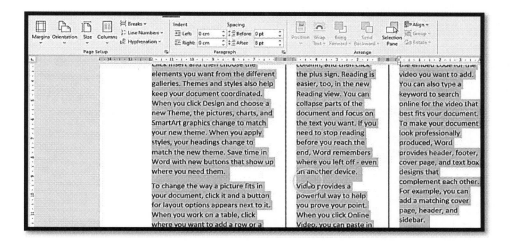

If you want to make it equal again, go back to "**More Columns**," make them all the **same width and spacing**, and it'll do the math for you automatically. You can also divide them into two columns if you choose.

Creating a four-column document

What if you want it to be divided into four columns? I'm going to demonstrate one small thing you can do with columns. You go to "More Columns" and change the "**Number of columns**" option to 4 to make it into four columns.

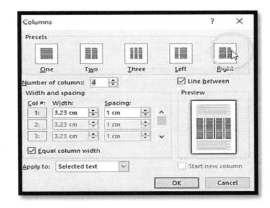

You'll see that there's also a "**Left**" and "**Right**" option, with a very thin first one on the left and a very thick first one on the right; you won't be able to use these options if you're doing 4-column.

A column on the left or right

Finally, let's take a short look at the Left and Right alternatives. If you go to the Columns drop-down and select "**Left**," you'll see that there's only a left column, but the rest of the text is still there.

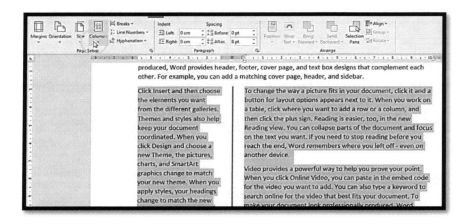

When you do it as a "**Right**," you'll get a large first column and everything on the right side.

Column Trick

Suppose you want a specific text to appear at the top of a column rather than in the middle. **Breaks** will be used to accomplish this, and they will be inserted at that specific point. Select the text, then go to "**Breaks**," under Page Breaks, and select "**Column**."

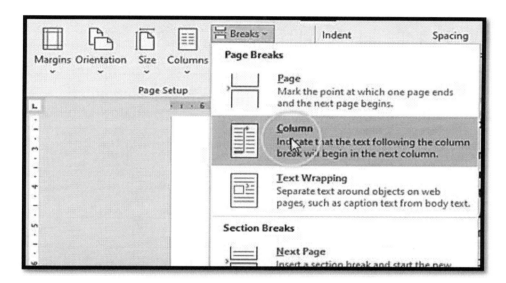

This shifts the text to the top of the page and moves everything down. You'll need to use a column break if you want to add additional text to the top of each column. That way, you can describe exactly how the columns should look, what should be at the top of each column, and how they should be brought up so that if you add additional text over here, it will not move up to the top since you already have what you want at the top.

A Quick Rundown

This concludes our discussion of columns. Remember to select the text you wish to convert to columns before going to **Layout**, **Columns**, and selecting your option or going to "**More Columns**" and using the options provided to you.

CHAPTER TWENTY
DOCUMENT GRAPHICS

In this chapter, we'll talk about inserting images from files or the internet into existing documents, as well as making the text flow properly around those pictures. We'll also go over the many options for modifying and editing any images in your document.

Adding Images

You can add pictures to a document in a few different ways. You can insert a picture saved to your hard drive or local drives, your desktop, or your pictures folder, into a document in one of two ways. The first is if you have a picture saved to your hard drive or local drives, and you've saved it to your desktop or your pictures folder, and the second is if you want to search for a picture available online and insert it directly into your word document.

From Your Local Drive

Let's take a look at the first option, which is inserting a locally saved image. It's worth mentioning that the photo will insert where you presently have your cursor in your document, so keep that in mind. Go to the **Insert** ribbon by clicking at the top of your page or the spot where you want the picture to be inserted, and you'll see "**Pictures**" and "**Online Pictures**" options in the Illustrations group.

- If you have an image stored locally or in a file, selects the "**Pictures**" option. If you click on it, your local drives will open up, and you can navigate through them to find the location where your images are saved.

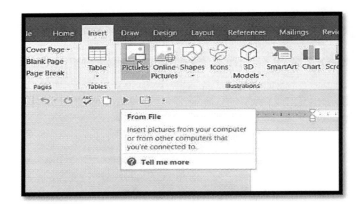

- You can now select it and then click "**Insert**," and your image will appear in your document.

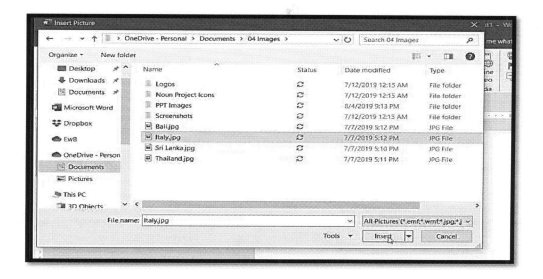

Inserting an Image from the Internet

Let's have a look at the second option, which is to insert an image from the internet. Return to your "**Insert**" ribbon and select the second option here, "**Online Pictures**."

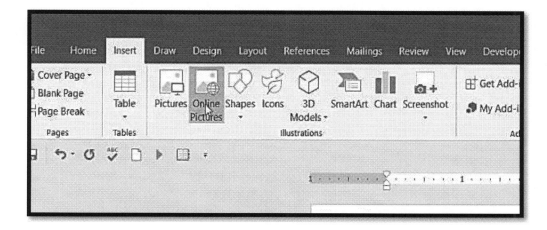

This will allow you to conduct a Bing image search using the keywords you enter in this field at the top. So, if you wanted to look for a photo of Italy, you could type in Italy and hit your Enter key, and it would look for pictures of Italy.

One thing to note is the "**Creative Commons only**" checkbox, which has a small tick in it. You have to be careful with photos because of copyright issues; you can't just go to Google and look for an image to use in your document, presentation, or whatever else you want to use it for. You should double-check that you have the authorization to use that image. So, what you're looking for in your photos is images with solely a Creative Commons License, which means you can use them without worrying about copyright issues. You can now select a photo you like and click "**Insert**," and your image will appear in your document. You can simply drag those handles in if you want to, and you'll notice that with these photos from the internet, you get a photo credit under it, but it also has a license, so you're okay to go. There's a lot more you can do with these images, which we'll get into later in this chapter.

Inserting Images into Existing documents

Now let's look at how to add images to a document that already has text in it. You saw how to insert a few images earlier, but it was only into a blank document. What's the difference if the document already has text? Let's see what happens. You already have your document and want to include an image anywhere within it. The first thing to remember is to place your cursor where you want to put the image and to select a photo from your local storage. So you'll go to the **Insert** menu, select "**Pictures**," and then navigate to your image. Select your image, then click "**Insert**" to place it in your document.

The comparison of mortgage rates nationwide reflects the market as 30-year fixed mortgages are

You can **resize** this. If you want it to fit on the page above, make it small but not too small.

Editing Images

When working with images, you'll notice a "**Picture Tools**" contextual ribbon appear, and you should be aware of what these contextual ribbons are for.

They only appear when you need them, so after you've clicked on your image, you'll see this Picture Tools ribbon with the Format sub ribbon, which contains all of the options you'll need to edit this image in your document. We'll go over some of these options right now.

Resizing an Image

If you wish to resize your image, look around the outside in the corners and in the middle for the resize controls or resize knobs. To resize the image, simply grab one of these controls and drag your image in. Now, if you hover over any of these at the top or bottom, you'll notice that they become a little diagonal double-headed arrow, which signifies that dragging them in diagonally will make them smaller.

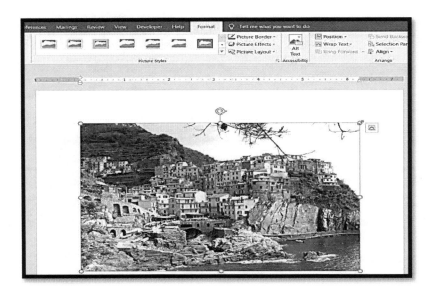

You can also utilize the side ones, although dragging them in would distort your image.

Image Alignment

If you wish to center this image on the page, go to your **home** ribbon and use the **Paragraph** group's alignment options. Simply choose "**Center**" to place the image in the center of the page.

Changing the position of an Image

You can also move this image from its present location to another in the document. Simply **click on your image**, **drag it up or down**, and **drop** it right **where your cursor is**, then let go of the mouse.

Changing the appearance of an image

For this, we'll start with the large group in the middle that reads "**Picture Styles**," and if you click the drop-down menu, you'll find that there are a lot of various styles you can use to change the look and feel of your image. You can get an idea of what they look like if you hover over them.

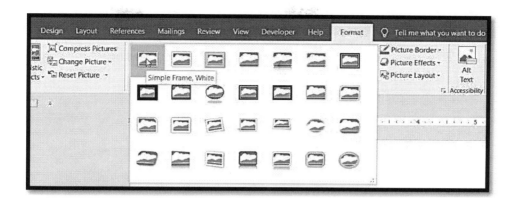

We have some **simple white frames** at the top, which create a great look. There's the **rounded rectangle**, which also has a reflection, creating a pretty wonderful effect.

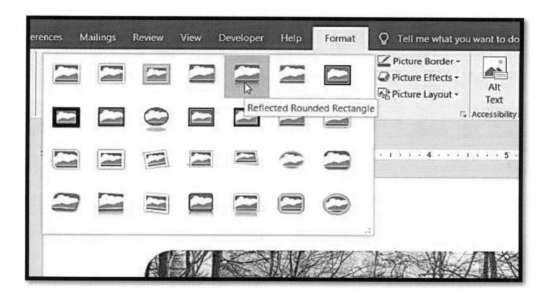

We have some **soft edges** and **Shadows**, and you can adjust things like the **Perspective** as well, tilt the image back, and modify the shape; there are a lot of things you can do here. Just keep in mind that you have a variety of picture styles to choose from.

Modifying an Image

Next to that Picture style, we have three options: "**Picture Border**, **Picture Effects**, and **Picture Layout**.

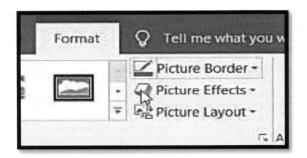

Adding and Removing an Image Border

If you simply want a plain border, **Picture Border** is the way to go. You can choose "black" from the palette and modify the border's weight to make it easier to see. As you'll see, the outside of the page now has a great plain black border.

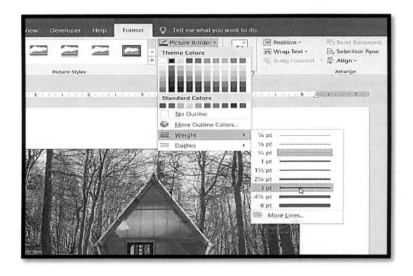

To eliminate your border, click "**Picture Border**" then "**No Outline**."

Changing the Image's Effects

You can use Picture Effects to add a **shadow**. Some of them are faint and difficult to notice, but you should now notice a small shadow across the bottom of the image. Inner shadows and Perspective shadows are also available, and some of these can be pretty dramatic. Just be mindful that you have shadow options.

Reflections come in a variety of forms. You may have noticed it in one of the image styles; they can be pretty effective, and there are a variety of methods to add a reflection.

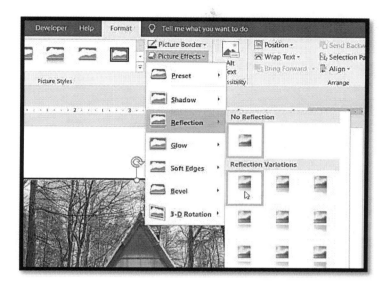

You can add a **Glow** to the outside if you wish, and you can choose from a variety of colors for your glow down here.

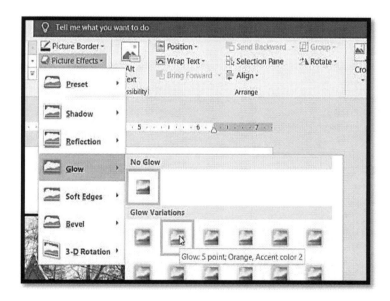

You could wish to add some **soft borders** to your image; however, some are more dramatic than others.

You can also give your image a **Bevel** effect.

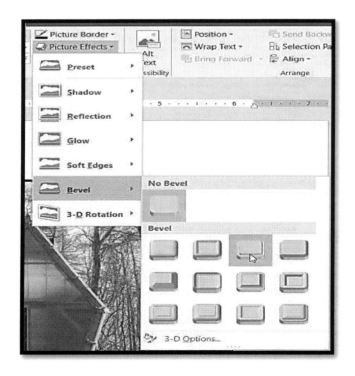

Finally, we have a **three-dimensional rotation**.

You can rotate your picture in a variety of ways if you want to, and it can be pretty attractive in some cases, so it's worth going into Picture Effects and playing around with those options.

Image layout

Then there's the **Picture Layout**. This could be useful if you want to make something that looks great with some writing over the top, and we have a variety of layouts here that you can hover over to see the many ways you can show a photo with text. That's a good one to use if you want the transparency to go over the top of a document.

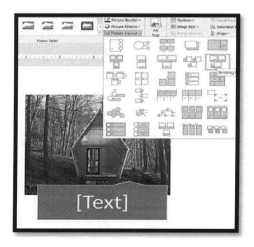

We've previously looked at a number of the other options on this toolbar in prior sections. You can change the position, wrap the text, align the image, and manually edit the height and width of the image, so rather than dragging these corners in, you might put in a precise height and width to resize this image.

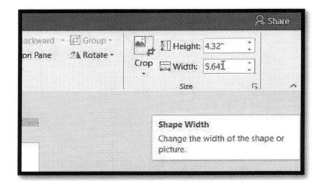

Wrapping Text around an Image

If you resize an image a little smaller, you can see that the text is above and below it, leaving white space on the side.

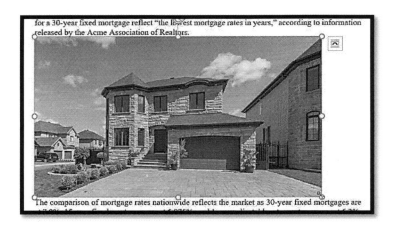

Now, you might just want to center that image and ignore the text above and below, but you should be aware that there are various text wrapping options available. You'll notice a small square with the words "**Layout options**" when you mouse over it. This allows you to customize how your object interacts with the words it's surrounded by. You can either click there or go up to your contextual ribbon, "**Picture Tools**" and the **Format** sub-tab and select "**Wrap Text**" from there.

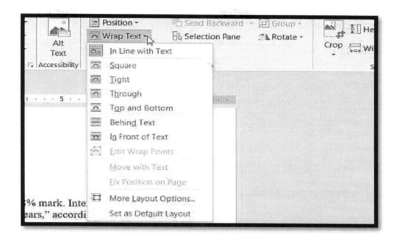

You'll see that the options you see are nearly identical to the Layout Options.

- You may now have "**In Line with Text**" chosen, which implies that the text will be placed above and below the picture. You do, however, have other options here: you have "**Square**," which you can see if you hover over it; with this one, the text flows around the outside of the picture.

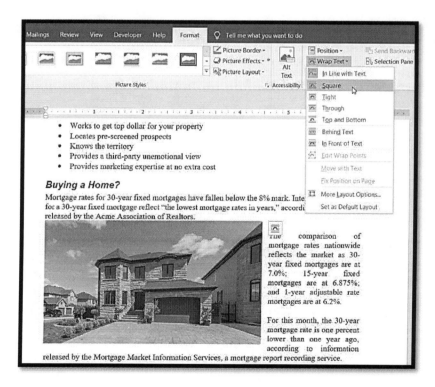

- If you select "**Tight**," the text will be a little closer to the picture edge or a little tighter to the picture.

- You also have the option of going "**Through**." If you select this, the text will run through the image if you move the photo slightly to the right. Although this makes it difficult to read, there may be times when you wish to use the "**Through**" text wrapping.

- There's also "**Top and Bottom**," which positions your text at the top or bottom of the image.

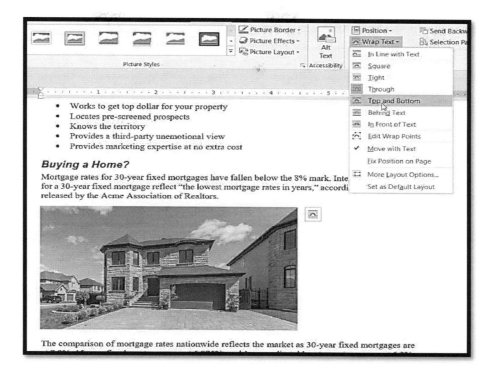

- We have a feature called "**Behind Text**," and if you enable it, the picture will appear behind the text.

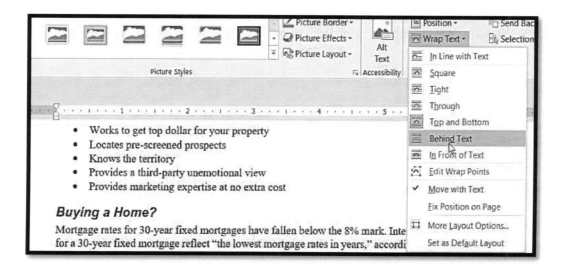

- It can be set to "**In Front of Text**," which means it will hide whatever is behind it.

You must ensure that you select the appropriate option based on your documents. If you're not happy with the way your text looks after you've wrapped it around your image, make some little tweaks. You can remedy this by making the image larger or smaller to fit everything on one line; it's up to you to decide how you want to handle it. It's worth experimenting with them to get your text to flow just the way you want it around, though, or in front of that image. Now, because there are so many, we'll look at some of the other options you have when it comes to images.

Getting rid of an image's background

Let's return to the first group so you can learn more about the "**Remove Background**" tool.

You will notice it reads **"automatically remove unwanted portions of the picture"** if you mouse over it. This would be beneficial if, for example, you wanted to eliminate the background from a picture and only keep the image.

Let's have a look at how it works because it's a little tricky.

- When you select "**Remove Background**," Word will try to figure out what you want to keep and what you want to remove, but it often can't tell what the background is and what you want to preserve, so it takes a guess. In the image below, all the items it's now going to remove are shown in purple, and you may alter this to keep or remove certain regions.

A background removal toolbar will appear at the top and will allow you to mark sections to keep or remove.

- If you say "**Mark areas to remove or keep**," you simply draw the pencil over the area you want to keep or delete, and as you know, it doesn't always get it exactly right, so you'll have to fiddle around with it a little to get it just right.

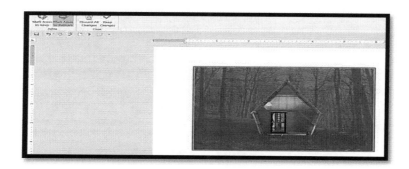

- Once you're comfortable with it, click the tick to say "**Keep Changes**," and there you have it, the background has been removed.

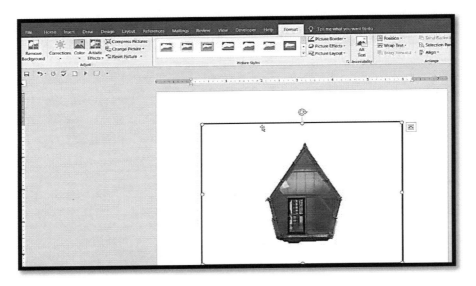

Correcting an Image

If you click a picture and go to the Format ribbon, you'll see some "**Corrections**" options.

This is commonly linked to your image's color, contrast, and sharpness. You have some **sharpening** options at the top here, as well as some brightness and contrast images, which, again, if you hover over, will modify the brightness of the picture.

Color is the next choice along, so if you want to recolor or modify the color of this picture, you can do so by selecting any of these options, and you can get even more colors or variants by selecting the option at the bottom.

Lastly, we have **Artistic Effects**. You can make your photo look like a drawing, a mosaic, a painting, or some scribble here. All of these are options that you can explore.

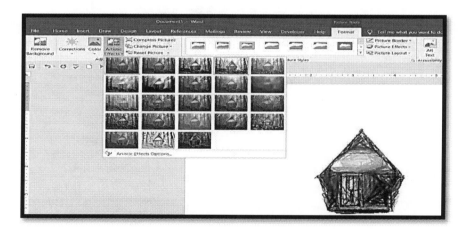

Compressing an image

One thing to keep in mind when using pictures in Word is that if you use a lot of them, your document will grow in size. It's always a good idea to compress your photos in your document to ensure that everything loads as quickly as possible and that you don't have any troubles, and we have the option for that right here.

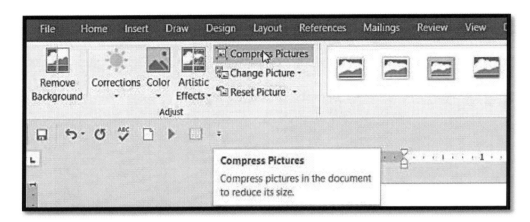

When you click "**Compress Pictures**," you'll be asked if you want to "**Apply compression only to this picture**" you've chosen. If you only have one picture in the document, this is acceptable; however, if you have a lot of pictures, you should untick this because it will compress everything in the document.

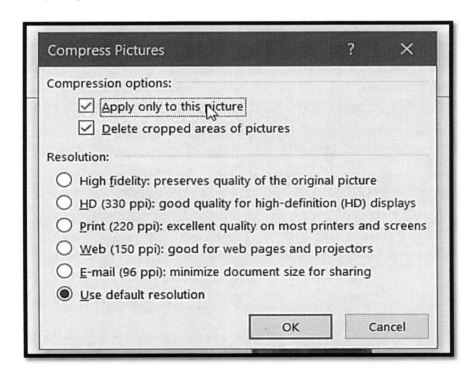

"**Delete cropped areas of a picture**" is another option available here. If you've gotten rid of the background on a picture, you haven't completely removed that from the document, and you could easily undo what you did with the "Remove Background" and restore it, thus the background is still there even though we can't see it. This option will erase any cropped sections of the image, which will assist in reducing the file size.

Changing a Picture

You also have the option to change a photo, so if you want to replace the current picture with something else, you can do so from a file, an online source, or an icon.

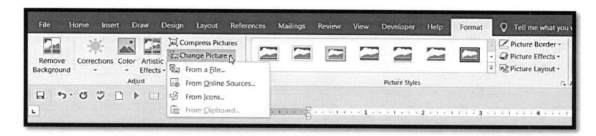

Restoring an Image

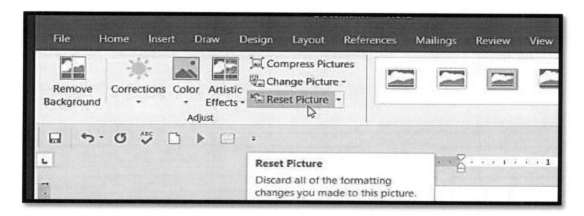

If you've made a lot of modifications to an image and don't want any of them, you can restore it to its previous state by resetting it.

CHAPTER TWENTY-ONE
COMMENTS ON YOUR TEXT

You'll learn the fundamentals of tracking changes and commands in Office 365 in this chapter. However, with small adjustments to some of the tabs, the same applies to several other versions of Microsoft Word. Turning on track changes, accepting and rejecting track changes, hiding tracked changes, adding and deleting comments, and comparing two documents are all covered in this section. If you printed a copy of your work and asked a friend to proofread it, they would most likely mark the faults in red ink and put any suggestions in the margins. Isn't it more convenient if you could do it electronically? You can do so with Word by using the "**Track Changes**" and "**Comments**" options.

Enabling Track Changes

We're going to **enable Track Changes** right now so you can see what it means. To do so, navigate to the top-left **Review** tab and select the "**Track Changes**" command.

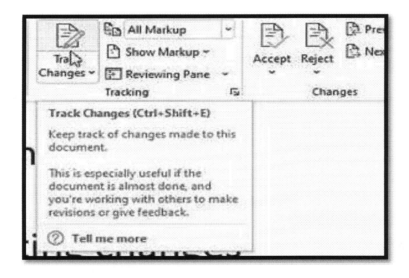

As you can see, it's now grayed out, indicating that any modifications you make will be monitored. With this command enabled, you can now make any modifications to the document and they will display as markup, which is Word's version of the conventional red pen. When you erase text, for example, it is not removed; instead, it is crossed out, and when you add more text, it is underlined, as shown below.

219

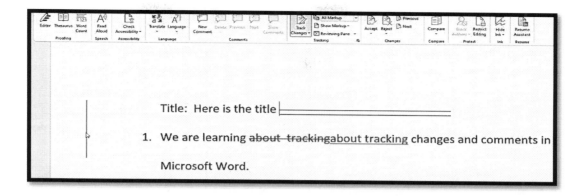

This allows the document's owner to see what modifications you've made before integrating them into the final draft.

Adding a Comment

By selecting the text, you want to remark on, right-clicking, and dropping down to the "**New Comment**" instruction, you can also write comments in the margin.

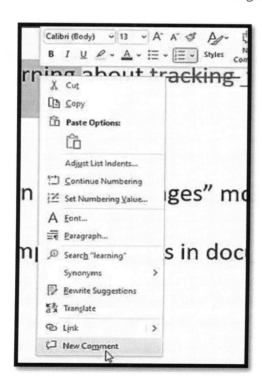

You can also go to the **Review** tab and select "**New Comment**." You can now add a comment, which the document's owner will see once you share it with them. When you're finished, simply click anywhere outside the comment to make it part of the others you're making.

Accepting or rejecting a comment

What happens if you're on the other side of the document? Let's imagine you're sending this document to someone else, that person has the option of accepting or rejecting the changes to make them permanent.

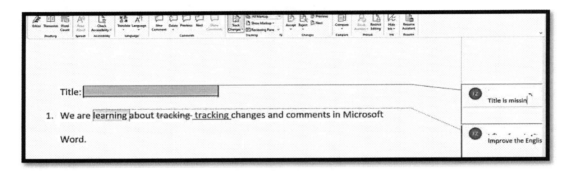

Looking at the changes made from the example above, you can accept or reject the comment by right-clicking on them.

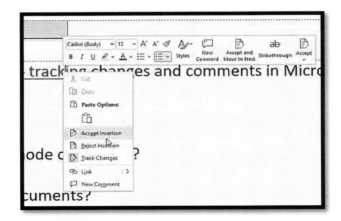

You can either perform this for all of the additions or subtractions at once, or you can do it one at a time. If you want to complete everything at once, select "**Accept all Changes**" from the "**Accept**" drop-down menu.

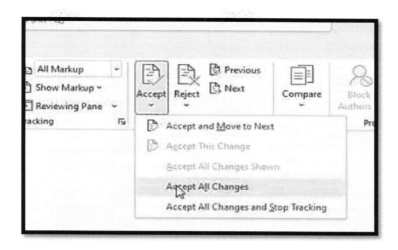

In general, accepting all modifications is not encouraged because the other person may not be as knowledgeable in the topic as you are, therefore you should carefully accept or reject changes. Except for the comments, all additions and subtractions will be done automatically as advised by your collaborator.

Commenting and Replying

You can either respond to the comments or mark the problem as resolved once you've addressed the issue.

You'll notice that it's now grayed out, indicating that you've fixed the problem. If you need to make any adjustments, you can click on the drop-down and reopen it by choosing "**Reopen**" if you need to add another comment.

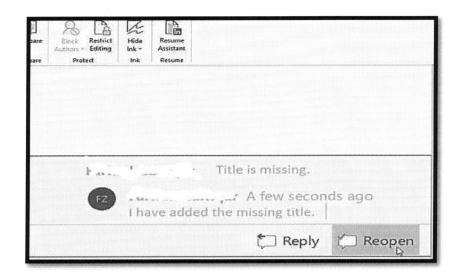

You'll get a hint that there are comments while working on your text. You can erase these comments by clicking on the comment box and selecting the **delete comment** button if you are satisfied that the changes made are acceptable to everyone.

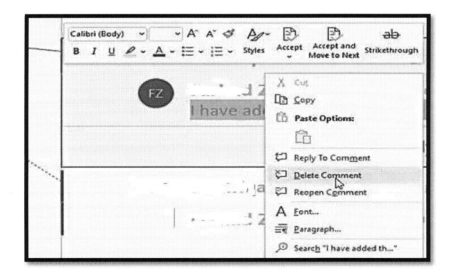

You can also do it from the **Review** tab by selecting **one after another** or **all of the comments** in the document to **delete**. However, if you need to make another modification, there is additional space here where you can simply make the adjustment and notify others that you've done so using the "**Track changes**" modes.

Organizing your document

Now that you've made all of the modifications, you'd like to see the document in its refined state; how can you achieve that? Remember that some markups in your document are visible while you're making modifications. By navigating to the "**Tracking**" group and clicking on the **Markup** options and drop-down, which contains **All Markups**, **Simple Markup**, **no markup**, and **Original**, you can remove these markups. You'll select "**No Markup**," and the document will be displayed in its final form.

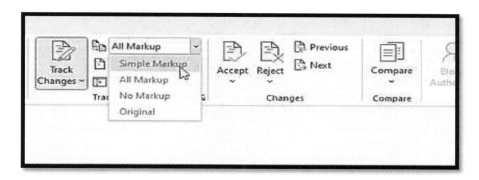

It's crucial to note, though, that the changes are still in effect because you haven't accepted or rejected them yet. As a result, when other people look at these documents, they'll be able to see the markups. After you've completed all of the modifications, you should accept the document before forwarding it. You can make modifications, edit the document, and add comments in this manner.

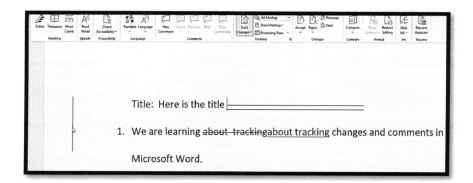

Another thing to keep in mind is that while making changes to your document, you may notice a **small grayed outline**; clicking on it will hide all of your modifications, and when you click, it will change to a red line, indicating that certain changes are hidden here. When you click again, it displays all of the adjustments you've made.

Comparing Two Versions of a Document

The next item we'll look at is how to activate track changes. Let's say you're working on a document with a coworker who made some modifications but neglected to switch on the track changes. You can use the "**Compare**" option here in such cases. You'll need two versions of the documents to use this "**Compare**" option: one is the original and the other is the changed version. As a result, you must choose between the original document and the edited version, which may have been created by someone else.

When you click "**OK**" after selecting both the original and revised documents, it will display three types of documents: one is **the original document**, the second is **the revised document**, and the third is **the compared document**, which is the version obtained by combining the two and will display the changes made.

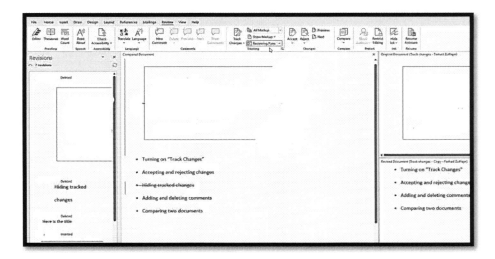

225

Tracking and Reviewing Changes

When you click on the "**Reviewing Pane**," another box will appear, detailing the changes made in the updated version.

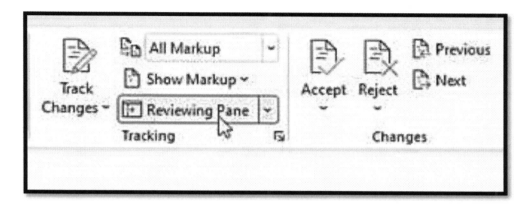

- In the example below, there were five bullet points in the original document that included '**hiding track changes**,' but your collaborator or partner has omitted this one bullet point from the revised version. It indicates that someone deleted the '**hiding track changes**' bullet point in the Compared document.

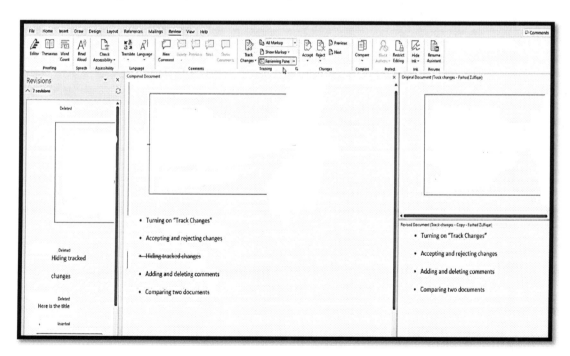

- The original document stated, "**How to Compare Changes in Documents**," whereas the revised version states, "**How to Compare Differences in Documents**," with "**changes**" substituted by "**differences**."

Even if someone forgets to switch on the track changes, you can still study and compare two documents if you have both the original and revised versions. If you're working on a large project with a large document, such as a 50 or 60-page document, it'll be impossible to look at individual changes without this track change option. That's why, whenever you're working with others, we recommend utilizing Track Change mode to keep track of updates and send ideas back and forth so you can collaborate on the same document with friends, family, or coworkers. Finally, once you've compared these documents, simply save this newly updated version, and it will appear on your computer after you've saved it.

CHAPTER TWENTY-TWO
MAIL MERGE

We'll look at Mail Merge in this chapter. What is a Mail Merge, and how does it work? Let's say you have a letter that you need to send to a group of individuals, but you want to personalize it with their names and other facts in each letter and all of these details are stored in another location, such as a spreadsheet or a database. You could either manually generate each letter in an attempt to personalize each one, or you could blend the data from the spreadsheet or database into your word document.

Two things are involved in mail merging

The Time-wasting Process

Take a look at the sample letter below, which is intended to be sent to persons who are attending an adventure camp and for whom we need to write their contact information. To personalize the letter, we'll need to know what class they're in, which team they're on, their team leader, and their campsite, all of which will be based on a database or spreadsheet, and that's what we'll send them.

You can also see that we have a spreadsheet below that covers all of their names, surnames, grades, and classes in one place. We could do this manually by copying this document and pasting it into another page of the paper, where we can now enter everyone's updated information. Then we can go through and update these elements one by one by hand; but this will exhaust us because we will be taking so long to complete a basic task. That would be a waste of time if we had to do it for every single person's letter, so how can we do it all at once? Let's have a look at it.

The Easier Way

First and foremost, we'll go to "**Mailings**," which is where we'll be working. All of our steps will be over here if we click on that. There is a "**Start Mail Merge**" option, as well as a "**Select the Recipients**" option, where we can edit which recipients we want to send to, **insert fields**, **evaluate the results**, and then **finish** them.

There are the stages we will discuss, and they're all right there for us to follow. We'll proceed from left to right, and it'll be really simple.

The Mail Merge process

1. **Starting a mail merge** is the first step. You must inform the Word processor that this document will be merged with another document.

2. Then you must **choose the recipients**, or, in other words, decide where you will acquire the information. Is this information coming from a spreadsheet or a Word document? Data from a text file or a database could be used.

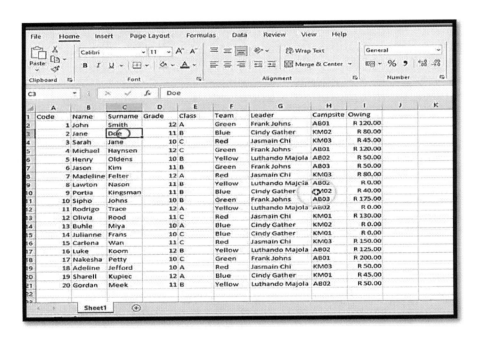

If you don't want to send the information to everyone in your source or the location where all of our data is stored, you can edit the recipients' list or only send it to specific persons on that list.

You can narrow it down a little so that you just utilize specific persons.

3. After that, you must **insert fields**. These are the fields you'll want to include in your document, and they'll come from either your source or your recipients. If you wish to put their names as fields or any other information about them that you've saved in your source document or the recipients', this is where you'll receive your fields and utilize them to insert them into the mail merge.

229

4. Then you can **preview** your results to make sure everything is working, and it will show you one of the first letters that are compiled from the first document with all the source fields, so you can see if it is in the appropriate format.
5. Once you're satisfied with the results, you can proceed to the **final merge**, which will create a new document containing all of the letters, each of which will be personalized with the information from the source.

With that out of the way, let's get right into it.

Creating the Mail Merge

Get Started

The first step is to **decide which type of mail merging to use**. You can do Envelopes and Labels, and when you do those, it will ask you for the size of the envelopes or labels. You can configure it so that it will automatically determine the paper size to make your life easier. These will be discussed in the next chapter, but for now, we'll focus on letters, which is what we've chosen.

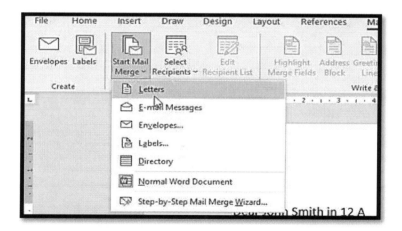

The Recipient List

Step two is to choose our recipients. We'll choose where we want to acquire the information for this letter from here. We can create a new list or make good use of an existing one. As you can see, we already have a spreadsheet with all of the information, which we'll combine with this document. Select "**Recipients**" and "**Use an existing list**" from the drop-down menu.

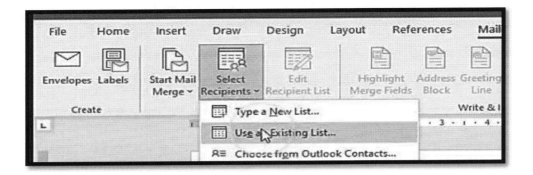

This will open file explorer, and all we have to do now is click on the data we want to open and then click "**Open**." We've now linked this document to that specific spreadsheet.

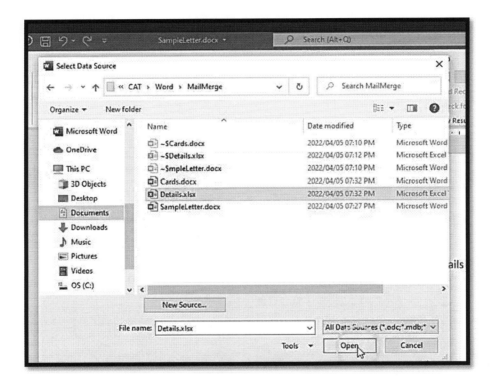

In a spreadsheet, you may have numerous sheets, thus it will ask which one you are using. Please keep in mind that if this were a **database**, it would ask you which **table** or **query** you wanted to use. Your source is dependent on what happens over here. Also, if your first row contains Column Headers, you can click the box at the bottom of this window to indicate that. If you're working with data on a spreadsheet, make sure it's right at the top and that the first heading is in A1 and flows across the page; this will make things much easier. We can now proceed to click "**OK**."

Making Changes to a Recipient List

If we only wanted to send data in one column, for example, we'd want to use this list but only for those individuals. If that's the case, we can come here and click "**Edit the Recipient List**," where we can see the entire list of names in our source and uncheck the ones we don't want to include.

If we wanted to, we could sort it or apply a filter. If you want to change your recipient list, you can use a variety of criteria.

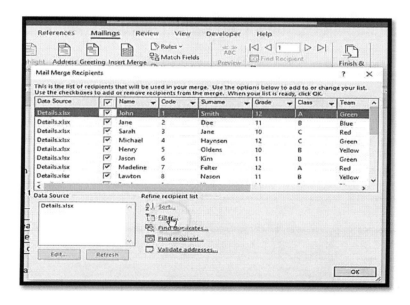

It may be sorting or deleting duplicates, rather than just excluding people. To continue, click "**OK**" after you've finished updating your list.

Inserting the Fields

Now that we have our recipients, we can go on to the third group. First, we need to make a list of all the headers in our recipient list, and now that we've linked this word document to that spreadsheet, when we go to "**Insert Merge Field**," you'll notice that all of those headings are now potential fields that we could enter when we click on the drop-down menu.

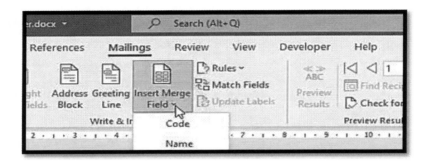

This means that if we want to enter anyone's name, we'll use the name field instead of the individual's name, and for the surname, we'll use the surname field, so whatever's in the surname block for each person will go into that particular location.

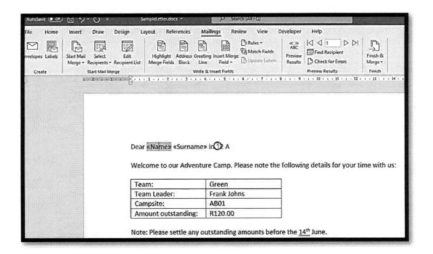

When you utilize the "**Insert Merge Fields**," you'll find that you can't just write in those weird little arrows, but you can see that it's gone gray when you click on it. Now, all we have to do is simply filling in the fields as we require them.

Previewing the Merged Documents

We've built our Mail merge, selected our recipients, and made any necessary edits; we've also entered these fields; we can now evaluate our results before doing the final merging.

If you click on "**Preview Results**," you'll see the page with all those small fields.

Merged at Last

Now that we've reached this point, we can move on to the next step, "**Finish & Merge**." By selecting this option, we get a list of different options for completing the process. We can **send emails** in bulk, **print documents**, or **modify each one individually**.

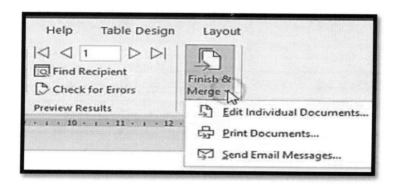

There are still some more options here if we chose to edit them individually. We could either do the first five records or the entire set. Now we can click "**OK**," and you'll notice that a new document has appeared.

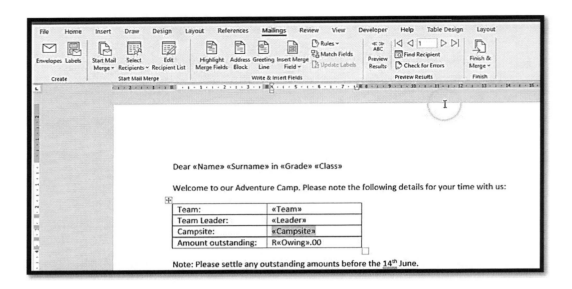

As you can see, all of the fields are filled in, but there are more pages to go down, and on page two, there's another individual with their information; as you continue down this document, you'll notice that it contains everyone's information. Keep your originals and save this as a separate document.

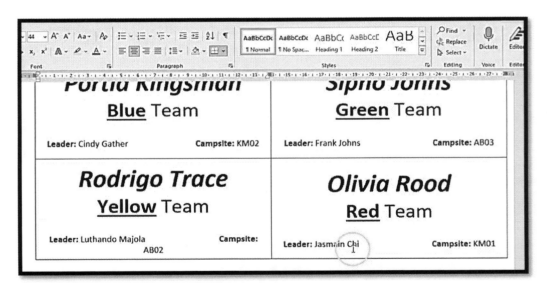

If you have numerous letters on the same page and want to proceed to the next record, you can go to "**Rules**" and play around with all of the rules, but in this case, you just need to click on "**Next Record**."

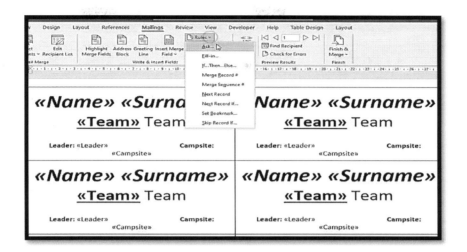

All you have to do now is put the Next Record on the back of each of these. You don't have to do it for the last one because it will be done automatically on the next page, but it must be done for all of them.

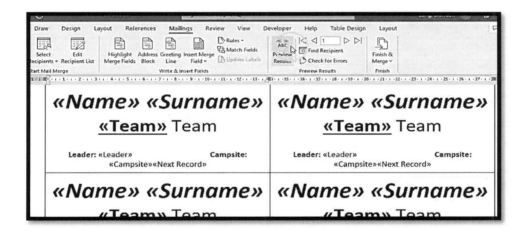

If you go to preview, you'll see a page with everyone's cards on it, and if we run out of records, it'll simply fill in the blanks. Hopefully, you now have a better understanding of how a mail merge works. If you choose, you can now print and laminate the document.

Keep in mind the following five steps: You go to the **Mailings** tab, **start the mail merge**, **choose your recipients**, and edit them, if necessary, after which you can **search your fields**, **preview** it to make sure it matches everything, and if it doesn't, go back to make the necessary changes, and then **Finish and Merge** and you're done.

CHAPTER TWENTY-THREE
LABELS AND ENVELOPES

Welcome to this chapter, where we'll go through how to work with envelopes and labels. We discussed mail merge in the last chapter, and you became familiar with the Mailings tab. We'll look at the first group in this chapter, which is about creating labels and envelopes. In this first section of this chapter, you'll learn how to work with envelopes in Word.

You'll see how to work with envelopes in Word in the first portion of this chapter. You can print any size envelope, and your Mailings ribbon displays all of your envelope options. We have two options in the first group, the "**Create**" group, if you click on there: **Envelopes and Labels**. In the next section of this chapter, we'll look at labels, but for now, let's begin with envelopes.

Working with Envelopes

After clicking "**Envelopes**," the Envelopes and Labels dialog box appears; note that this is the same window that you'll use for both envelopes and labels, and the two tabs at the top are for envelopes and labels.

You'll be on the Envelopes tab right now, and you'll notice that the first thing you need to do is type in a delivery address for the envelope's front.

You have a little drop-down just here that will allow you to select something from your Outlook address book, but you can also manually type in a delivery address that you've already copied to your clipboard, and then the second large box we have here is a return address; it's always good to put this in if you can so that if the letter doesn't get delivered for whatever reason, the letter will have a return address. You've got your return address in there, and you've got your delivery dress, which is wonderful, and you'll be able to see where those two elements will show when you print the envelope in the preview window on the right-hand side. If you don't want a return address, you don't have to have one. If you wish to remove it, you can click the "**Omit**" checkbox just here, and if you check the preview again, you'll see that it's now gone.

There's also a checkbox for "**Add electronic postage**" here. If you add it, a popup may appear, stating that you'll need to install electronic postage software before you can use this function, which you can get from the Microsoft Office website.

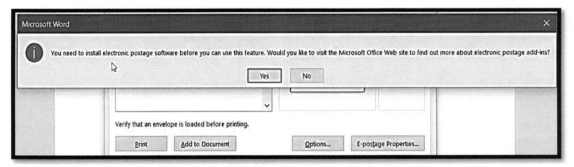

Electronic postage allows you to add a barcode to the top of your envelope, which the post office could scan and use to determine how to route your mail. Just be mindful that the option exists, and if you think it will be useful to you, you might want to look into getting the Word add-in for electronic postage. We have this tiny button next to the Preview window to the right that reads "**Feed**" and shows you how to feed your envelope into the printer. You can see that you feed it in from the bottom, with the return address on the left-hand side if it is closest to you. That's just a handy little diagram to keep you from putting your envelope in the wrong direction.

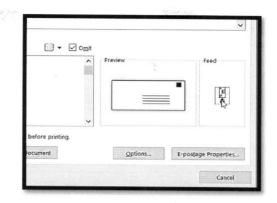

Let's have a look at some of the other options available. You can select the size of your envelopes by clicking the "**Options**" button.

Yours may have a default size of 10, which is a common envelope size, but you can measure the size of your envelope and select the appropriate size from the drop-down menu.

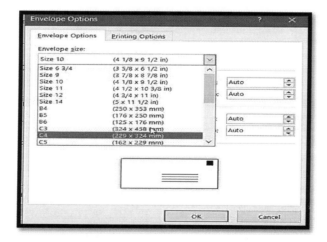

If you like, you could also modify the font for the delivery and return addresses, as well as the spacing, which is how far the delivery address and return addresses appear from the left and top. You'll see a preview of your changes as you make them, so you can see how they'll look.

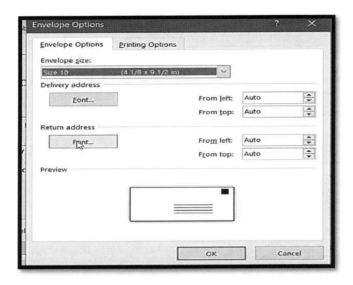

There's also a **Printing options** box, which displays the various feed methods available when feeding envelopes into the printer. You can **rotate clockwise** or **clockwise** and choose "**Face Up**" or "**Face Down**." Before you print your envelope, keep in mind that you have some more customization possibilities.

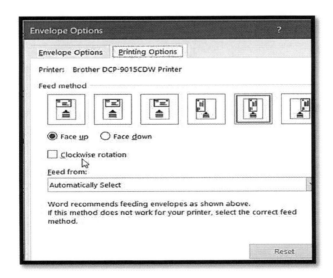

You'll need to add an item for the "**E-postage Properties**" option, so if you've added electronic postage, this will also be active.

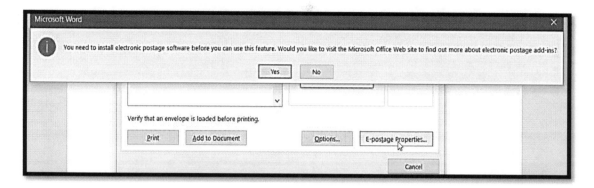

Finally, you have the option of **printing** from a printer directly. You can simply print when you've loaded your envelopes.

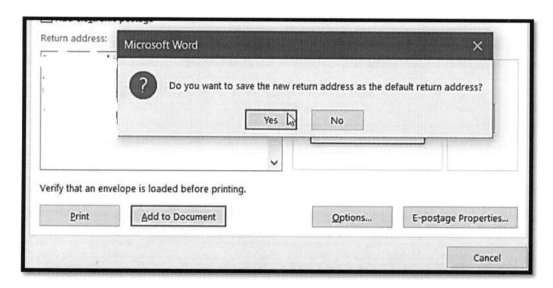

Alternatively, you can choose "**Add to Document**," which will prompt you to save the new return address as the default return address when you click it. This can be handy in some cases, especially if you're printing the same thing over and over. You're going to say yes, and there's your envelope waiting for you.

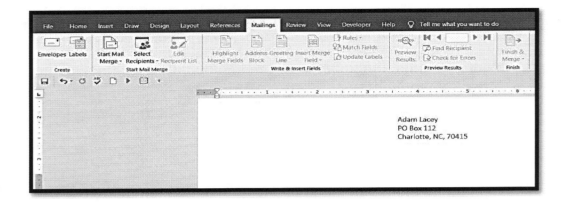

You might want to go in now and make some changes, such as slightly moving that address up, which you can do because it's simply a text field. The good thing about this is that you have your envelope at the top and then space at the bottom to enter your letter or document, so you can print everything at once. You can put your envelopes in one feeder and then put your plain letter paper or A4 paper in another tray and print the document right away. Envelopes are rather straightforward to put up.

Working with Labels

We looked at how to print and customize an envelope in the previous section, and now we'll look at how to print labels. When we talk about labels, we're talking about those adhesive sheets of paper that you can peel off and place onto packages or whatever else you choose, and Word has a great feature for organizing and printing labels. If you go back to the **Mailings** ribbon and look in the first group, you'll see a "**Labels**" option, which you should select.

You'll see that this is the identical window that we dealt with in the last section; it's only that this time it's defaulting to the Labels tab.

You would type your address in the address field, and then select what you want to print from the drop-down menu. You have the option of printing a whole page of the same label (with this address on every label) or simply a single label. You might be wondering why you'd want a complete page of the same label; well, if you're printing a full-page, having a couple of sheets of pre-printed labels with your company address on them is a fantastic idea. If you choose a single label, you'll need to tell Word where it is on the page by identifying which row and column it belongs to. Let's have a look at our Label options for a moment. Your printer information is the first part at the top, and this is where you tell Word where your labels are located.

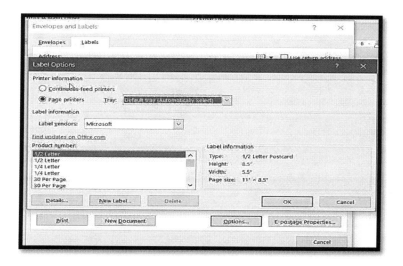

Then you must choose a label from the various options available on this page. The "**Avery US Letter**" is a popular label vendor, and there are a variety of labels to choose from.

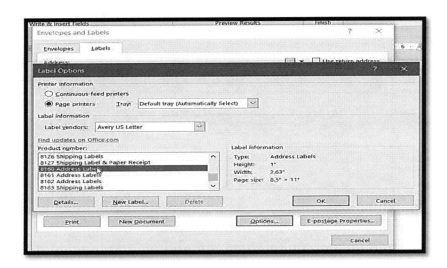

When you click on the **numbers**, you'll see the label information on the side, which will tell you the precise height and width of the label as well as the page size, so you can browse through and locate the one you need. "**8160 Address Labels**" is a popular choice. You have the option of **printing directly from the printer** or **creating a new document**. Now that you have that address on all of your labels, you can just load them into the printer and print them off.

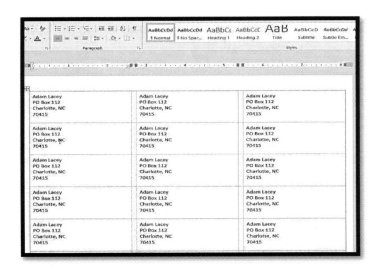

That's fantastic; however, because you chose full-page, each label has the same name and address, as you can see in the image above. You might be asking how to get different names and addresses onto distinct labels, which is where **Mail Merge** comes in.

CHAPTER TWENTY-FOUR
WRITERS' TOOLS

In this chapter, we'll look at various tools that can help you stand out as a writer. As a writer, you'll need to be familiar with these techniques to make your work much easier to read and comprehend for your audience. So, without further ado, let's get started.

Adding a Formula

If your table contains any numbers or numerical data, you can include a formula that adds them all together. First, add a blank row at the bottom, and then go to the Layout ribbon and add a "**Formula**" to your word table under the "**Data**" group.

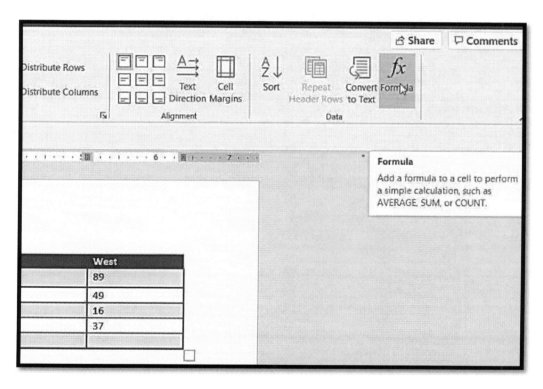

It recognizes that you have numbers above the point where you clicked and automatically enters the formula. So, it equals sum, followed by "Above" in brackets; "**=SUM (ABOVE).**" When you click "OK," the sum is added.

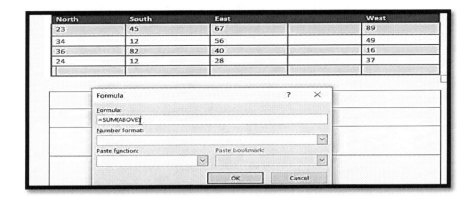

North	South	East	West	
23	45	67		89
34	12	56		49
36	82	40		16
24	12	28		37

North	South	East	West
23	45	67	89
34	12	56	49
36	82	40	16
24	12	28	37
117	37.75		

In Word, you can utilize roughly 18 distinct functions in formulae, and all of them are listed in the **"Paste Function"** drop-down menu. If you'd rather do an average computation than a total, you can do so by selecting ABOVE, BELOW, LEFT, or RIGHT, depending on where your numbers are present.

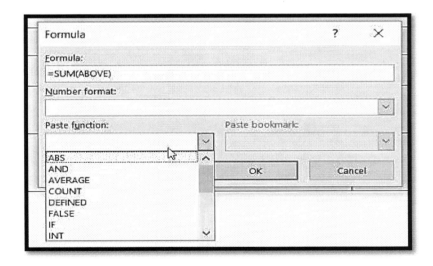

For example, all you have to do is delete the sum function and select **AVERAGE**, then type in "**ABOVE**" and click "**OK**" to get the average.

247

Collaborating With Others

In this section, you will see how you can **collaborate on a Word document** with other people without needing to send attachments back and forth. In the past, if you've wanted to collaborate on a document with others you needed to send an attachment back and forth and what typically tends to happen is someone might say document one then someone responds with their edits and its document two and maybe someone else had a version of document three and then you have to merge them all and you just end up in this really bad situation of different versions and just a versioning mess. Luckily with Microsoft Word, you can now work together on a document that's in the **Cloud**. In this section, you will learn step by step how you can do this in Word and these same things apply to the other office apps.

Uploading your File

In the past what you would have done is if you need help on a document, you would have emailed it to someone and then they would have made some edits and they would send it back but if you have multiple people doing that it becomes very complicated. What you want to do is to get other people to help you with this and the best way to do that is to **get this document into the Cloud** so everyone can work on the same version of the file. The version you have on your desktop is referred to as a **Local copy** because it's located on your computer; a **Cloud copy** is something that everyone can access. That's one of the benefits of putting a file in the cloud, not only is it safer in the cloud, because if something happens to your PC you would lose this file on your desktop, but other people can also access it as long as you permit them to access it and then you can work on that file together all at the same time. To do that within Microsoft Word there is an option up here in the top right-hand corner that says "**Share**".

You go ahead and click on that and now what it says is to upload a copy of your document to OneDrive to share it with others so if you want to share this document you need to put it in the Cloud.

What you could do is once you upload it you could remove the copy or the local file that's on your computer. This probably makes sense because if you have one in the cloud and one on your computer it might get confusing you have multiple copies of the file. You can check that box and get rid of the copy on your computer once you put it in the Cloud. It also gives you the option to attach the file as either a PDF or as a Word attachment to an email but once again you could end up with version issues where one person makes updates and then that doesn't match your version. Instead, what you should do is get this file in the cloud and to do that you're going to select your account here and what it's going to do now is to upload this file to OneDrive.

Granting Permissions

Now that it's placed the file in OneDrive you can now share this file with others and you have a few different options in terms of the permissions that you can set here. You can allow anyone with the link to edit it or only people in my organization to edit it. You could also allow editing or make it read-only so other people can't edit it. You can also set an expiration date on when they won't have access anymore, you can even set a password to a file or you could prevent downloading of the file; there are lots of different controls you could use.

249

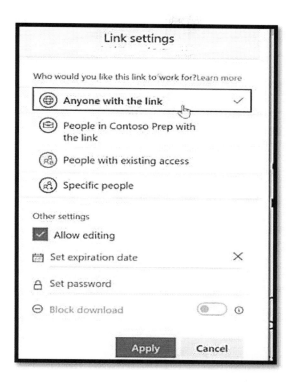

After applying these settings, you can type in the email address of someone you want to send it to and then Microsoft will send an email to that person with a link to the document. You can also copy the link to the document, paste it where you want to share it, and then they can access the document.

Accessing your Shared Files

Now the file is in the Cloud if you want to know where the file went, on the website **office.com**, what you are going to do is click on **OneDrive**. This is where you can see all of the files that you have saved in the cloud.

Once it's uploaded your file to OneDrive, not only can you share directly from Word, one of the things you could do is right here next to the name of the file you also can share it from here and the same dialog that you saw in Word pops up here within OneDrive also allowing you to share the file.

Editing a Shared File

Let's say a friend of yours has asked you to help out with a document and shared the file link with you. What you are going to do is paste in the URL of that document and this is going to now open up the Word document and you can start working on the document.

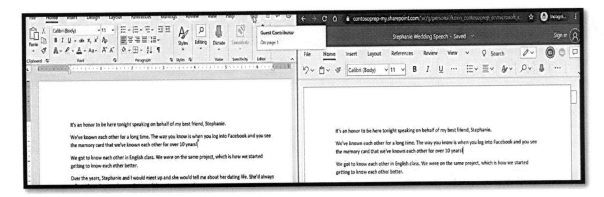

If you share this document with someone, as they start typing on the document from their window, you can see all of the edits that are happening in real-time. Up here in the ribbon as well, you can see who else is within the document.

If they are logged in with their account, you'd also be able to see who exactly is within the document. This summarizes how you can work together with others on a document in real-time and as mentioned earlier, this isn't just limited to Microsoft Word; you could also use it with Excel, or PowerPoint, you could share your file with others and then you could work together on content so you don't just have to work alone in isolation.

Inserting Special Characters

You'll learn how to type foreign letters and special characters that aren't on your keyboard in this part. We utilize an English keyboard by default unless we are in a place where there are keyboards that are specific to that country's language. You may occasionally need to enter foreign letters or special characters that are not present on the keyboard you're using at work, school, or even at home, but thanks to **ASCII (American Standard Code for Information Interchange)**, we can do so. This simply refers to a readable text that is not in binary form, and with the help of ASCII codes, you can overcome the difficulty of writing foreign characters; of course, there are a variety of **ASCII** codes available. To overcome this difficulty, we will look at options that are already available to us. The **Character map** is what it's called. If you type "**Character map**" into your Windows search area, you'll get a list of results.

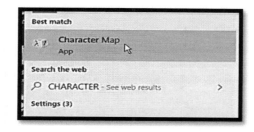

This is a system tool that can be found even in far older versions of Windows, and it provides you with a list of readily available foreign and unusual characters.

Inserting Characters such as Π, Ñ, Ç, and Ũ

Let's say you are trying to type a Spanish character which is the letter N with a special character at the top (Ñ). You may need to write a Spanish name with a particular character that isn't available on the English keyboard at work. To find it, go to the Character map you've already opened and look for it. Now **click on that character**, then on the "**Select**" button here, then on the "**Copy**" button beside it, and this character will be copied to the clipboard once you click on the Copy button. This works for both uppercase and lowercase letters.

Now all you have to do is paste it into your document. As you can see, you've used this character map to enter the foreign character you require. This character map offers a lot of lists of characters from various languages if you scroll through it. Consider the letter U with a special character at the top (Ũ). If you wish to use it in your document, follow the same steps. Another well-known character is the letter C, which has an "S" sound (Ç). After you've found it, select it, copy it, and paste it into your document. The Russian special letter n (П) is located farther down.

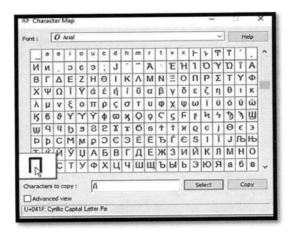

Hopefully, this gives you an idea of what the Character map can do and how it can help you overcome the difficulty of needing to use foreign letters or accented vowels in documents like Word. You've also seen how to insert these unusual characters into your document; explore these options to learn more about foreign characters.

CHAPTER TWENTY-FIVE

PUBLISH YOUR DOCUMENT ON MICROSOFT WORD

In this chapter, we are going to learn how to publish and print a document. Before you print a document, you must look at it and make sure that everything is in order. This chapter will also cover how to export a document and create a PDF

Introduction

After writing, editing, formatting, and proofreading, the last step in document preparation is to put it on the Internet. Publishing is a broad term that includes printing a document on paper and making an electronic document that you can share on the web.

Document on Paper

When you finish your document on Microsoft Word, you can choose whether to make a paper copy of the document, which is also called a printout or a hard copy.

Previewing Before You Print

Before you print, look at what the document will look like. Even if your document is supposed to look the same on the screen as it does on paper, you might find little mistakes like missing page numbers, blank pages that don't belong there, and so on.

Therefore, you must get a look at things before you print. To see your document, first, you have to save your work. Then click on the **Ctrl+P** key (The Ctrl+P keyboard shortcut is the most common way to print). Another way to do this is to click the File tab and choose Print from the File screen's left side. The Print screen comes up, like the one shown in Figure 1.

Figure 1: An image of the Print screen

If you want to see a preview of each page, click on the forward and backward buttons at the bottom of the page. To read more text, use the zoom slider at the bottom of this page to make it bigger. The zoom slider that lets you change the size of the text is shown in chapter 1, figure 5. You might want to look at the layout of footnotes, headers or footers if you're using them in your text. The goal is to find anything that's not appealing before you print. When things need to be fixed, you can click the back button or press the Esc key to get back to your text.

Printing the Whole Document on Microsoft Word

To print a document, ensure the printer is on and ready to print. It is faster to print when the printer is on, so make sure it is turned on. Save your document and then click on the **Print command** on the File tab or press Ctrl+P. Choose Print from the **File tab**. The Print screen comes up. Look at Figure 1. Click the big Print button. The print screen closes and the document comes out from the printer **Note:** Fortunately, you can keep working while the paper is printing. Also, you should not use the Print command again if nothing comes out. It's very likely that the computer is still thinking or sending information to the printer, and that nothing has gone wrong. It's likely that if you don't see an error message, everything will likely print out at some point.

Printing a Certain Page

To print a particular page that you want. Take these steps:

- To print, you need to move the insertion pointer so that it's sitting somewhere on the page that you want to print.

- To make sure you're on the right page, look at the page number on the status bar
- Press the keys Ctrl+P. The Print Range button is next to the Settings button on the right shown in figure 1, it says Print All Pages.
- The menu has a print option called **"Print This Page,"** which you can choose from.
- The Page Range box at the bottom of the Print screen can also help you check the page number.
- Then print.
- That single-page prints with all the formatting you put in.

Printing a Range of Pages

On Microsoft Word, you can print a range of pages including odd number pages, even number pages, or a mix of different pages from your document. To print a group of pages, go to the Print screen or press the keys Ctrl+P.

The Pages text box shows up as shown in figure 2

- To print pages 5 to 9, write 5-9.
- To print pages 3 through 9, type 3-9.
- To print pages 4 and 8, type 4, 8.
- To print pages 3, 5 to 9,15 to 17 and 19, type 3, 5-9, 15-17, 19.
- Print All Pages is now turned into Custom Print if you type any value into the box.
- Print when you're ready. Only the pages you tell the printer to print come out of it.

Figure 2: An image of the Print screen with an arrow pointing at the page box

Making Copies of a Page that are Printed on Both Sides

On Microsoft Word, you can print your document on both sides of a sheet of paper. Take these steps:

- Right after you save the document, press Ctrl+P.
- Click the **Duplex Printing button** on the Print screen to make two copies of the same thing.
- Choose "Print on Both Sides, Flip Pages on Long Sides," then click "OK."

Short Sides isn't worth it if you don't plan to bind your document in that way.

Odd and Even Pages are Printed on Both Sides of the Paper

If you have a printer that doesn't print on both sides of the paper, what would happen? If that's the case, you can print all the odd pages in your paper. Turn the paper over and put it back in the printer again. In the next step, print all the even pages. This means that the text will be printed on both sides of the page. **Note:** It's a good idea to print only one odd-and-even page first, to make sure that when you put the paperback in, it's in the right orientation.

Printing a Block on Microsoft Word

When you print a document with Word, you have a lot of different options for how it looks. Make sure you have marked a block of text on the screen. Then, ask the Print command to print only that block of text. This is how:

Mark the text you want to print

See Chapter 6 for all the instructions on how to block a text on the word document.

- Press Ctrl+P to bring up the Print screen.
- The Print Range button is next to the Settings button on the right.
- When you go to the menu, choose the Print Selection item.
- To see the Print Selection option, you need to select at least one block in your document.

It's time to print.

The block you chose prints in the same place and with the same formatting (headers and footers) as if you had printed the whole document.

Printing More Than One copy

This simply means making more than one copy. When you print a document with Word, you can choose how the paper looks. If you want to print more than one copy of your document, you can do that, too. **Follow these steps to print more than one copy:**

- Press the keys Ctrl+P. Word opens up the Print dialogue box as shown in figure 1.
- In the Copies box, choose how many copies you want to print.
- Click on the **Collate check box.** If the check box is selected, this indicates the copies will be collated.
- Click the Print button and click OK.

Note: As a rule, Word prints one copy of a document after the other. This is called collating, and it is how things are put together. However, if you want Word to print five copies of page 2 and then five copies of page 3 and so on, choose the option from the Collated menu button and type in the number of copies you want of each page the collated option is indicated with an arrow in figure 3 below: Then click on print.

Figure 4: The Collation Option

Choosing a Different Printer

Your computer may be able to use several printers, such as one that is connected directly to your computer, as well as some network or wireless printers.

To choose a specific printer, such as that fancy color printer, you should follow these steps:

- Press Ctrl+P to bring up the Print screen.
- Make sure you click the "S**elect Printer button"** next to the Printer title.
- The button shows the name of the printer that Windows has chosen as the default one.
- Choose a different printer from the list and click on it.

Note: Not all printers have names that are easy to understand. Also, not every printer on the list is a real printer. Several of them are printers that print documents like Microsoft Print to PDF. To add printers, change their names, or set them as the default printer,

Cancelling a Print Job

You can cancel a print job in Word by running to the printer and pressing the **Cancel** button. At times, there is an icon with a red X on it. When you touch that button, the printer will stop. The button stops the document from printing, but it might not stop the printer right away. The Cancel button doesn't work on some slow printers. You can try to use Windows to stop a print job on a printer with slight issues. **Follow these steps:**

- D**ouble-click** the little printer icon on the right end of the taskbar to open the printer.
- Select the job that you want to delete from the list.
- Choose either the Document Cancel command or the Document Cancel Printing command to cancel the document or print job.
- Click **"Yes" or "OK"** to stop the job.
- Then shut down the printer's control window now.

Note: It may take a while for the printer to stop. This is because printers have their memory, and even though you cancel it, some pages of the document may be stored and keep printing even after you have cancelled it.

Publishing Your Document Electronically on Microsoft Word

Some documents don't need to be written on paper at all. They are sent to the publisher electronically, and they can be changed right on the screen. When you buy an eBook, you don't need to print it out. And sometimes, documents can be better spread by email than by paper. It's all part of putting your document online and making it public.

Convert a Document to PDF Using Microsoft Word

The best way to convert your document to PDF on Microsoft Word is as follows:

- Open the document you want to convert and then click the "**File" tab.**
- Select the "S**ave As**" option on the backstage screen
- From the Save As screen, select where you would like the PDF to be saved (OneDrive, This PC, a particular folder, or wherever).
- Choose where to save the converted PDF
- Click the drop-down arrow on the right side of the "**Save As Typ**e" box and select "PDF" from the drop-down menu.
- If you want to, you can change the filename at this time. When you're ready, click the "Save" button.
- Change the name of the file (if you wish) and then click the "Save" button

After saving the PDF, you'll be returned to your Word document, and the new PDF will open automatically in your default PDF viewer.

Other Ways to Make a PDF from a DOCX File

If you don't know how to convert a file to or from PDF, use a service like Small pdf, which has free tools for doing so. It's possible to use services like this that have some restrictions or require a fee for full access, but they can be very useful for converting PDFs when you need to do so a few times.

Close Your Document

When you're done you can close your document by simply clicking **Ctrl + W** or clicking the File button and closing the window.

CHAPTER TWENTY-SIX
TIPS AND TRICKS FOR WORD

This chapter will show you how to make more efficient use of Microsoft Word. These include new features and advanced tips. Let's get started learning about today's Word and some of the features you might not be familiar with.

Dark Mode

Do you know you can turn on dark mode on Microsoft Word 2024 especially at night to give your eye a break? To turn on dark mode, go to the top left corner and click on the **File** Menu. Within the file menu, scroll down to the bottom left corner and click on Account. This opens up the account screen and right in the middle, there is a section called **Office Theme.** By default, it's always on the colorful screen which tends to be bright. Click on the drop-down arrow to see other colors (dark grey, white, black) you can select dark grey or black to make your screen dark. **Note**: When you change the office theme, not only will it affect word, it affects all other Office apps (excel and PowerPoint). When you go back to the word, all the ribbons tabs are dark but the document still looks bright. To change this; Go to the **Design tab,** on the right-hand side, click on the page color. Click on the theme color, and choose the dark color. Your document color changes to black and word change your font color automatically to white. **Note**: It doesn't affect your document when you want to print. It comes out in its standard color (white).

Figure 1: The Dark Mode Theme on Word

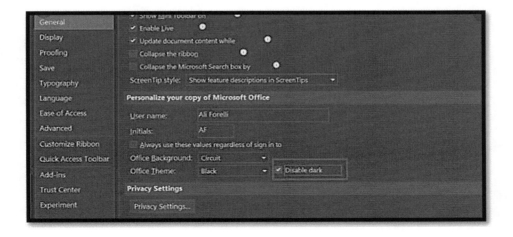

Turn Your Word Document into an Interactive Web Page

You can turn your document into an interactive web page that looks great on any device. To do this; click on the File tab. Then click on the option called Transform. On clicking it, it opens a pane on the right-hand side where you can transform your document into an interactive web page. There are lots of styles, you can choose from, select any one and click on transform. Then you can see a preview of your word document as an Interactive web page.

Figure 2: The Transform Icon

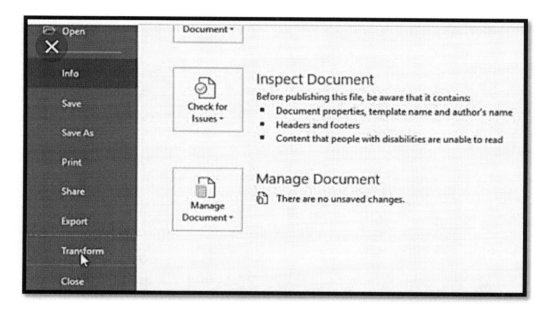

Note: To make any changes, click on Edit above and you can Modify the look of your webpage, you can also review the navigation and share (share this sway)

Convert Photo or Document PDF to an Editable Word Document

You can convert from PDF with ease and edit your files without restrictions. To do this; Go to the File Menu and click on Open. Navigate to where you have your PDF file on your computer and then open it. You get a prompt telling you that it wants to convert your PDF file to a word document. Click on OK. Then you can go through and edit it.

Using Equation/Formulas in Microsoft Word

Formulas and Equations are not limited to Microsoft Excel alone. You can use formulas in Microsoft word. All you have to do is, click on the **Layout tab**. Within the Layout ribbon, over on the far right-hand side, there is an option for Equation. Click on it and it opens a formula dialogue box. You have to select the formulas you want to use, fill in the figures into each box and click on Ok and you'll get the value. **Note**: On the paste functions button, there are lots of different calculations you can run also.

Figure 3: The Equation Button

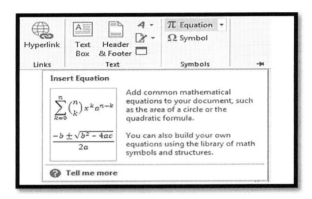

Sort List in Word

To sort the list on Microsoft word. First, select all the lists and click on the **Home tab,** and right in the middle there is an option as **sor**t. Click on it and the sort text box opens. There are different options like the sort by option (by paragraph, headings, and field) and the text option (Ascending or Descending order), Number option, or the date option. Then click on OK and it is automatically updated.

Figure 4: The Sort Icon

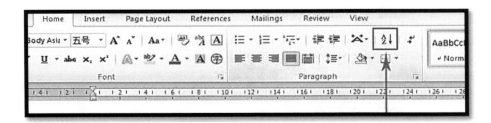

Collaborate with Others

In Microsoft word, you can easily collaborate with others on a document at the same time. In the past, to work with others on a document, you have to email someone else an attachment, they make an edit and send it back then you have to all the edits together and work on them. Fortunately, it is now a lot easier. To do this: On the top right-hand corner, there is an option for Share. Click on it and it opens the share dialogue box, you can share it with others. By default, it says anyone with the link can edit. When you click on it, you can define specific persons to share it with. You can go to the Settings and edit as you want. Then type in an email address and copy the link to share with anyone. If you want to call out someone or ask a question or you want them to work on a Sentence. All you have to do is highlight the sentence. And on the top right-hand corner, there is a button on Comment. Click on it and click on New Comment. It opens the Comment box at the right-hand side of the document and you can type in your comments. You can put @ to select a specific person to direct the question or sentence to. Then they will get a notification about that specific section of the document. Then when you click on the specific person's name, you can share your document with the person.

Pin Document

You pin your document so you can easily and quickly get back to them in the future. To do this: Click on the File tab and this brings us to the word backstage. Within the home view, you can see all your recent documents. If you select the document and hover around it, there is a pinned icon (figure 5). Click on it and click on Pinned.

Figure 5: The Pinned icon

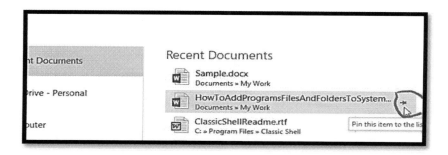

Whenever you want to get back to where your document is, just click on Pinned as shown in figure 6 and the document appears

Figure 6: The Pinned Document

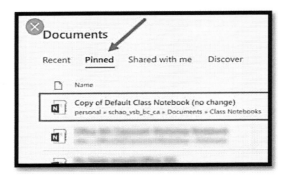

How to Rewrite a Text

On Microsoft Word, you can rewrite a text or a phrase. To do this: Highlight the word and right-click on it. There is an option as Rewrite Suggestions. When you click on it, different ways to write the highlighted or selected text will be displayed. Select your preferred choice and it is updated on your document.

Figure 7: Rewrite Suggestions icon

Resume Assistant Powered by LinkedIn

This is a feature created by LinkedIn on Microsoft word that helps you write your CV or Resume. To use this feature: click on Review. On the right-hand side, there is an option called Resume Assistant. Click on it and it opens a pane for resume Assistant. Then you can fill in the required field. There are also some bullet points to help you with the skills, you can learn from them to put yours together. When you're done, click Ok and your resume is ready.

Translator

Microsoft Word comes with a built-in translator. To use the built-in translator, go over to the Review tab and under language, there is an option to Translate. Within the submenu, you can translate selection or translate an entire document. When you click on Translate Selection, it opens the translator in the right-hand pane. Then select some text select the language you want and click on Insert.

Figure 8: The Translator button

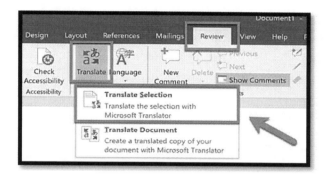

Citation

Microsoft word makes it easy to work with citation. To insert a citation on any quote, click on the Reference tab and click on Insert citation (figure 9). First, you have to add a new source. Click on Add New Source. This opens up the create source dialogue box and you can add information related to what the source is (book, journal article, report, conference proceedings, etc.) (figure 10). Then you can fill in the Author, title, year, city, and publisher. Once you've finished typing in all the information, click on Ok and it will be updated in your document.

Figure 9: The Insert Citation button

Figure 10: The Create Source Dialogue Box

Also, to insert a work cited section. Go to the citation option, there is an option for Bibliography. First, select your style, and next click on bibliography. (Figure 11) Within here you can insert a few different build-in formats and the works cited on your doc will be updated on your document.

Figure 11: The bibliography section

Format Painter

First, select the formats you want to copy, then go to Home Ribbon and click on the format painter. This then copies the formatting and there is a big brush close to your cursor. Then highlight the text you want to apply in the same format and it is automatically updated on your document.

Figure 12: The Format Painter icon

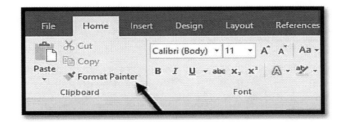

Read Aloud Voice

This is a feature that reads out your selected text. First of all, select the text and click on the Review Tab. And select the Read Aloud option, it automatically reads out the selected text on your Word document. There is also a backward, pause, and a forward option you can select from. You can also further change the voice to either a male or female.

Dictation

On Microsoft Word, you can dictate your Words and Microsoft word listens to your Words and types them in. Click on the Home Tab and then click on the Dictate button. As you dictate your words, Microsoft word types it in. There are also Settings options where you can turn on auto Punctuation. There are language options also on the Dictation button.

Figure 13: The Dictation Button

Convert Word to PowerPoint

Open your document and click on the File menu, then click on export. There is an option for export to power presentation (preview). Click on it and it fetched lots of themes for your presentation. Click on any design you want and click on Export. A few seconds later it is open, click on open presentation. Your PowerPoint is ready.

Figure 14: Export option to PowerPoint

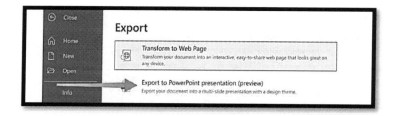

Text Prediction

This has been built-in words that you can turn on or off. Text prediction suggests the next word as you type on your word document. To put it on, go to the Review tab and click on Editor. On the drop-down arrow, click on text Prediction and turn it on. Then as you type, it predicts the word you want to type before you finish typing.

Autosave Option

Go to File and click on Options. Click on Save and you will see an option to 'save auto recover information every time' adjust the time and then mark the box.

Drop Cap

A drop cap is a large letter at the start of a paragraph as seen mostly in newspapers that covers two or more lines in your document as shown in figure 15 below. To create a drop cap, place your cursor on the paragraph that you want to format with the drop cap. Then select the Insert tab on the ribbon. Next, select the drop cap button in the text group and choose an option from the drop-down menu (None will remove an existing drop cap, the Dropped option will drop the first letter to about lines, and the In Margin option places the drop cap in the margin next to the paragraph and the drop cap options open the dialogue box with customization options)

(figure 16). Choose any option of your choice. You can go further to choose additional options such as the font, lines to drop, distance from text, etc. Adjust it according to your choice. After making your choices, select the Ok button and the drop cap will appear in your text immediately.

Figure 15: Example of Drop Cap

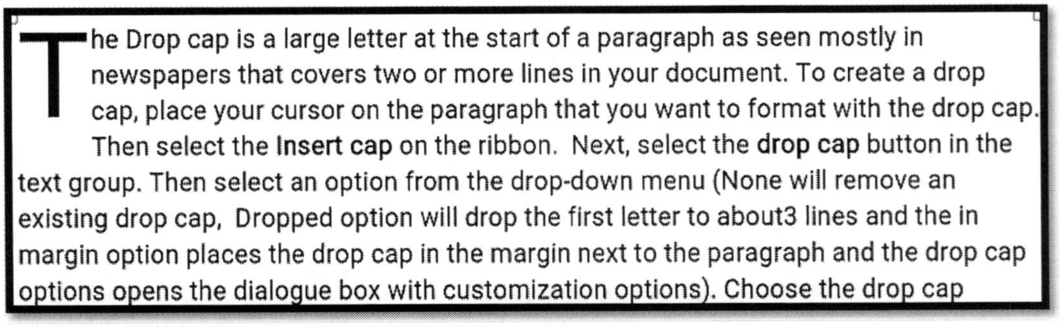

The Drop cap is a large letter at the start of a paragraph as seen mostly in newspapers that covers two or more lines in your document. To create a drop cap, place your cursor on the paragraph that you want to format with the drop cap. Then select the **Insert cap** on the ribbon. Next, select the **drop cap** button in the text group. Then select an option from the drop-down menu (None will remove an existing drop cap, Dropped option will drop the first letter to about3 lines and the in margin option places the drop cap in the margin next to the paragraph and the drop cap options opens the dialogue box with customization options). Choose the drop cap

Figure 16: The Drop Cap options

Lock Your Document on Microsoft Word

Open a blank document input your write-up and goes to the Save Option on the File Tab. Choose a location to save it and type in your document name. To lock that document, go to the Tool option beside the save option. Click on the drop-down arrow and click on the General option, it will require a password if you want to lock it, input a password and click Ok. It will ask you to reconfirm your password, type it in and click OK. That document has automatically been locked. To open it again, it requires your password. Alternatively, click the File tab and select Info. Choose the Protect Document button. There are different options (Mark as final, Encrypt depth a password, Restrict Editing). Choose an option and answer the question that appears on the dialogue box, then click Ok and your document is locked.

Bookmark in Words

Bookmarks are used for documents that contain several pages; you can add several bookmarks so that you can identify this bookmark easily for future reference. First, select the headings with the paragraph that you want to bookmark. Then go to the Insert tab and click on the Bookmark option under links and the bookmark window will appear on your screen. Give the bookmark a name in the popup window and click on Add. Once you're done, click on the File Option. On the file option window, click on the Advanced tab and scroll down to the Show document content section. In that section, check the show bookmark option and click on the Ok button to save the changes. The brackets will mark the area you bookmarked. Once you've added several bookmarks, click on the bookmark options again and the window will show you all the bookmarks you have. If you want to go to a particular bookmark, select that bookmark and click on the Go to Button. To delete a bookmark. Click on the bookmark and select Delete.

Figure 17: The Bookmark Option on Word

Side-to-Side Page Movement

You can arrange your document on Microsoft word to a side-by-side view. To do this; click on th**e View tab**. Select **side-to-Side** on the Page Movement group and it is automatically updated on the word document. Note that on this view tab, the zoom command becomes inactive and the horizontal scroll bar becomes more useful as you can use it to go through each page.

Accelerate the Ribbon

The keyboard accelerator can be used to access commands in the Ribbon. (Press **F10** key to access the Ribbon accelerator as a shortcut method) The best way to do this is to use the **Alt** Keys. When you click on Alt keys, letters in boxes appear on the Ribbon and each box contains one or two letters, which are the accelerator keys.

Note: You can click on a letter or the two letters in sequence to "click" a specific part of the Ribbon. To disable the accelerator mode, click on the Alt key again.

Click-and-Type

This is another feature of Word 2024. The click-and-type is used to stab the mouse anywhere on the page and information can be typed in immediately.

Insert Video on Your Document

You can easily insert videos on Microsoft word, 2024. To do this; go to the **Insert tab** and click on Online Video. Before that, get the embed code or URL of the web page of the video. Then select where you want the video to be pasted on your document and click the **Insert tab,** select online video and paste the URL you copied then click Insert.

Figure 18: Online Video button

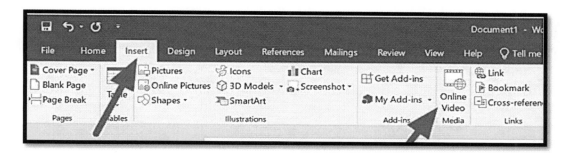

Hidden Text

Some texts are not visible on a document; they are hidden text. The only way to make this text visible is to click on the **Home Tab** ribbon and then on the **Paragraph group,** click on the **Show/Hide** command which looks like the paragraph symbol. When you enable it, the hidden text shows up in a document with a dotted line as shown below

----

Document Properties

To access a document property. Click the **File** tab and choose the **Info** option. The document Properties are displayed on the right-hand side which displays the document size, pages, word count, and other options. You can click on the **Properties button** and select **Advanced Properties** to see more options.

Document Version History

To View Previous Versions of Word Documents; click the "File" button on the Ribbon and select "Info." On this tab, click the "Version History" button and it will open up the Version

History pane on the right. This Version History pane lists all major documents revised by date, time, and author. To view any version of a document, click "Open version." This will open that version of the file and you can view the version of that document.

The Common Keyboard Shortcut for Shift Key

- Shift + F1: Review text formatting
- Shift + F2: Copy the selected text
- Shift + F3: Change the case of the text (uppercase to lower case)
- Shift + F4: Perform a Find or Go To action again
- Shift + F5: Move to a previous revision
- Shift + F6: Go to the previous pane
- Shift + F7: Launch the Thesaurus
- Shift + F8: Shrink the current selection
- Shift + F9: Switch between field code and its results
- Shift + F10: Display a shortcut menu
- Shift + F11: Go to the previous field
- Shift + F12: Save a document
- Common Keyboard Shortcut for the Alt Key
- Alt + F: To use backstage view open the file page
- Alt + H: Move to the Home tab
- Alt + M: Opens the Mailing tab to manage the Mail Merge task
- Alt + N: Open the Insert tab
- Alt + P: Open the page layout tab
- Alt + R: Open the Review tab
- Alt + S: Open the Reference tab
- Alt + F4: Close Document
- Alt + F5: Restore the document window size
- Alt + F6: Switches to another document
- Alt + F7: Find the misspelt word or grammatical error
- Alt + F8: Open the Macro dialogue box
- Alt + F10: Display the selection task pane.
- Alt + F11: Display Microsoft Visual Basic code
- Alt + Backspace: Undo the last action

Common Keyboard Shortcuts of the Control Key

Ctrl + A: To select all text

Ctrl + B: To apply a bold format to the selected text

Ctrl + C: Copy selected text

Ctrl + D: Open font window to change font

Ctrl + E: Align selected text to the centre

Ctrl + F: Open the Find Dialogue box to search for words

Ctrl + G: The Go-to dialogue box to search for a specific location in the current document

Ctrl + H: Open the Replace dialogue box to replace text

Ctrl + I: Italics

Ctrl + J: Align the selected to justify the screen

Ctrl + K: Insert a Hyperlink

Ctrl + L: Align text left

Ctrl + M: Indent a paragraph from the left/ Hanging indent

Ctrl + N: New Document

Ctrl + O: Open other documents / open the dialogue box to select a file to open.

Ctrl + P: Print

Ctrl + F1: Open a task pane

Ctrl + F2: Display the print preview

Ctrl + F4: Close the active window

Ctrl + F6: Switch to another open Ms word document

Ctrl + F9: Insert an empty field

Ctrl + F10: Maximize the document window

Ctrl + F12: Close the open command

Ctrl +]: Increase size of selected text

Ctrl + [: Decrease size of selected text

Ctrl + 0: Add/ remove 6pt of spacing above the paragraph

Ctrl + 1: Add a single space between two lines

Ctrl + 2: Add double space between two lines

Ctrl + 5: Add 1.5 space between two line

Ctrl + ↓ Moves the cursor one paragraph to the down

Ctrl + ← Moves the cursor to one word to the left

Ctrl + Q: Add Space before paragraph / Remove paragraph formatting.	Ctrl + → Moves the cursor to one word to the right
Ctrl + R: Align Text Right	Ctrl +↑ Moves the cursor one paragraph upward
Ctrl + S: Save	Ctrl + Backspace: Delete one word to the left
Ctrl + T: Left indent / to create the Hanging indent	Ctrl + Delete: Delete one word to the right
Ctrl + U: Underline	Ctrl + End: Move the cursor to the end of the page
Ctrl + V: Paste	Ctrl + Home: Move the cursor to the beginning of the document
Ctrl + W: Close Document	Ctrl + Enter: insert a page
Ctrl + X: Cut selected text	Ctrl + Insert: Copy selected text
Ctrl + Y: Repeat / Redo	Ctrl + Spacebar: Reset highlighted text to default the font
Ctrl + Z: Undo	Ctrl + Tab: Insert a tab character
	Ctrl + = Set selected text as subscript

The Editor

The editor is for you if you haven't thought about your spell checker in the last 10 or 20 years. It's the next version of Word's spell-checking. It's on the right-hand side of the **home** tab.

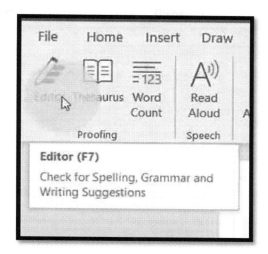

Also, the spell check button has been replaced with Editor under the **Review** tab. When you click it, a pane will appear that examines everything on your page. We have traditional spelling here that organizes your words; you can even read aloud, and you can go back with the arrow at the top.

If you want to double-check your grammar, you'll see that it's properly highlighted and structured. You can jump to the next position by using the forward arrow here, and you can also read aloud.

Then there's the Suggestion, which is the difference between the classic and general effects.

- **Clarity** is a new idea that uses natural language processing, and the recommendation here gives you clarity in altering how your paper appears.

There are many additional things to learn here, and if you select "**Settings**," you can go down and enable whatever you want in Editor Right here.

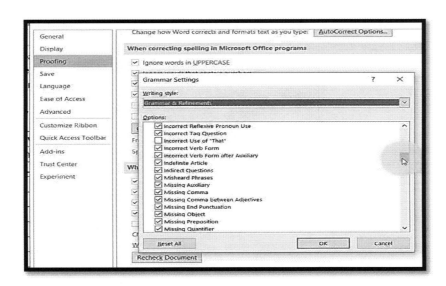

You can experiment with a variety of new concepts, and Editor can verify everything for you, including grammar, clarity, conciseness, formality, and much more.

Speech-To-Text

A "**Dictate**" button can be found on the **home** tab, much to the right.

When you click this, you will be able to type using your voice. You simply click it to turn it off again, and if you want to change the language, you can do so by selecting it from the drop-down menu.

Focus Mode

This allows you to concentrate solely on the information, rather than the user interface. A "**Focus Mode**" button can be found in the View menu.

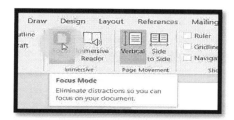

If you click that, it removes all other material immediately, and if you go to the top here, you can also change the background, and if you click away, the toolbar vanishes.

To turn off focus mode, go up here and click "**Focus**," which will remove it and return it to normal Word mode.

Immersive Reader

This was created with everyone in mind to aid in reading, and it's now included in Word to help make documents even more accessible. The **Immersive Reader** button is located on the View tab, next to "**Focus**," and is comparable to Focus mode.

When you click on it, a special toolbar called the immersive reader contextual toolbar appears. You can reduce visual congestion by increasing text line and word spacing and clicking "**Text Spacing**" here to space out the text and letters; this can aid with reading speeds and comprehension for some people. Increase the size of the text below to make it a little bigger. You can narrow the column if you want, as some individuals prefer only a few words per line. You can also alter the background color. Keep in mind that there are numerous solutions available.

You can select to read aloud since line and word highlighting will assist you to read those words out loud. You can control the pause, jump forward and backward, choose the voice type, and change the reading speed faster or slower while it is reading aloud. Breaking words into syllables is one of the last things we have, so if you click "**Syllables**," you'll see the words are automatically broken into syllables; for some people, this can help with decoding the phrase, and it's just a simple switch you can turn on and off. Finally, there's "Line Focus," which allows you to focus your gaze on a single line, three lines, or five lines. This can help those with ADHD, students, dyslexia, or cerebral palsy manages just one line at a time or three lines, depending on your preference. If you close this, the document will revert to its original state. This is also beneficial when it comes to co-authoring. There are a few people who use the immersive reader when collaborating on a document; they can have settings that are unique and private only to them; it's like a custom layer over the content that doesn't modify the document structure at a core level.

LinkedIn-powered resume assistant

Resume Assistant can be found on the right side of the screen under the **Review** tab. When you select this, a pane appears that provides you with inspiration and tips for writing your Resume.

Whatever you put in, it extracts some of the top skills from LinkedIn and then provides articles to assist with resume building. Additional language refinement for Resumes is another option; if you choose it, Word will provide you with additional refinements as you type.

It even suggests jobs, and if you click to explore more positions on LinkedIn, it launches LinkedIn with the terms you entered. It creates a wonderful link that connects Words to LinkedIn in a useful way.

Convert a Word Document into a Web Page (SWAY)

This is a relatively new feature that few people are aware of. If you go to File, select "**Transform**" from the drop-down menu.

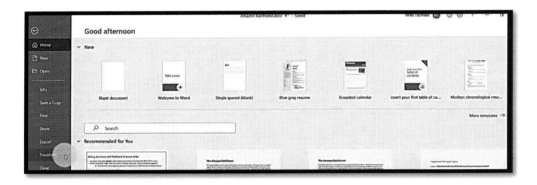

This will bring up the transformed page, which will generate a sway. You can see there are many various styles here; simply click to see a preview, and SWAY will create a beautiful web page for you that concentrate on the formatting so you don't have to. Click "**Transform**" to create a stunning web page with only a few clicks, and Sway will handle all of the formatting for you.

If you click the "**Share**" button, you can share it with others, go into Sway and edit it, and there are also options to duplicate it, save it as a template, print it, and many other things.

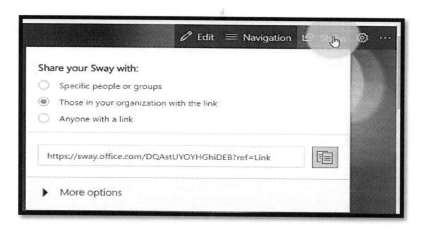

Translate Your Word document to another Language

You can translate a single selection or the full document by going to the Review tab in Word and dropping down the "**Translate**" button.

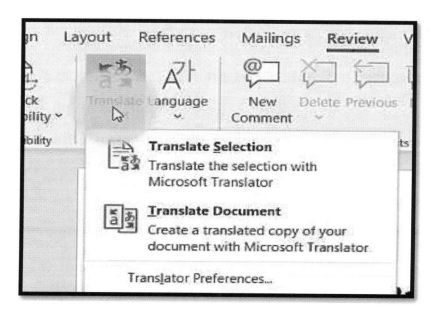

It brings up a pane on the right here that allows you to translate from one language to another, and if you scroll down, you'll see that there are over 70 languages available.

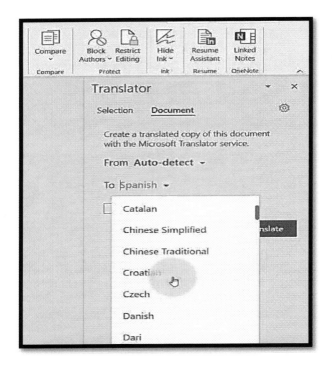

If you click "**Translate**," a new document will be created in the language you selected.

Real-time sharing and collaboration

Many people believe that Word does not enable real-time co-authoring; nevertheless, it does, just as well as Google Docs, and can accommodate a large number of individuals. If you go up to the "**Share**" button and click it, a window will appear where you can type in the name or email address of the person to whom you want to send a link so they may open it and work with you. You can pick who you want to **view** and **change your document**, **set an expiration date**, **create a password**, and **block downloads**, among other things.

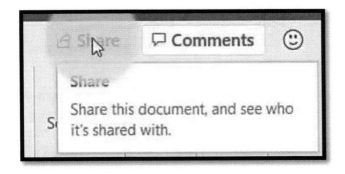

283

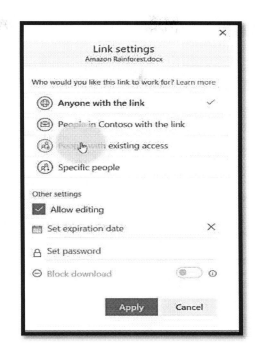

This is something to test out because Word supports more than 30 individuals typing in real-time. It works with Word on the desktop, on the web, and on the iPad all at once.

@ Mentioning someone's name in a document

This is a widely used method on numerous social media networks. If you wish to highlight a statement and @ mention someone, go to the **Review** tab, **write a new comment**, and type the **@ symbol** over here, and that person's attention will be drawn to it.

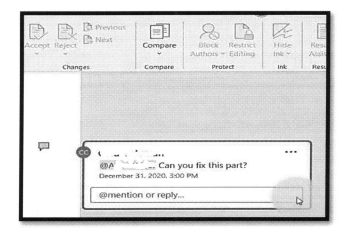

When you hit send, it will @ mention that individual, and they will be able to respond to your comment.

Save and open a file as a PDF

If you go to the **File** menu on your Word document to save a copy, **select PDF** from the drop-down menu, **choose a location,** and hit "**Save**," the document is saved as a pdf and opened using a pdf viewer.

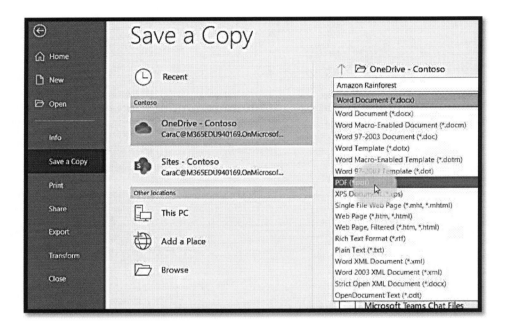

You can also **open a PDF in Word** and do the opposite. Go to the **File** menu, select "**Open**," and then **browse to a pdf file** on your local drive. When you open it, it prompts you to convert it, and the entire pdf is now open in Word; you can choose text, delete it, and even do things such as translate the document, utilize Immersive Reader, and all of the other things you saw before are now available in that pdf that you just opened in Word.

The Office Lens for Photo

This is about **taking a snapshot** of anything with the free Office Lens mobile app, having it **OCR** it, and **sending it** into a usable Word document. On iPhone or Android, Office Lens is available for free. You'll select your document, take a photo, resize the image, touch "**Confirm**," and then tap "**Done**."

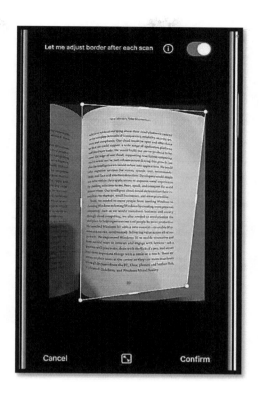

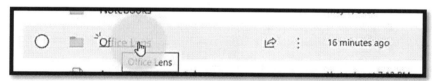

When you open it, you'll notice that the entire page has been OCR'd, and if you scroll down, you'll see both the text and the original image. You can open this on Word desktop by selecting "**Open in Desktop App**" from the "**Editing**" menu. You'll receive that document on Word desktop, which means you can take a photo of anything, import it into Word using Office Lens, and do whatever you want with it.

Tools for drawing and inking

When you go to the **Draw** menu, you'll notice a lot of options. You have pens, erasers, and the ability to conduct Ink replay. After selecting a pen, you can choose from a variety of thicknesses: thin, medium, or thick. You can now draw on the page, and if "**Draw with Touch**" is enabled, you can draw with your finger.

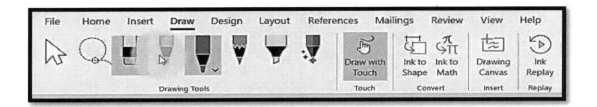

You can also write a word in ink, and if you choose this and use "**Ink Replay**," it will write that word back to you, with a small slider to go backward, forwards, or pause it. This is very important for things like writing and math.

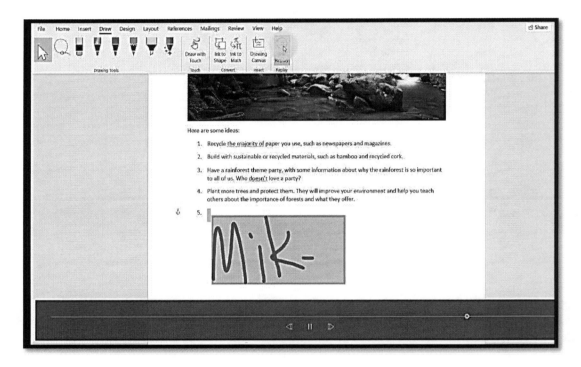

Also, if you choose "**Ink to Shape**" and draw anything like a triangle, it will snap into a little nicer shape.

Clipping from the screen (Screenshot)

This is now a feature of Word. If you go to the **Insert** menu and select **Screen clipping**, you can take a screenshot of a photo as it calls up the browser, disables it, and you just click, draw your square, and it pops it straight into Word.

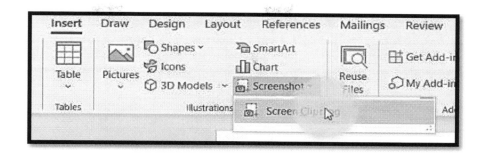

The Accessibility Checker built into Word

This can make your document more accessible to those who might read it. Select "**Check Accessibility**" from the **Review** tab and the Accessibility Checker will appear.

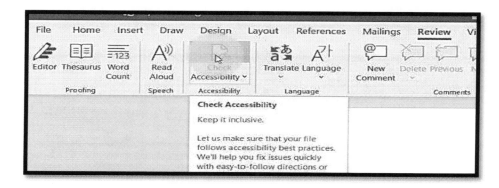

When you return to Check Accessibility, you'll see a few more options, including Focus mode, the navigation window for navigating the page, Alt Text, and the Accessibility Checker.

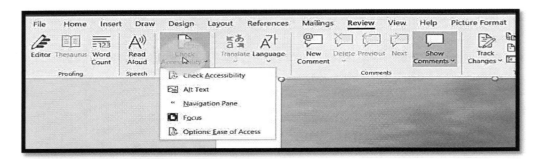

Many of them are quite useful, and if you want to explore all of them, go to "**Options Ease of Access**," where you'll find a lot of options to explore in the Ease of Access settings for Word.

Inserting Video from the Internet into a Word Document

If you go to the Insert menu here, you'll see "**Online Video**," which you can click to paste a link to, say, a YouTube or Vimeo video.

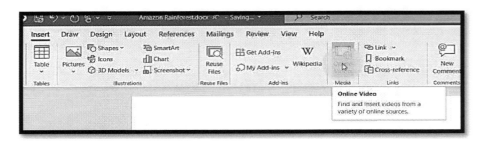

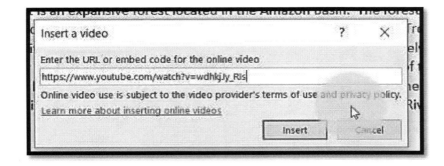

Just make sure you've read and agreed to all of the provider's terms of service and privacy policies. Now, if you click Insert, the video is automatically inserted into the page. It's ready to use, whether you want to size it or play it.

Interesting Points of View to Include in Your Word Document

You can make it look more like a book by going to the View menu and selecting the **"Side to Side"** option. This allows you to scroll left and right and slide the pages, making it look like a book.

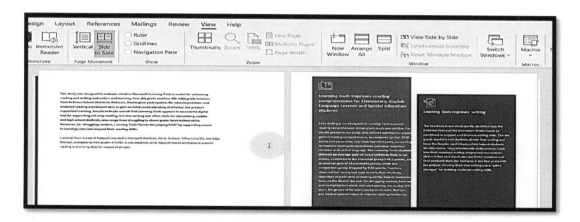

More fascinating, if you select **"Thumbnails,"** it will appear like a PowerPoint slide sorter, and you may now select a page or scroll around.

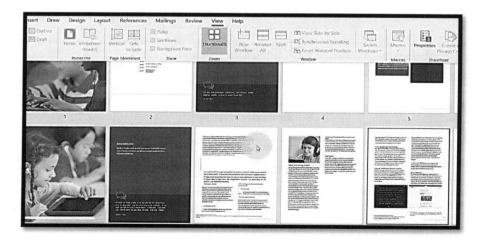

Instead of scrolling through a 40-page document, which might take a long time, the Thumbnail view allows you to quickly navigate through it and transition to a new page.

Built-in Icons, Images, Stickers, and Illustrations

These are quite similar to the PowerPoint high-grade ones. You can see all these different icons with different categories if you go to the **Insert** menu and click "**Icons**." It defaults right here to icons.

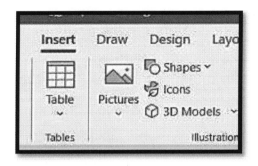

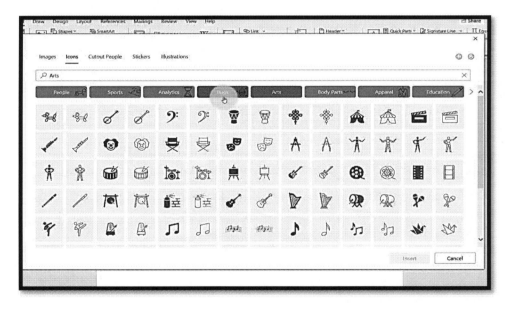

There are also some lovely royalty-free photos that you are free to use. There are also "**Cutout Individuals**," which are quite easy to choose from if you need some people in your text. Stickers come first, followed by artwork. When you're inserting different objects into your Word document, you'll have a lot of options to pick from.

Word Templates Included

Although they are of excellent quality, many people are unaware of them. When you go to the **File** menu, you'll notice a variety of templates at the top.

If you click "**More templates**," you'll get a list of more templates. You can browse through the many categories by scrolling down: business, cards, flyers, letters, and education. Clicking on any of these categories will bring you a variety of attractive documents that you can use to get started with and then update and modify later.

Reducing the size of a Word document

This is a little more advanced, but it's useful if you need to reduce the size of particularly large Word documents. Many people are unaware that this one exists. You'll go to the File menu and select "**Options**" in the lower-left corner. Next, select "**Advanced**," then scroll down through the advanced options until you see "**Image Size and Quality**." This allows you to customize your document's default saving patterns.

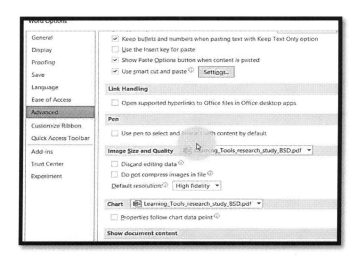

You can do this for all documents or other documents, a single document, the one you're working on right now, or just leave it as the Learning Tools document if you drop it down. If your document has a lot of photographs, this can help you trim it down by allowing you to adjust how many pixels per square inch is saved, which can make your document considerably smaller. This chapter wraps up the book, and with these tips, you'll be well on your way to mastering Microsoft Word.

As a way of conclusion, these are necessary things to note about Microsoft word 2024;

- Always remember to save your work on Microsoft Word
- Be very vigilant when using the space bar
- Don't abuse the enter key
- To make your work easy and fast, use most of the keyboard shortcuts.
- Avoid manually numbering your pages and using the bullet in the wrong way
- Do not force a fresh/ new page and always remember the undo icon.
- Make sure your printer is in a good condition before you click on the print button to print any document

CHAPTER 27

ADVANCED DOCUMENT COLLABORATION

Multiple users can collaborate on a Word document, Excel spreadsheet, or PowerPoint presentation using Microsoft 365, OneDrive, or SharePoint. Co-authoring is the process of collaborating with multiple people at the same time. Co-authoring is available for documents that are saved in either Sharepoint or One Drive.

Below are the basic things you need for effective collaboration with other people;

- **A shared storage area**: Co-authoring is made possible by shared storage spaces like OneDrive, OneDrive for business or education, SharePoint, and SharePoint Server.
- **Applications that offer support for co-authoring**: Co-authoring is supported by Word and PowerPoint on all platforms and in versions higher than Office 2010. Co-authoring is also supported by the most recent version of Excel for Microsoft 365 and the Excel mobile apps.
- **A co-authoring-friendly document**: Only contemporary file types, such as.docx (Word), pptx (PowerPoint), and.xlsx (Excel), are compatible with co-authoring.
- **Edit permissions for co-authors:** The documents must be accessible to and editable by each co-author.

27.1: Real-Time Co-Authoring

Simultaneous Editing with Multiple Users

Word now allows users to co-edit a document simultaneously and remotely. This feature is also referred to as real-time collaboration. This is a response, of course, to the increasing trend of apps becoming more collaborative—particularly productivity apps. You can collaborate with others on a document using Microsoft Word. In every industry, this promotes increased productivity and fosters a more cooperative work atmosphere. You will learn about every detail of utilizing real-time collaboration for a Word project in this section. When it comes to delivering a document for review, approval, and comment from superiors or coworkers, having this real-time collaboration capability saves a ton of time and eliminates numerous steps from the workflow. Hence, several people can view the document simultaneously in real-time and make any necessary comments or edits there and then, saving time compared to exchanging emails back and forth. Most importantly, they do not need to be in the same space. Anywhere in the world, they can collaborate.

- You have to save your content to SharePoint Online or OneDrive first. Next, select the **Share option in Word**

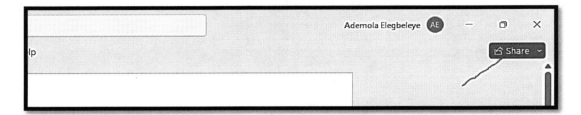

- **And input the email addresses of the recipients of the document**.

You have to provide them the ability to edit the document if you want them to work with you on it. After that, you may include a remark or message to go along with the share invitation. The **Automatically Share Changes option** can also be changed. For real-time updates of your changes as you make them, you can set it to Always. You could also decide to when you open the document and want to share the alterations you made, ask to be prompted. To share your modifications as they happen, you must select "**Yes.**" This allows for co-editing in real time. An email message will now be sent to the individuals you invited to share the document with you. After that, Word Online or their version of Word will open with the document. They may allow you to view their updates as soon as they are made if they consent to sharing the changes automatically. Along with tracking the changes, you can also observe when they are added to or removed from the document. When you save a document while simultaneously amending it, as is frequently the case when co-editing, Word will highlight any conflicts so you may decide which to preserve. Word locks the area you are editing to stop someone from overwriting your changes, which is another way to avoid this. To prevent collisions, this editing order operates on a "first-come, first-served" basis.

Tracking Changes in Real-Time

Since business and legal documents for instance form relationships, record significant decisions, and function as legal records, they must be exact, understandable, and well-structured. However, writing in these disciplines is hardly done alone. The final document is a result of the contributions of multiple authors, resources, and tools. Small changes can make a great item extraordinary or alter its meaning. It's critical to monitor a document's development and the source of any modifications to comprehend how and why the document evolved and ensure that its objectives are not compromised. The Track Changes feature in Microsoft Word is a great way to monitor the evolution of a document. It offers a concise, well-organized list of every modification performed throughout the editing process. Additionally, it facilitates writers' visualization of revisions, which enhances individual and group revision. Track Changes can be very helpful whether you're writing alone, in a team, or even collaborating with another group to develop a single document.

This function facilitates the management of numerous versions of a document, enables a methodical examination of revisions, and ensures that nothing was changed accidentally. This feature allows formatting adjustments, moves, deletions, and additions to show up in the text as different colors. It is simple to identify which sections of the paper have been modified and how thanks to this visual assistance. This thorough documentation may be necessary to preserve integrity and correctness. Writers can provide input right next to the pertinent information, saving a back-and-forth email exchange. Collaborators can ask questions, provide revision suggestions, and justify changes without interfering with the primary document by using the Comments function. When clearing metadata, you can (and should!) remove all comments to avoid accidentally including internal discussions when transferring a document outside of your company. This function is a fantastic method to clear up any misunderstandings and enhance communication regarding the writing and editing process.

Document version control with track changes and compare

Keeping track of several versions of a document can be difficult during the revision process. You don't have to start from scratch or lose important change logs when you can track changes and observe how the document has developed. You may ensure that everyone is working on the most recent version of the document and lower the possibility of error or miscommunication by keeping modifications contained within the same document. You can determine what has changed between two versions of a document by using the Compare and Merge Changes capabilities, even if your co-authors neglected to use Track Changes before making their revisions. It is possible to generate a change log from one or more documents in the past, merge several iterations into a single document, examine all of the changes, and select which should be retained and which should be deleted. It's an effective technique to keep control over the progress of your work and produce a final, cohesive product that combines the greatest ideas from the entire team.

Track changes for Team Collaboration

When you work together on a paper, you are combining a variety of viewpoints, concepts, and abilities. Each co-author may identify distinct flaws or provide original ideas to enhance the finished work. With Track Changes, it's simple to combine these different viewpoints into a single document while maintaining the original text that served as the proposal's inspiration. People feel heard when ideas are added visually without instantly erasing and overwriting the work of others, which encourages accountability and teamwork. When more than one person is reviewing the same document, Track Changes records who made what modifications. Team leaders may easily identify who has made revisions by seeing which reviewer's changes are colored differently and by using reviewers' usernames or initials to indicate who has contributed. This ensures that everyone's contributions are valued and taken into account. It also aids in the creation of a finished document that is coherent and conveys the desired meaning.

Track changes for co-authoring with opposing groups

To foster a sense of collective ownership and dedication to the finished result, opposing parties could collaborate to produce a document. Additionally, co-drafting helps foster a culture of openness and compromise. Track Changes and Comments facilitate co-drafting and produce a cohesive manuscript. In negotiations, where the process of drafting and commenting is part of discussing substantive components of a settlement, the capacity to accept or reject revisions can also be crucial. While keeping track of changes allows everyone to make suggestions, not all of them have to be carried out. After considering each other's ideas, each group can make a decision based on its objectives and areas of interest. This feature ensures that no decisions are made without agreement, fostering the endeavor's collaborative spirit. With Comments, both parties can agree or disagree with suggested changes, make clarifications, and suggest alternative language. This allows for greater complexity and granularity without raising the possibility of misunderstandings.

To track changes in Microsoft Word, follow the steps below;

- **Open the document**: commence by opening the document you would like to permit the tracking changes feature for. Note that for collaboration, this should be a document that you have already shared.
- **Get track changes enabled:** Move to the **Review tab**

That can be found on the Word toolbar and then choose the **Track Changes button** to aid with switching on this feature.

Once completed, it will also initiate the recording of modifications made to the document.

- **Make due changes**: As necessary, add, remove, or alter text in the document. The modifications will be automatically monitored and presented with various formatting, such as strikeouts for deletions and underlining for insertions.
- **Review the tracked changes**: You can simply navigate through the document to view the recorded changes. The changes will be apparent, along with the name or initials of the individual who made each alteration, making it simple to identify those who contributed.
- **Accept or reject changes**: You can simply navigate through the document to view the recorded changes. The changes will be apparent, along with the name or initials of the individual who made each alteration, making it simple to identify those who contributed. You can also choose to get tracking changes locked.

Lock Tracking

Prevent other authors from turning off Track Changes.

Enter password (optional): [   ]

Reenter to confirm: [   ]

(This is not a security feature.)

[OK] [Cancel]

Below is an indication of the various types of tracked changes;

- **Formatting changes**: You may easily change the look of your work with formatting adjustments. To make your material look visually appealing and readable, experiment with font styles, text sizes, and paragraph alignments. Use italic or bold font styles to highlight key information. Apply strikethrough and underlining to indicate additions or deletions. Modify the indentation and line spacing to create coherent paragraphs. You may maximize the impact of the layout by using formatting tools. By employing bullet points, subheadings, and headings, you may also manage the structure. This directs readers and gives your paper a polished, well-organized appearance.

- **Insertions and deletions**: Insertions allow you to infuse your work with fresh energy. You can add motivating thoughts to your work by only adding a word or a paragraph. This feature makes it easy to add new concepts and keeps texts consistent. You can improve your writing by making deletions. Your writing will be clearer if you cut out any unnecessary words or phrases. This strategy aids readers in maintaining undivided attention on the main point. It enhances readability and draws attention to your ideas more. In teams, both insertions and deletions improve communication. It is simpler to identify changes made by other people when they are tracked. Accept these resources to realize the complete potential of our combined knowledge.

- **Comments and annotations:**
  - **Comments**: Users can remark on specific passages or pose questions. Collaboration is enabled since these comments are visible to other users who have access.

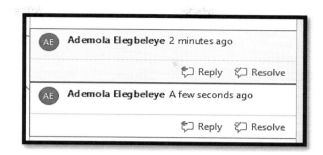

○ **Annotations**: Similar to comments, annotations are meant to draw attention to certain content. They can be applied to offer context, highlight important ideas, or make change suggestions.

○ **Replying to Comments**: Users can respond to comments made by others, which keeps discussions focused and orderly.

○ **Annotating with Formatting**: Users can annotate annotations with bold, underlining, italics, or color highlighting using tracked modifications. This highlights specific issues or illustrates needed improvements.

To navigate and also review tracked changes, follow the steps below;

● Launch **the document in Microsoft Word.**
● Choose the **Review tab at the upper part of the screen.**
● Permit the Track Changes feature by choosing the **Track Changes button**.
● Move through the tracked changes with the use of the **Previous and Next buttons in the changes group.**
● Have a review of each individually by choosing it and then read the comment or the edit made to the document.
● Accept or reject the alterations made with the use of the **Accept or Reject buttons** in the Changes group.

27.2 Advanced Commenting Features

Resolving Comments

You can add notes to the document's content in Word by using comments. If you share the document with others, the comments are shared along with it and are preserved with it. Comments are quite helpful when editing and proofreading a Word document. Different people can post comments and respond to those of others. It's simple to remove every comment after you're done.

The Ribbon's Review tab is where you'll locate the specific comment tools.

- Comment-specific tools are available in the **Comments group under the Review tab.**
- Tools for tracking changes and comments are available under the Tracking group under the **Review tab**. You can use the tools in this group to modify the way comments appear.

Adding comments in Word

You can create or insert comments from two distinct locations using Word's built-in capabilities. In Word, follow the steps below to add a comment:

- **Choose the text you would like to comment on;**

  o The text selection will be identified as the scope of the comment. Word will designate the previous word, if any, as the comment scope if no text is selected.

  o Make sure you select the exact text that your comment refers to—don't, for example, select full paragraphs—so that other people can comprehend it as easily.

- **Once the above has been done, follow any of the steps below;**

  - Choose the **Review tab in the Ribbon > Comments group > New Comment.**

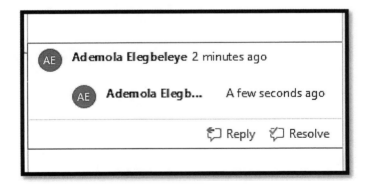

  - Choose the Insert tab in the **Ribbon > Comments group > Comments.**
  - With the use of the keyboard shortcut press Alt + Ctrl + M.

Depending on your preferences for comment display, the entered comment shows up in the markup area (also known as the balloon area), in the margin, or in the Reviewing Pane.

- Type your preferred comment in the inserted comment.
- When you are through, tap the **Esc key** to go back to the document text or you can also choose to select in the document. Keep in mind that selecting the text you marked in step 1 above will happen when you press **Esc.** Pressing Esc, if you have DocTools CommentManager, will move the insertion point after the scope you have chosen, allowing you to continue typing without having to deselect the comment scope first.

Adding a comment as a reply to another comment

You can add two levels of comments in Word. Initial comments and responses to initial comments. **To respond to a previous comment:**

- To respond to a comment, **click inside its text.**
- Below the comment text, click the **Reply icon.**

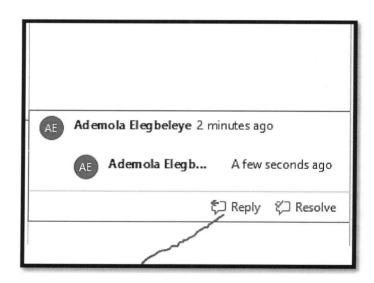

Alternatively, right-click within the remark and choose Reply to Comment.

- Type the comment text in the reply that has been inserted.
- When you're done, click **inside the document or use the Esc key to get back to the document's content.**

Comment responses are nested beneath the corresponding comment. The same comment can have many replies added to it. Even if a reply has been written as a reply to another reply, they will all appear on the same level and be displayed as replies to the first-level comment.

Resolving a Comment in Word

You can designate a comment as resolved in Word. This will result in the comments' font color(s) appearing pale. You may be able to keep track of which comments still require attention by marking them as resolved. **To get a comment marked as resolved, follow the following set of instructions;**

- To designate a remark as resolved, click **inside the comment text.**
- Underneath the remark text, click the **Resolve symbol.**

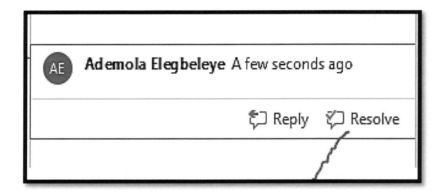

- OR Choose **Resolve Comment by doing a right-click in the comment.**

You may see that the Resolve command and icon are grayed out, meaning that they are inoperable and cannot be utilized. Continue reading to learn why this occurs and how to fix it. **The conditions below get the Resolve feature grayed out;**

- Word 2010 or a previous version was used to produce the document or to save it last.
- Compatibility mode is selected for this document. Newer Word features cannot be used if the document is in compatibility mode. The Word window's Title bar will display the text "Compatibility Mode" following the file name.

You can alter the document to make all of the features from your Word version available to address the issue. To update the document to the Word version you have, use one of the following techniques. Resolve will become available as a result.

- Choose **File > Info > Choose Convert** and then get the document saved.
- Choose **Save As**. In the dialog box for Save As, ensure that the option to Maintain compatibility with previous versions of Word is switched off then choose **Save**.

Depending on how it was formatted, a document's conversion may cause formatting modifications. For instance, when converting to the most recent format, tables made in Word 2010 and older may have different widths (due to changes in how cell margins are handled). It is not possible to remove all resolved comments in one go with Word's built-in capability. You must go over each resolved comment and remove it one at a time. Take note that you may simply **click a button** to remove all resolved comments with the DocTools CommentManager add-in.

Hiding a resolved comment

A comment that has been resolved using Word's Resolve feature is indicated as resolved and appears darkened. But until you remove it, the comment is still present in the document. Until all comments have been addressed, you might want to retain the resolved comments in the document. To avoid being distracted while resolving the remaining comments, you might wish to conceal the ones that have already been resolved. The improbable circumstance that every resolved comment has a single, unique author and that no unresolved comments have been added by that author is the only way to conceal resolved comments using Word's built-in features, and without concealing other comments.

- You could deselect the author in that case by going to **Review > Tracking group: Display Markup > Particular Persons**.

Commenting for Collaborative Editing

The growing need for cooperation in the workplace led to Microsoft Word's expansion to include comments for the sharing and modification of notes and ideas. With this, you and the rest of the team may collaborate on Word projects more successfully while utilizing cutting-edge tools like @mention notifications and other capabilities. It was initially included in Word's web application, but it's now accessible in Word on Windows and MacOS!

Below are a few features that you ought to take note of while making use of this amazing experience;

Explore your view of comments

By default, comments appear on the right side of the page. You won't have to worry about missing any current comments on the work being done on the paper to concentrate on your content.

Resolve comments

The comments are transferred to the Comments pane when you choose the **resolve option.** Later on, you can always verify and locate them there.

Access Comments pane

Click the **Comments button** in the upper right corner of your Word window to navigate from the default, focused view of comments to the right of the page and the **Comments pane**. This area is referred to as the "Collab corner."

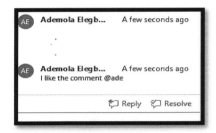

Engage others

After you've finished modifying them and hit the **Post button**

Other people can view your comments. @mention can be used to include other people in the discussion. Any user you name will immediately receive notifications when the comment thread is updated.

Follow the steps below to get the above explained with ease;

- Select the text you wish to comment on, then press **Ctrl+Alt+M** to start a document thread.
- After typing your remark, click **"Post."**
- To comment, stand out, and emphasize the material it references, choose any **comment inside the document.**

Click the box that says **"@mention or reply"** to respond to an already-posted comment. This will allow you to reply to a comment thread with@mention. To finish the response, type @ followed by the person's name that you wish to interact with, and then click **Post**. To declare a comment thread as resolved, choose "..." on any comment thread, and then choose Resolve thread to make it official. Later on, if you need to check the resolved remarks, click the **remarks button located in the Word window's right corner to open the Comments pane.**

Advanced Commenting Options

Modern comments

By enabling contemporary features like @mention alerts and other capabilities, modern comments set the foundation for a more enhanced Word collaborative experience for you and your teams. It unifies the way that comments function across Office on various endpoints, ensuring that you and your team always have a uniform experience when using Word, Excel, or PowerPoint on any platform. First featured in Word for mobile and web, modern comments were iterated depending on user feedback. It is currently being rolled out to production on Word for Mac and Windows! **Below are some of the various things that modern commenting can help you to achieve;**

Stay in control

You no longer need to be concerned about others seeing your comments before you've completed editing them thanks to contemporary comments. Once you have composed a new comment or response, you can share it with others by clicking the **Post button** or by using the keyboard shortcut **Ctrl + Enter (Windows) or Cmd + Enter (MacOS).** A reply or comment can now only be updated by the original author.

Flexibility in how you see and interact with your comments

Comments in Word are automatically positioned to the right of your page. Contextual comments are displayed alongside the page content in this view to assist you in concentrating on the input that is most pertinent to the section of the document you are currently working on. You may view a comprehensive list of all comments in your document, including those that have been resolved, in the Comments window. To go between the Comments pane and the contextual view, just click the **Comments icon** located in the Word window's upper right corner.

Resolve comment threads

In documents, comments typically express queries, viewpoints, or reservations about the content. You can mark a post as resolved by using the comments feature once things have been answered. To keep you focused on what's active, resolved comment threads won't show up in the contextual view, but you can still locate them in the **Comments window**.

Improved @ mentions in comments

Names have been appended to comments by users for years. Using@mention to reach out to several colleagues in your company or institution is now easier if you're an enterprise user working with cloud files. To comment, select some text, click the **Comment option**, type your message, and @mention the people you want to read it.

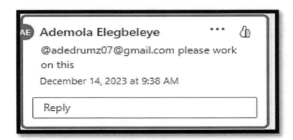

Anyone you've @mentioned in a comment will receive an email notification when it is posted. Also, the person who initiated the comment thread will be notified. Email notifications alert your collaborators to new activity in the comment thread and provide them with an overview

307

of the text of the document where the remark was made, along with the comment you submitted. If they wish to see more contexts, they may select a link in the notification email to open the document and go directly to the comment. Alternatively, they can react to your comment directly from the email.

Furthermore, you will also be able to get the following done with the use of modern commenting;

- **Quick Edit:** it is now much easier for you to get into the edit mode for a comment by simply displaying the edit icon in the comment.
- **Ctrl + Enter & Cmd + Enter awareness:** To encourage their use for making comments, these keyboard shortcuts are now displayed in the comment.
- **Comment anchor connection**: To make it easier to understand what a comment is referring to, the text and content that are highlighted in comments have been changed. This makes it fairly obvious that comments will be explicitly linked to the information that is addressed.
- **Tracked changes; showing revision inline**: You can now quickly learn how to use the "Show All Revisions inline" setting to display track changes on the canvas rather than in between the comments when you have a document with comments and track updates.
- **Image support**: Current comments will now show pictures that are already there without requiring you to enter the Revisions window.
- **Font colors**: modern comments will now reveal the font formatting that is currently being used.
- **Selection interaction improvements:** now you can enlarge and also get to read another comment while a draft comment is still in progress.

27.3 Version History and Document Comparison

Reviewing Document Versions

It is now very simple to keep track of changes made to any document and roll back to earlier versions using Microsoft Word. You will discover how to access and retrieve earlier iterations of a Word document. There is a need for you to ensure that the files are saved on OneDrive first before you attempt to view them.

- To start with viewing older Word document versions, clicking **the file name in Microsoft Word's top bar** is the quickest way to accomplish this.

- Once done, choose **Version History.** As an alternative, you can also choose to select the **File button** from the top menu bar. Once done, choose **Info and then click on the Version History icon.**

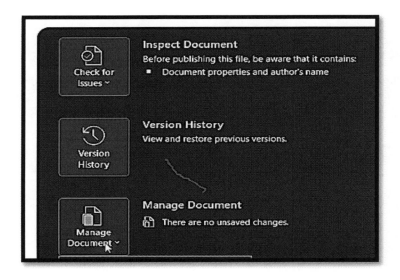

The **Version History pane** will appear on the right after doing this. Your document's most recent version will be shown at the top. Word also neatly organizes your edits according to when they were made, which greatly simplifies finding previous iterations of lengthy documents.

- To examine any version of a document, select **"Open version."** This will cause that file version to open. If the document has a Previous Version label above it, you may verify that it is an older version.

- You can choose the **"Compare" icon** to view the changes made on the same line. This will transfer the previous version of the file to a new document and indicate the modifications made from earlier iterations of the document.
- You will get to locate the exact modifications that have been done there. To start with, you will choose the up arrow icon that can be found beneath **Revisions.** With this, you will be able to see the exact kind of changes that were made to the document and the number of revisions that were made in the current version that is being opened.

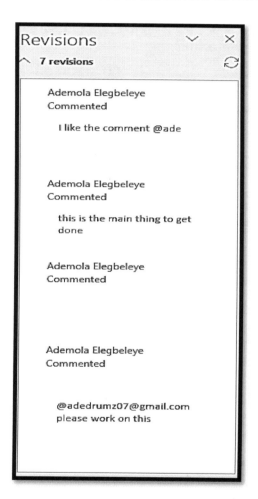

- To have more detail as regards the changes that were made, navigate down in the left pane. This will highlight all of the modifications. There are some paragraphs on the right with a vertical red line next to them. This is merely a straightforward method of indicating that this version of the text has changed. Additionally, there's a means to view more specific modifications by locating the **Review menu.**

- Choose the downward arrow close to Simple Markup in the tracking section.
- Choose **"All Markups."** This will make the details we were looking for clear. The deleted text is indicated with a red font and strikethrough. Red highlights and underlining are added to the additions.

Once you are done with all of the above set of instructions, you are free to save the document if there is a need for you to do so.

Restoring Previous Versions of Word Documents

Now that you have the choice to compare an earlier version, you will exit this document and go back to the prior one. To restore this to the most recent version of your Word document, click the **"Restore"** option here. If this is not what you want to accomplish, you can always use the same procedure to restore previous versions by going to the **Version History window**.

Comparing Changes over Time

You can use Microsoft Word's Compare Documents feature to determine the exact differences between two similar copies of the same document, such as a draft manuscript or basic contract, and an updated or edited version. This function is particularly popular in the legal field since it can produce what is called a blackline comparison. However, this can be very helpful in other professions as well if someone made modifications and saved a fresh version of the document without using Word's Track modifications feature. When I used to compare two documents, I would arrange them side by side on a small screen and painstakingly go over each text, sentence by sentence, for flaws. That procedure, as you might assume, turned my face into a frightening scrunch, and worse, it was a human error waiting to happen. Comparing documents in Microsoft Word's desktop application is quite simple, albeit it's not immediately apparent. This is the simplest method to follow.

(Note: The Word web version lacks a built-in feature for document comparison.)

- Launch **a new Word document.**
- Choose **the Review** that can be found in the upper ribbon.
- Choose **Compare documents** after you have chosen **Compare.**

- **Make an update of the fields below in the Compare Documents window;**
- ○ **Original document**: select the initial document you would like to employ for comparison.
- ○ **Revised document:** select the other version of the document you would like to employ in your comparison.
- ○ **Label changes with**: for a much easier way to check for differences, choose to assign a label; for instance, the name of the writer so you will be able to mark changes in the revised document with that.
- ○ **Naturally**, Word will show the modifications between the two documents in the main document. In case I ever want to go back to the original version, I prefer to compare papers in a new document. Choose a **New document** in the **Show Changes area** to accomplish this. (If you are unable to see this option, select **the down caret [V].)**
- Once the above steps have been completed, choose **OK.**

After that, Word combines the two files and notes any discrepancies as comments in the Markup Area (next to the document). Microsoft Word also highlights text variations and applies a red font color when you're just browsing the document. Once you are done comparing, you should see a three-pane Word document. **Follow the steps below to make use of it;**

- The compared document is shown in the center pane. You are free to make any necessary edits, and it includes every modification made to the amended document.
- The original and updated documents are stacked on top of each other in the right pane. These materials are available for reference only and cannot be altered. It is noteworthy that the center and right windows scroll simultaneously as you go through the document.
- Every modification made to the amended document is listed and summarized on the left page. Any change you click will cause the right and center panes to instantly navigate to that section of the content.

- You are free to accept, reject, and make more adjustments. Make sure you save this new file once you are happy with the document.

Merging documents after comparison

Assume for the moment that you wish to combine all of the modifications made in the second version with the original document's content—minus all markup. Here's how to swiftly complete this task after comparing the two documents.

- On the **Review tab**, select **Accept by clicking the down arrow (V).**
- Select **"Acknowledge All Changes."** Alternatively, to carefully examine each modification and combine certain edits, click **Accept** and move on to the next step.

Word incorporates modifications from the Revised document (the second file) into the Original document when you compare two documents in a new document. Additionally, this is how to combine Word documents without first comparing them.

- Select **Review** from the top ribbon.
- After selecting **Compare**, select **Combine Documents.**

- Choose the two documents you wish to merge from the **merge Documents window that opens.**
- Press **OK.**

Activity

1. Share a document with your friends or colleagues at work and work on the document with them at the same time.
2. Track the changes your friends must have made to the document.
3. Resolve some of the comments made by your colleagues if need be.
4. Take a look at the previous document before it was modified and then compare the various changes that have been made.

CHAPTER 28

ADVANCED FORMATTING TECHNIQUES

28.1: Advanced Page Layout Options

With Microsoft Word, you may arrange the page layout of your document to present information in a way that promotes readability. Setting margins and page size, deciding on the page orientation, adding features like columns, and segmenting a document into sections so that various formats can be applied to different portions are all included in the page layout. The Layout tab's tools provide access to these features.

Custom Page Sizes and Orientations

Page Setup

Located inside the **Page Setup command group, the Layout tab**

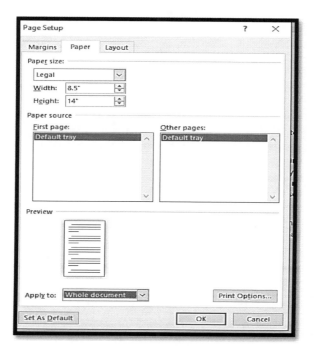

Offers tools and commands for modifying the general page setup of your document. Setting up a page usually entails adding features like section breaks and columns in addition to modifying the paper's size, margins, and orientation. Although there are recognized guidelines for document formatting, they can differ depending on the business and target audience. A 12-point typeface (Calibri, Times New Roman, and Cambria are a few popular fonts) and one-inch margins on all sides (top, bottom, left, and right) are customary for business reports, like your market trends report. To help organize and divide the content, most reports also include divisions and section headings. The reports may have different line spacing, but single, 1.5, or double spacing will be used the most frequently.

Every one of these components affects readability and plays a crucial part in presenting the document to its target audience, which are business professionals. Certain typefaces are more suitable for a particular type of document or are simpler to read than others. For published corporate reports, you can use a style guide (a handbook for consistent stylistic and editorial treatment) such as the Modern Language Association (MLA) style or the Chicago Handbook of Style, however, many companies do not rigorously adhere to a manual of style for internal reports. The employee or supervisor is typically in charge of deciding on the ideal formatting and design for reports such as your market trends report. Ask coworkers in charge of these events if they have any formatting or style requirements for reports that will be delivered outside, like at a conference. Setting up the paper with the intended audience in mind is crucial.

Page Size

Knowing page size is especially crucial if you work for a multinational company. Standard page sizes change between nations, thus it's useful to be aware of potential variations in documents between different company locations. For instance, whereas Europe and East Asia generally use the A4 format (8.25 inches wide by 11.75 inches long), the United States utilizes the conventional letter size, which is 8.5 inches wide by 11 inches long. The Size command also has a drop-down choice of default page sizes, similar to margin selection. You can make your custom page size or pick one of these possibilities. Be aware that materials other than regular pages, including envelopes, are included in the size selections.

Follow the set of instructions below to alter the size of the page. It is worth noting that Word has a lot of predefined page sizes that you can choose from;

- Choose your preferred **Size command from the Layout tab.**

- A drop-down menu will be shown. The current page size will also be highlighted. Choose the preferred predefined page size.
- The page size of the document will be altered.

You not only can choose the predefined page size, but you can also choose to customize the page size in the Page Setup dialog box;

- Choose **Size from the Layout tab**. From the drop-down menu, choose **More Paper Sizes.**
- You will see the **Page Setup dialog box.**
- Choose the **OK button** after you have modified the values for Width and Height.
- Once the above has been completed, the page size of the document will be altered instantly.

Columns

The column format is a common one in print media like newspapers and magazines, where a page's text is divided into several vertical columns. In some Word document formats, including newsletters or brochures, columns are preferred. They can also be helpful if you have a lengthy list of abbreviations and would like to maximize the amount of white space on your page by using columns rather than having a lot of space. Word provides numerous choices for building columns. You can choose among popular column layouts by selecting a part of the text, and then selecting it from the Columns drop-down menu. Equal-sized columns or selections with one narrower column on the side of a bigger column are examples of menu options.

- Select **Columns and then More Columns** if you would want more than three columns on a single page or if you would like to tailor a column to have a specified width. An outline of the document's appearance is displayed in the dialog box. As can be seen in the dialog box, a line can be drawn between the columns.

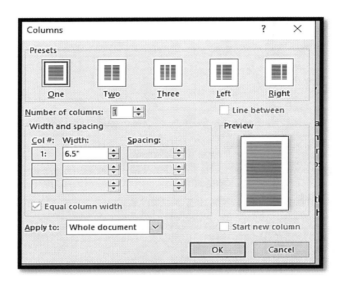

Orientations

The term "page orientation" describes the vertical or horizontal orientation of a page. Word is pre-configured with a vertical layout known as portrait mode. Regular text documents, such as business reports and correspondence, are best suited for this layout. Known as "landscape orientation," the horizontal arrangement is most effective for texts that contain tables and graphs that would not fit well on a vertical page. You can modify the orientation of your entire document or just specific pages or parts by using the Orientation command in the Page Setup command group.

To make certain modifications to the page orientation, follow the steps below;

- Choose the **Layout tab.**
- Choose the **Orientation command from the Page Setup group.**

- A drop-down menu will be displayed. Choose either **Portrait or Landscape** to alter the page orientation.

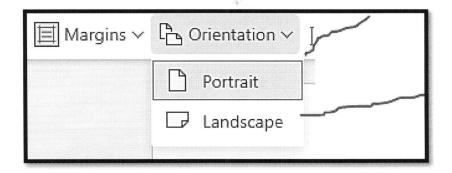

- The page orientation of the document will then be altered.

Line Spacing

Line spacing is the amount of space between text lines as you read through a document. Double-spacing, which is frequently necessary when preparing documents for a class assignment, may be familiar to you. Word, on the other hand, uses single spacing by default. Use the Line and Paragraph function from the Paragraph command category on the Home tab to adjust the line spacing. If you want to alter the spacing between already typed texts, just select the text and adjust the line spacing to the appropriate value. Before entering any text in the document, you can also adjust the spacing. There may be variations in the document's line spacing. It's not required to be constant. Anytime you wish to adjust the line spacing, just select the text to be adjusted and use the Line Spacing tool on the Home tab to choose a new spacing. However, bear in mind that the document you are preparing ought to be professional. It is not a good idea to change the line spacing in the report because that could make it harder to read.

There may be variations in the document's line spacing. It's not required to be constant. Anytime you wish to adjust the line spacing, just select the text to be adjusted and use the Line Spacing tool on the Home tab to choose a new spacing. However, bear in mind that the document you are working on ought to be professional. It is not a good idea to change the line spacing in the report because that could make it harder to read. You can adjust the indentation of lines of text, the spacing before and after paragraphs, and the space before and after lines of text using the Line Spacing Options tool.

Section Breaks

Word sections are quite helpful for writing lengthy papers. With the use of sections, the user can divide a document into separate sections—for example, front matter, body text, and back matter—and format and style each one differently while keeping the entire text on the same page. In a lengthy report, sections are also crucial for setting page numbers and constructing a table of contents. Longer publications, such as comprehensive reports, books, and manuals, are more likely to be divided into front matter, body content, and back matter. Prefaces and forewords, the table of contents, and the title page are usually included in the front matter. The document's primary text is found in the body. A lexicon, index, appendices, and references might be found in the rear matter. Having sections in a document lets you apply distinct styles, such as page numbering, page orientation, and formatting, to each individually, regardless of how you divide it up. Take a look at a document where the main material starts on the third page and there are separate sections for the table of contents and title page. The primary material should begin on page 1, but you don't want a page number to show up on the title page. This can be accomplished by using a section break.

- First, add page numbers to your document by selecting the Page Number option under the Insert menu.
- Navigate to the Layout tab, click the **Breaks drop-down menu**, and choose the **Next Page section break to insert a section break**. On the following page, this will open a new section. Next, select the location for your page number to display. It'll be in the lower right corner. Next, select **"Start at 1"** from the dialog box that displays by performing a right-click on the page number in that new section. This function allows you to apply several page numbering schemes, like Roman numerals for front matter.

Having distinct sections within a document also allows for better integration of various graphics. When working with graphics that are best suited for landscape orientation, for example, this can be useful. You can alter the orientation for a particular section, just like you do with the page numbering.

Advanced Margins and Gutter Settings

Margins

Every page in a document has a margin, which is the space between the content and the edges of each page. Margin enhances the readability of a page and provides room for notes, bindings, and other elements in printed papers. You can come across projects that require unusual margins, bespoke margins, or various margins on separate pages.

- Go to the **Layout tab to change a page's margins**. When you click the **Margin icon**, a drop-down option will show up.

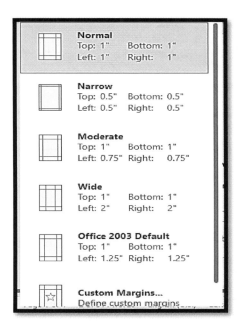

The prepopulated settings allow you to change the default margin, which is Normal (1 inch on both sides), to accommodate other layouts with smaller margins. Select the **Custom Margins option** located at the bottom of the drop-down menu if you wish to adjust the margins yourself.

There are a variety of predefined margin sizes to choose from;

- Choose the **Layout tab**, and then select the **Margins command.**
- A drop-down menu will be shown. Choose the predefined margin size you wish for.
- The margins of the document will be altered immediately.

You can also choose to customize the size of your margins in the Page Setup dialog box;

- From the Layout tab, choose **Margins.** Choose **Custom Margins from the drop-down menu.**

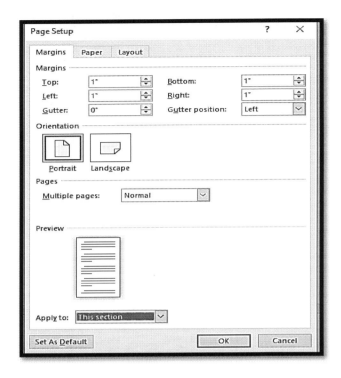

- You will get to see the **Page Setup dialog box.**
- Modify the values for each of the margins and then select **OK.**
- Once the above has been completed, there will be a change in the margins of the document.

Alternatively, you can click the small arrow in the lower-right corner of the Page Setup group and select the Layout tab to access the Page Setup dialog box.

Choosing a Pre-set Margin

The pre-set margins in Microsoft Word provide an easy way to arrange your content. After you make a selection, the text and images will line correctly. You can adjust margins to suit your needs as they vary from narrow to wide. This is how you do it:

- Click **Margin on the Page Layout tab.**
- There's a drop-down option that has various margins. To preview each option, hover over it.
- Select **the appropriate margin by clicking it.**

Every margin option provides a unique set of benefits.

- **Narrow margins**: They work well with lengthy materials. They conserve room for things like papers and reports.
- **Moderate margins**: they are quite useful for daily documents such as letters or memos.
- **Wide margins**: They facilitate reading by providing lots of white space surrounding the text. Excellent for handouts or presentations.

Select the appropriate predetermined margin for polished outcomes and straightforward information delivery. Try out different alternatives to determine which works best. For easier layouts, Microsoft Word has pre-set margin options.

Take these actions to fix any margin problems you may be having with Microsoft Word:

- **Check page layout**: On the **"Layout" tab**, select **"Margins."** Make sure the margin option you have chosen fits your needs.
- **Adjust margin setting**: Click **"Custom Margins"** from the **"Margins" dropdown menu** if the default margin settings aren't appropriate for your needs. This is where you can specify the widths of the top, bottom, left, and right margins.
- **Check page orientation**: Change to portrait mode and make the necessary margin adjustments if your document is in landscape mode and the margins don't seem right.
- **Remove manual formatting**: Go to the section in question and choose **"Normal" from the "Quick Styles" menu** if you have manually changed the margins for that particular section of the page. The margins will return to their initial values as a result.

To ensure that your newly applied margins are applied correctly, always save your document after making any changes. Additionally, make sure you have the most recent version of Microsoft Word installed, as older versions of the program may have compatibility problems that impact margin settings. For instance, one user reported that after updating Word, their margins became problematic. They discovered that the update had caused a glitch that resulted in the margin settings reverting to the default values. This problem was resolved by reinstalling the program.

Margins to default

It's simple to return margins to their original settings. The steps are as follows:

- Open the webpage or document in an HTML or text editor.
- Locate the CSS attributes that pertain to margins, such as margin-top, margin-bottom, margin-left, and margin-right.
- Put values on "auto" or "0." To view the changes, save and reload the webpage or document.

This can assist in fixing layout problems and create a more unified look and feel. To improve this even more:

- Examine whether any CSS rules are superseding the default values for margin.
- Modify margins separately for each piece.
- Examine the file or webpage using many browsers.

Margin adjustments help to enhance the document's appearance and aid in improving readability. This is a necessary ability for anyone working with Microsoft Word documents.

Gutter Settings

The area on the left, top, or inside of the document that is not part of the page margin is known as the gutter margin. Its function is to give additional room for binding written items like manuals, novels, and other such publications. This extra space guarantees that your text will stay intact and leaves enough room for binding.

Size and position of Gutter Margin

Consult the provider that will bind the document to find out the gutter margin size, as it may differ depending on the firm or page count. Gutter margins typically measure 0.5 inches if you're doing it yourself.

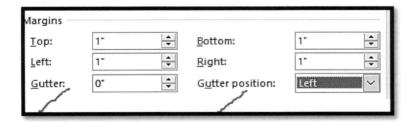

- In Word, you can adjust the gutter margin to the desired size; however, you can only adjust the gutter margin's position while using the Normal page setting. This gives you the option to set the gutter margin to the left or top.
- You can still add the gutter margin size if you choose the **Mirror Margins, 2 Pages per Sheet, or Book Fold settings, but by default, the location is inside or on the left.** Additionally, you'll see that for these document types, the Gutter position setting is grayed out.

Both the Mac and Windows desktop versions of Word have the gutter margin option. Although you can add the functionality on the desktop using Word on the Web or the Word mobile applications, you cannot add or modify gutter margins with them. Books, manuals, pamphlets, catalogs, and related products are examples of printed documents that should include a gutter margin, as previously noted. If you intend to print the document and bind it with a ring, spiral, comb, or other comparable binding method, you can also include a gutter margin. This type of binding is commonly seen on portfolios, legal documents, training materials, and study aids. The Word desktop version for Windows and Mac both allow you to set a gutter margin in the same manner.

- Navigate to the **Layout tab** in Word while your document is open.
- In the Page Setup group, select the **Margins drop-down option and select Custom Margins from the list at the bottom.**
- Verify that you are on the **Margin tab of the Page Setup dialog box.**
- To specify the size of the gutter margin, use the **Gutter setting located in the Margins section.**

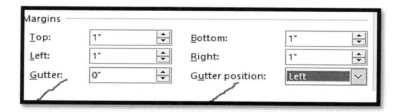

- The Gutter position is another option available to you if you select **Normal from the Multiple Pages drop-down box.** Select **from the Top or Left.**
- The Preview appears on the right side of the screen on Mac and near the bottom on Windows as you make changes. A checkered pattern in black and white is displayed at the gutter margin.
- When you're done, click **OK.**

Upon revisiting your document, you will observe that the gutter margin has been added beyond the margin. After adding the gutter margin, you can easily remove it by going back to the margin parameters.

- Return to the Layout tab, and select **Custom Margins** from the drop-down option. To save the modification, choose **OK** after setting the **Gutter size to "0" in the Page Setup box.**

28.2 Advanced Table Formatting

With the use of Advanced Table Formatting, you can conditionally change a table cell's appearance based on where it sits on the table. For instance, you can make the text in the top row bold or alter the background color of even rows. This can highlight specific areas of the table and significantly increase how readable your tables are.

Built-in-styles

Table styles can be used to provide Advanced Table Formatting to a table. You have the option of making your style or selecting from the several pre-built ones.

- Navigate to the **Table Design tab** to accomplish that. A selection of the available table styles can be seen in the gallery. The arrow at the bottom appears as you move the pointer over the gallery. To see every table style and to expand the view, click on it.

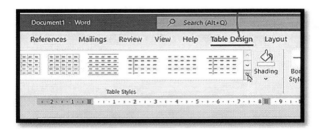

Custom formatting

- Select the **New Table Style...** Choose **from the expanded gallery pane to make a custom table style**. However, keep in mind that Tables have multiple sections to which formatting can be applied. These sections include;

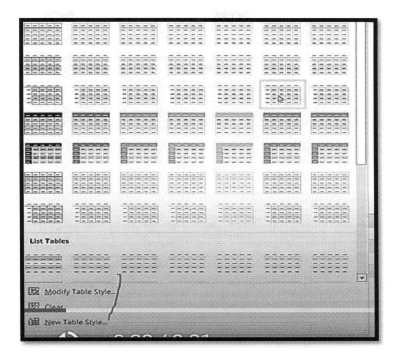

- ○ Header row
- ○ Total row
- ○ First column
- ○ Last column
- ○ Banded rows and columns
- ○ Corner table cells

Checkboxes in the Table Design tab also allow each table to toggle whether the formatting of a specific region should be applied to it. **Note also that by default, the formatting of the following region is usually enabled;**

- • Header row
- • First column
- • Banded rows

Complex Table Designs

One type of chart that arranges and displays data in rows and columns in Microsoft Word is a table. Compared to simple text explanations, it facilitates the quick grasp, comprehension, and analysis of information. There are multiple options in Microsoft Word for inserting or creating tables. Furthermore, you have fine-grained control over the look, feel, and formatting of Microsoft Word tables. Table charts come in very handy for a variety of Word projects, be they for business, education, or personal usage.

Making a basic table

You can design a basic Microsoft Word table in the following way;

- Choose the **Insert tab, and then select the Table button on the ribbon**.

The panel labeled **"Insert Table" appears**. To indicate the number of columns and rows you are interested in creating, drag the cursor over the squares. To apply, click **on the preferred one.**

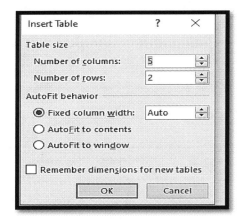

You can also decide to choose the Autofit behavior you would like the table to have. There are various choices available for you to choose from;

- **Initial column width**: By default, the width of your page window is divided across the number of columns in the table by the Auto setting. Alternatively, you can set a distinct column width.
- **AutoFit to contents**: this option alters the size of the column width depending on the width of the content that is on the inside of the column.
- **AutoFit to the Window**: this choice shares the columns evenly across the whole width of the page window.
- **Set as default for new tables**: If you want the configurations to be applied to every new table you create, check this option.
- Click **OK** once you're satisfied with the options you've chosen.

Drawing a Table

In MS Word, a table can be drawn. With this feature, you get to bring in all your creative measures in designing not just a complex table but one that is bespoke! This is a helpful feature if you want to design a more complex or asymmetrical table with different-sized rows and/or columns. To draw a table simply, choose **Insert > Table > Draw Table.** To begin drawing your table, **click and drag the cursor with your mouse or trackpad**. You can start by sketching the table's outermost border.

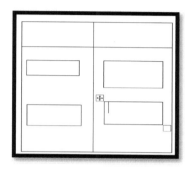

Next, make rows and columns inside the table by clicking and dragging the cursor. Click **anywhere outside the table when you're finished.** If you make an error, you can remove a line from the table by selecting **Layout > Eraser.** To erase a line, click and drag the eraser along it. The line that is going to be removed shows up as a thick red line. To erase, let go of the mouse or trackpad. Once you are finished, click **outside the table.**

Converting Text to Tables and Vice Versa

Transforming text into a table is an additional method of creating a table. This implies that non-tabular data from a plain text file (TXT) or CSV file can be transformed into a table.

- The non-tabular data should first be copied and pasted into your Word document.
- Choose **Insert > Table > Convert Text** to Table while the text is selected.
- The panel labeled Convert Text to Table opens. Choose **the settings that you want to use**. Press **OK.**
- After that, a table is created from the text.

The opposite is also possible; turning a table into text.

- Choose which cells to convert or the entire table. Click **the Layout tab** after that, and then select the **Convert Table to Text icon.**
- The table-to-text conversion panel appears. Here, you can choose how to divide text that is currently displayed in different columns. Click **OK** once you've made your choice.

You can also choose to make nice designs for your table by editing it just the very way you would like to have it.

Add row and column

- Adding a column or row: You can click inside a table cell to add a row or column. To insert, **right-click the mouse and select it.**
  - **Columns to the Left**. Adds a column to the left of the current column
  - **Columns to the Right**. Adds a column to the right of the current column
  - **Rows Above**. Adds a row above the current row
  - **Rows Below**. Adds a row below the current row
  - **Cells** … Inserts a cell and shifts the rest of the cells either to the right or down from where the cursor is
  - **Table** … Inserts a table inside the current cell

As an alternative, placing the cursor in any of the cells, you can choose the Layout tab. Once done you can then make any choice of the following buttons that can be found on the ribbon;

- **Insert Above**. Inserts a row above the current cell.
- **Insert Below**. Inserts a row below the current cell.
- **Insert Columns to the Left**. Inserts a column to the left of the current cell.
- **Insert Columns to the Right.** Inserts a column to the right of the current cell.

When you get to the last cell in the last row of your table, you can finally add a new row. Just hit the tab to bring up a new row.

Delete a column or row

To eliminate a cell, row, column, or table, select the Layout tab > Delete option. Choose from the options that display:

- Delete Cells …
- Delete Columns

- Delete Rows
- Delete Table

To make changes to a table you've drawn, follow the same procedures. Alternatively, you can add or remove rows and columns using the **Layout tab**.

Merge cells

To display information more clearly, you might occasionally want to combine cells. Click and drag the **cursor to select the cells you want to merge to do so.**

- Click the **Merge Cells button on the Layout tab,** or right-click on the cells you want to merge and choose **Merge Cells from the menu.**

Split cells

Cells can always be divided back into separate cells after they have merged. After moving the cursor inside the combined cell, select **Layout > Split Cells.** Or, you can select **Split Cells with a right-click on the mouse.** The Split Cells panel appears in either case. Indicate how many rows and columns you wish to divide the cell into. Press **OK.**

Table styles

Using a preformatted table style is the simplest way to format a table. Place your cursor in any table cell.

- On the **Table Design tab, click it.** After that, click **the arrow to make the Table Styles group larger.**

When you click on a style, it is instantly applied. Any style that you've chosen can be altered. Once more, select **Table Design, and then expand the group called Table Style and select Modify Style.** The panel to Modify Style opens. After making the desired selections, click **OK.** You have complete control over how your table will look by using the Table Design tab. select the **Table Design tab and click any relevant ribbon buttons**.

Table Styles and Themes

Your Word tables can be formatted quickly and consistently by applying table styles. Word comes with many pre-made table styles, or you can design your own. Table styles can be edited by changing table properties, character formatting, paragraph formatting, borders, and shading. Table styles are very helpful if your document has a lot of tables.

Note: Depending on your Word version, screen size, and Control Panel settings, buttons, and Ribbon tabs may appear differently (with or without text). Ribbon tabs may have different names in later Word versions. Table Design, for instance, could be displayed under the Table Tools Design tab.

Each Word document has a theme, which consists of a color scheme and font choice. The color theme guides the selection of colors for table styles. The Themes, Colors, or Fonts drop-down menus on the Design tab in the Ribbon allow you to choose between document, color, and font themes: To format your tables with the colors of your choice, you can also design your unique color schemes. Your document's overall appearance is determined by its theme, which is a collection of fonts, colors, and effects. Using themes is a great way to quickly and simply change the overall tone of your document. Even if you weren't aware of it, you have been using the Office default theme. Each theme has unique theme elements, even the Office theme. You should find that your document looks good and that the colors complement each other if you are using theme elements. This will save you time when it comes to document tweaking. But there's yet another excellent justification for using theme elements: All of these elements will change to match the new theme when you switch to one. With just a few clicks, you can significantly alter the document's appearance, and it will typically still look good. Recall that you can only get updated colors and fonts if you are using theme colors or theme fonts. Your text will remain unchanged when you switch themes if you select any of the default colors or non-theme fonts. This can be helpful when designing a title or logo that must remain consistent over time.

Display gridlines

Turning on gridlines is a good idea when working with tables. Borders are a format that can be printed. Printing gridlines is not possible.

To make grid lines visible:

- In a table, make a click.
- Select either the **Table Layout or the Table Tools Layout tab**.
- Select **"View Gridlines."** All Word documents will continue to have gridlines.

When you click on a table, the **View Gridlines option** shows up on the Table Tools Layout or Table Layout tab.

Applying a table style

It is preferable to use table styles rather than manually or directly formatting each table in a Word document that has several tables that you want to format consistently.

To give a table a table style, do the following;

- In the table, make a click.
- In the Ribbon, select the **Table Design or Table Tools Design tab**.
- In the Table Styles gallery, click the **More down arrow on the bottom right**. There's a drop-down menu.
- Navigate **through the different table styles**. As you navigate between the various table styles in the gallery, the formatting of the tables will alter.

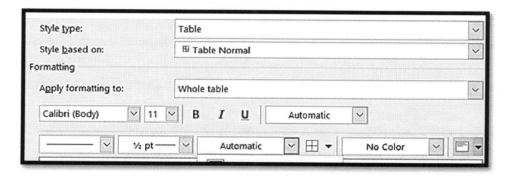

- Select **the desired table style by clicking on it.**

Note: Custom cell formatting for individual cells, row height, and column width are not included in table styles. The table style will be overwritten if a user applies manual or direct formatting (such as fills and borders) to a table on the Table Tools Design or Table Design tab.

Apply Table Style Options

After choosing a table style, you can check or select various Table Style Options, some of which are impacted by the formats of the chosen table style.

You can use the following six table-style options: First Column, Last Column, Banded Columns, Header Row, Total Row, and Banded Rows. If you choose different Table Style Options, you might not notice any differences in the table formatting if you have chosen a plain table style.

When you click on a table, Table Style Options appear as follows on the Table Tools Design or Table Design tab:

Follow the steps below to choose the Table Style Options;

- In the table, make a click.
- In the Ribbon, select the **Table Design or Table Tools Design tab.**
- Header Row can be checked or unchecked in Table Style Options. The header row will be formatted distinctly from the body rows if this option is checked.
- Check Total Row in Table Style Options. The final row will be formatted distinctly from the body rows if this choice is checked.
- To change the shading of a row or column, select or deselect **Banded Rows or Banded Columns in Table Style Options.**
- If you would like the first or last column to be formatted distinctly from the other columns, select **First Column or Last Column under Table Style Options.**

Modify a table style

In a Word document, you can change a table style, and all the tables that use that table style will also change.

Changing a table's style

- In the table, make a click.
- In the Ribbon, select the **Table Design or Table Tools Design tab.**
- In the Table Styles gallery, click the **More down arrow on the bottom right. There's a drop-down menu.**
- To change the table style, click **Modify**.

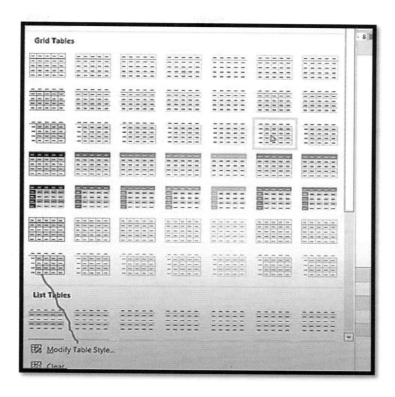

A dialogue window opens. Moreover, you can choose Modify with a right-click on a table style.

- Choose **the item you wish to change (e.g., Header row) from the Apply Formatting to the drop-down menu.**
- Choose **the font, font size, font color, fill, and border that you want.**
- Choose the next element you wish to edit from the **Apply Formatting to drop-down menu.**
- Choose **the font, font size, font color, fill, and border that you want.**
- Continue with the remaining elements.
- In this document or in new documents created using this template, select **Only**. The modified style will only be available for the current document if you choose Only in this document. The table style for upcoming documents based on the current template (usually the Normal template) will change if you choose New documents based on this template.
- Press **OK.**

To select different options, like Font or Paragraph, you may choose **Format at the bottom of the dialog box.** If you make changes to a table style and the tables that use it stay the same, the table may have been formatted manually or directly, overriding the table style. It might be necessary for you to click on the **Clear Formatting button located on the Home tab within the Font group after selecting the table.** In a table style, Table Properties can also be changed. Table properties consist of row configurations, cell margins, and table alignment.

Create a new table style

Additionally, you can design a unique or novel table style.

To design a unique table style:

- In the table, **make a click.**
- In the Ribbon, select the **Table Design or Table Tools Design tab**.
- In the Table Styles gallery, click the **More down arrow on the bottom right. There's a drop-down menu.**
- To use a table style as your base style, click on it.
- In the Table Styles gallery, click the **More down arrow on the bottom right. There's a drop-down menu.**
- To change the table style, click **New Table Style**. A dialogue window opens.
- In the Name box, give **the new table style a name.**
- Choose the formatting that you want.
- In this document or in new documents created using this template, select **Only**.
- Press **OK.**

The newly created table style will show up under Custom in the Table Styles gallery (at the top of the gallery). To remove it, simply right-click on it within the gallery and choose **Delete Table Style.**

28.3 Advanced Graphics and Multimedia Handling

The hardware or software that enables a computer to display and alter images is referred to as graphics. The images themselves may also be implied by the word. For instance, because they enable the computer to print images, plotters, and laser printers are considered graphics devices. By using graphics, you can increase the amount of information and add interest to your documents, spreadsheets, and presentations. All of Office 365's programs use the same commands and tools for adding and modifying shapes, images, clip art, and SmartArt graphics. From improving the appearance of Web pages to serving as the presentation and user interaction layer for fully functional Web applications, graphics are used for a variety of purposes. There are numerous applications for graphics, which means there are numerous technologies available.

Images and Multimedia

Word is more than just a text creation and editing application. It comes with everything you need to create some artistic page layouts. Even though it lacks the power and feature set of a professional page layout program such as Adobe InDesign. Know what you have and how to use it, and you can still look very professional.

Pictures and Online Pictures

Both "Pictures" and "Online Pictures" accomplish the same task. The ability to insert pictures from your computer is the only distinction when you select "Pictures." Nevertheless, you can upload pictures from the internet, including clip art from Office.com, Bing, or OneDrive, when you select "Online Pictures."

Drawing Tools

Drawing tools include curves, lines, shapes, flowcharts, diagrams, and WordArt. The Word document you are working on contains these items. To alter and enhance these objects, you can apply borders, colors, patterns, and other effects.

Picture Tools

You are free to click on anything in a Word document to make changes, and the appropriate tab will appear on the Ribbon. The picture tab is called "Picture Tools." As you work, we can see that you can make adjustments to the image. For example, you can adjust the color, contrast, brightness, and border. The placement and formatting of your text will also greatly influence the final appearance of your documents. Since Word isn't the final step before publishing online, you don't need to worry as much about how words wrap or where they go in our documents. However, these will be important if you're creating something WYSIWYG (What You See Is What You Get), such as for a print or PDF publication. Additionally, you have several options for altering your pictures inline, including resizing, rotating, and moving them. You can see these controls in the following image, many of which you may be familiar with.

Shapes

Microsoft Word has built-in shapes that you can use to create callouts, boxes, stars, and other shapes. All you have to do is draw the shape on a blank area of the page after clicking on it. It doesn't matter if it's flawless or exactly how you want it once it's in your document; you can edit it as much as you like.

- To create a "new drawing canvas," select the option located at the bottom of the "Shapes" menu. This will open a shape box that functions similarly to a text box. On this drawing canvas, you can create drawings using these shapes. This facilitates the creation of flowcharts and diagrams.

SmartArt and Word Art

There are some similarities between WordArt and SmartArt, particularly when you use WordArt to create something and then modify the text. One or the other is acceptable, but not both. Nonetheless, since one frequently leads to the other, we'll talk about them together in this section. Consider SmartArt as ready-made drawing canvases that you can incorporate into your document and customize to your preference. Simply choose a method of organization, such as a cycle, process, or list. You can choose just anything you like, be it even a continuous block process. Also there are always the normal grab handles that are used for modifying the size of the image and layout options which enable the wrapping of text just the way you like.

Chart

Everyone enjoys looking at charts. Visual representations of data sets can be achieved through charts, and Word provides a wide range of chart types, including pie, bars, columns, and many more.

Check out the screenshot to see the number of options you have:

Chart formatting and modification are simple. As you might expect, the "Chart Tools" tab appears when you click on a chart in your document. This is the Ribbon tab specifically designated for charts.

Text Box

Text boxes in Word resemble tiny islands. No matter what you do to the rest of the document, once you add a "Text Box," it cannot be removed. It resembles nesting one document inside of another. This is useful if you want to display something in your work "as is" while still having the option to modify the document's overall formatting. Anything you've copied won't change.

Adding Picture in Document

To incorporate an already-created image into your Word document, follow these steps. You are expected to have a picture on your computer before you add this one to your Word document.

- Choose the area where you would like to include a picture.
- Select the **Insert tab** and then choose the **Picture button** in the illustrations group, the dialog box for insert pictures will then be shown.

- With the use of the box, you will be able to select your preferred picture. Once you choose Insert, the picture you select will be included in your document.

You have several options for experimenting with your inserted picture. You can quickly style it, adjust its size, or change its color, for instance. Simply click on the image you inserted to test it out. Word will then present you with a variety of formatting options under the Format tab. If you'd like, you can experiment with adding additional graphics, like screenshots, SmartArt, charts, Clipart, and various shapes.

Adding WordArt in Document

WordArt allows you to insert fancy words into Word documents. You can back up your text in a variety of ways. To add WordArt to your document, follow these steps.

- Select anywhere in your document where you would like to include WordArt.
- Choose the Insert tab option and choose the **WordArt option** that can be found in the Text group; with this, a gallery of WordArt will be shown.
- To select a WordArt style, just click on any of the images in the gallery. You can now modify the text you've added to suit your needs and enhance its appearance with the various options. Try it out by double-clicking the **WordArt you've added.** Word will then present you with many formatting options on the Format tab for your image. The most frequently used options are Shape Styles and WordArt Styles.

For experimentation, you can alter the insert WordArt's shape styles, colors, WordArt styles, and other elements.

Interactive Multimedia Elements

Digital content that combines text, audio, video, images, and animation with other forms of media to create dynamic and immersive experiences is referred to as interactive multimedia. In addition, it is utilized in e-commerce, news, architecture, gaming, advertising, healthcare, and education.

Enhanced engagement, better learning outcomes, increased accessibility, personalization, improved audience retention, and increased revenue are unquestionably advantages of employing interactive multimedia. It is worth noting that elements of interactive media can also be incorporated into Microsoft Word to ensure that your documents appear more appealing and fun to read!

There are five main elements of interactive multimedia and in this section, you will learn about each one of them;

Text

- The fundamental component of multimedia is text. Text types, sizes, colors, and background colors are all used in it.
- Text is mostly used in multimedia for menus, titles, headlines, paragraphs, lists, and other elements.
- Text can be used in a multimedia application to link other screens or media. You refer to this as hypertext.
- The programs that are most frequently used to view text files are Microsoft Word, Notepad, WordPad, etc. The majority of text files have extensions like DOC, TXT, etc.

Graphics

- It is a digital depiction of non-textual data, like a picture, chart, or drawing.
- The multimedia application is visually appealing. They aid in the explanation of concepts through still images.
- Bitmaps, or paint graphics, and vectors, or draw graphics, are the two types of graphics that are used.
- **Bitmaps graphics**: They also go by the name of raster graphics. An array of dots known as pixels is used in bitmaps to represent images. Large file sizes are produced by bitmap graphics, which depend on the resolution.
- **Vector graphics**: These are computer-generated images created with software that only needs a small amount of memory and represent images using geometrical formulas.

Videos

- The electronic capture, recording, processing, storing, transmission, and reconstruction of a series of still images that depict moving scenes is known as video technology.
- Photographs that give the impression of full motion when they are replayed at 15 to 30 frames per second.
- Video can be effectively conveyed through multimedia applications by embedding it, and this allows for the addition of a personal element that other media cannot.
- Promoting movies, TV series, and other non-computer media that have commercials that have historically included trailers.
- Video gives the audience a sense of the personality of the speaker.

- Video shows moving objects. For instance, a scene from a movie. Video is a great medium for product demos of tangible goods.

Audio

- Audio in multimedia refers to playing, recording, etc.
- Audio is a crucial part of multimedia because it makes the content easier to understand and more conceptually clear.
- Speech, music, or any other sound is considered audio.

The use of sound

Music

- Background
- Attention grabber
- Sound effect

Speech

- Narration
- Instruction

Animation

- The quick presentation of a series of pictures of two-dimensional artwork or model positions to give the impression of movement is called animation.
- It is an optical illusion of motion caused by the persistence of vision phenomenon, and there are several methods to produce and exhibit it.
- Animation is a major component of many multimedia entertainment titles, especially those geared toward children.

Animations can be used for the following;

- Attracting attention.
- Provide information about the state of a process
- Demonstrations
- Interactive simulations

Advanced Image Editing Within Word

Word is a commonly used office program that is typically used to edit text documents. However, did you know that you could use it to edit photos as well? It enables you to edit the inserted pictures to suit your needs in addition to allowing you to insert pictures into documents to improve the way the text is understood. This section will go over how to edit a picture in Word in detail.

Inserting a Picture

You can use the instructions listed below to add an image to Word:

- Type Word into the toolbar, locate, and select the **"Insert" option**.
- After selecting the desired picture, click **"Picture" and you're done**. (Generally speaking, the cursor is located where the added image is.)

Once you have inserted the picture in your document, you are free to do any of the following as it pertains to editing the picture you have inserted.

Change Color

Usually, Word allows us to change the color of an added picture so that it better fits the context. After selecting the newly added image,

- Select the **"Picture Format" button** from the toolbar and click the **"Color" options** drop-down box. The image's color parameters, including color saturation, color tone, recoloring, more variations, transparent color, etc., can be changed here.

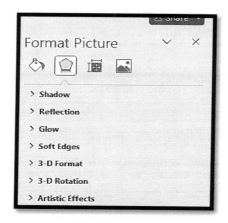

Add Border

The inserted picture can look more beautiful by setting the border. Adding a border to an image can be simple with these steps:

- Put in the image that will have a border.
- Select the **"Picture Format" menu.**
- Locate **"Picture Border"** and select it using the drop-down menu that appears to this button's right. The border's dashes, weight, and theme colors can all be adjusted.

Locate the Picture

The steps that follow will allow you to reposition the image as you please.

- Select **Picture Format from Picture Tools.**
- Click the **Position button**. Word's default format embeds the picture into the text, but we can change this at will using the "Wrap Text" option. You can also simply click **"More Layout Options"** to adjust the picture's position to suit your needs.

Cut Out

In Word, there are two primary methods for achieving clipping:

- When you click **on the image,** a clipping button will show up beneath the function key on the right. To accomplish clipping, click the **button** and use the mouse to drag the black line at the edge.
- Select **"Picture Format" from the toolbar and select "Crop" from the drop-down menu.** It is your choice to cut it freely or crop it according to aspect ratio, shape, etc.

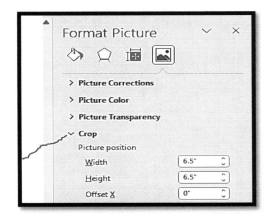

Adjust the Width and Height

Likewise, there are two methods for adjusting the inserted image.

- The first is to find the height and width of the page directly in the upper right corner and **type the value you wish to modify there**. The second method involves picking the image directly, using the right mouse button to select **"Format Picture."** The toolbar will appear on the right; adjust its width and height.

By modifying the width and height, you can alter the image's size.

Compress the Picture

There are just a few easy steps in Word to compress an image: Place the image in the picture tool,

- Choose **Picture Format > Compress Pictures, then adjust the Resolution and Compression Options.**

Artistic Effects

Microsoft Word can, as is well known, be enhanced with creative words to draw readers in or improve the viewing experience. The artistic effect that comes with Word can also be applied to the picture that we inserted.

- Select **Artistic Effects after clicking the image.** Select **your favorite or click "Artistic Effects Options" > on the right, a toolbar will appear.** There are seven different categories of special effects to pick from, including Glow, Reflection, and Shadow.

Embedding Online Videos and Interactive Content

With the help of the Insert Online Videos feature in Microsoft Word, you can incorporate videos from websites like SlideShare.net, Vimeo, and YouTube into your Word documents. This is a great way to include multimedia content in your documents, like interesting presentations, product demos, or instructional videos.

This is the way you do it;

- Launch **the internet browser.**
- Go to **the video that you wish to embed.**
- Vimeo, YouTube, and SlideShare.net are just a few of the websites from which videos can be inserted into Microsoft Word.
- Take **a copy of the URL.**
- To insert the video, **open the Word document that contains the video.**
- In the ribbon, select **the Insert tab.**
- Select **Online Videos from the group of media.**

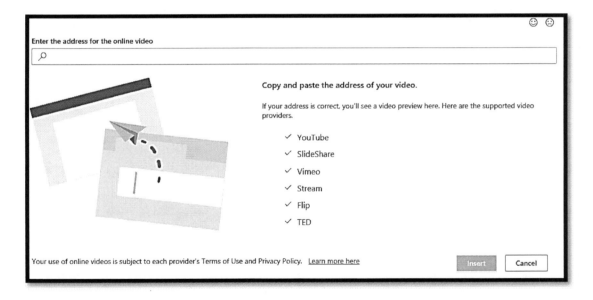

- Paste the URL of the desired video into the Insert Video dialog box.
- Press **the Insert button.**

You can now see your video in your document. You can adjust the size and position of your video after it has been inserted.

- Choose the video thumbnail. Make sure you pick the thumbnail of the video rather than the center Play button.
- To change the size of the video thumbnail, use the resizing handles.
- You can also rearrange your video by choosing a different layout.

Activity

1. Distinguish between custom page sizes and orientations.
2. Work in your Word document with the use of advanced margins and gutter settings.
3. Combine the use of table styles and themes in your Word document.
4. What are interactive multimedia elements?
5. Edit images in Microsoft Word.
6. Embed online videos and other interactive content in your Word document.

CHAPTER 29

AUTOMATION AND MACROS

29.1 Introduction to Macros

What are Macros and how do they work?

Word users can create macros by writing code in Visual Basic for Applications or by using the built-in macro recorder. Macro creation is shared with others and can be stored as an add-in, template, or document. Microsoft Word macros are frequently used to perform complex editing operations, automate formatting tasks, and insert frequently used text or graphics. Macros can increase productivity by lowering the amount of manual labor required to finish a task. To put it simply, a macro is a set of commands and instructions that you can use as a single command to complete an action automatically. You can complete the same tasks with macros, saving you from having to complete each step by hand. You can then save it, assign a shortcut to it, or add it to the taskbar for instant access. Spending less time and effort on repetitive tasks can be achieved by using Microsoft Word. Macros can be used to automate routine tasks, which will ultimately save users time and effort. By creating your macros, you can modify Word to suit your requirements and preferences. Macro automation can reduce the chance of errors and inconsistent formatting in your documents by handling time-consuming formatting and editing tasks. Macros can help ensure consistency by employing the same styles and formatting consistently across multiple documents. Automating complex document processes, applying styles, and formatting text are just a few of the numerous tasks that macros can perform.

When formatting lengthy documents, such as a thesis or dissertation, it can take a long time. By building a macro that applies formatting styles to the document's headings and paragraphs, you can save hours of tedious manual formatting. Macros allow you to give special keyboard shortcuts to frequently used Word commands and tools. This is particularly useful for mouse-accessible functions that are hidden in menus or difficult to use. Macros can be used to automate a variety of repetitive tasks, such as replacing text, adding page numbers, and inserting tables. By building a macro to automate these tasks, you can save yourself the trouble of having to perform them manually each time. Planning thoroughly is the most crucial step in creating effective Word macros. This planning means being clear about the jobs you want the Word macro to accomplish, how it will make your next work easier, and the scenarios you want to use it for. Once you have this in mind, schedule the precise actions. This is important because the recorder will record everything you do and add it to the macro. Word will consistently create the same entry and then remove it when you run that macro, for example, if you type something and then delete it. This leads to an untidy and inefficient macro. Depending on the task's complexity, Microsoft Word supports two different kinds of macros: (1) keystroke macros and (2) scripted macros (also known as Visual Basic for Applications, or VBA). Even though VBA is a strong scripting language that frequently serves as a template for document assembly and supports conditional logic in macros, it is devoid of essential features for complex document assembly.

The absence of tri-state logic in VBA for document assembly is a significant scripting flaw. Conditional logic with document assembly may need to be based on a third state, null or unknown, in addition to one of two states—true or false—in a variety of scenarios. Stated differently, act A if the condition is true. Perform B if the condition is false. And take action C if the condition is unknown. Tri-state logic is essential in scenarios where a template user might not provide any response at all. Put differently, act C if the question remains unanswered. HotDocs is a RAD (Rapid Application Development) platform that was created specifically for document automation. Unlike VBA, it can easily handle tri-state logic and a variety of other scripting tasks related to document automation, like repeating text blocks with automated punctuation and creating documents by aggregating and inserting subdocuments. HotDocs automatically generates questions for variables used in the document, stores, and reuses answer files, and lets a template user go back and forth in a template interview. And that's only a sampling of the features that Word macros cannot provide, but HotDocs can. Keyboard macros are excellent for a variety of repetitive jobs. The functionality of Word can be significantly expanded with the help of the robust language VBA. However, when combined, they still fall well short of HotDocs' functionality unique to document assemblies.

Recording and Running Simple Macros

Creating and executing macros in Word allows you to automate routine tasks. A macro is a collection of instructions and commands that you can combine into a single command to automatically complete a task. When performing repetitive tasks, group the steps into a macro to save time. You start by recording the macro. After that, you can use a keyboard shortcut or a button on the Quick Access Toolbar to launch the macro. Depending on how you configure it, yes.

Record a macro with a button

- Choose **View > Macros > Record Macro.**

348

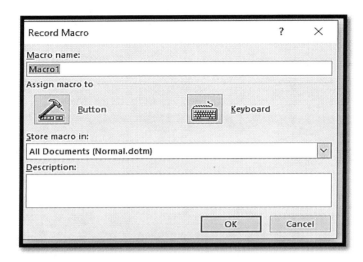

- Give **the macro a name of your choice.**
- To make use of this macro in just any new documents you create, ensure that the Store macro in the box says All Documents (Normal. dotm).
- Choose **a Button** to run your macro immediately just when the button is tapped.
- Choose **the new macro option (it will be named Normal.NewMacros <your macro name>), and choose Add.**
- Click on **Modify.**
- Choose a button image, insert the name you like, and then choose OK twice.
- It's time to write down the steps now. For each task step, click **the commands or press the keys. Word logs all of your keystrokes and clicks.**

Note: While you're recording your macro, use the keyboard to select text. Mouse selections are not recorded by macros.

- To put an end to recording, choose **View > Macros > Stop Recording**. The button for your macro will be shown on the Quick Access Toolbar.

Once the above-described steps have been completed, run the macro by selecting the button.

Recording a macro with a keyboard shortcut

- Choose **View > Macros > Record Macro.**
- Insert **your preferred name for the macro.**
- Make sure that All Documents (Normal. dotm) is selected in the Store macro in the box before using this macro in any new documents you create.
- To get your macros up and running when you tap a keyboard shortcut, choose **Keyboard.**

- Insert a combination of keys in the **Press new shortcut key box.**
- Verify if anything else has been assigned that combination already. Try a different combination if it has already been assigned.
- Make sure that the Save changes in the box are set to Normal in any new documents you create if you want to use this keyboard shortcut.DoTM.
- Press **Assign.**
- It's time to write down the steps now. For each task step, click **the commands or press the keys**. Word logs all of your keystrokes and clicks.

Note: While you're recording your macro, use the keyboard to select text. Mouse selections are not recorded by macros.

- Choose **View > Macros > Stop Recording** to put an end to recording.

Once the above set of instructions has been completed, press the keyboard shortcut keys to get the macro running.

Run a macro

You can initiate a macro by selecting it from the Macros list, by clicking **the button on the Quick Access Toolbar, or by using the keyboard shortcut.**

- Choose **View > Macros > View Macros.**

- Choose the macro you would like to run in the list that can be found beneath the Macro name.
- When the above has been done, choose **Run.**

Make a macro available in all documents

A macro can be added to the Normal. dotm template to enable it to be used in all new documents.

- Launch the document that has the macro in it.
- To view macros, select **View > Macros.**
- Select **Organizer.**
- Choose the macro you would like to include in the Normal. dotm template and choose **Copy.**

Add a macro button to the ribbon

- Select **File > Options > Ribbon Customization.**
- Click Macros under Choose commands from.
- Select **the desired macro by clicking on it.**
- To add the macro, click **the tab and custom group under Customize the ribbon.**

Click **New Group** if you don't already have a custom group. After that, select **Rename and give your custom group a name.**

- Select **Add.**
- Choose **Rename** to make a choice of a picture for the macro and insert the name you want to make use of.
- Choose **OK twice.**

Write a macro from scratch in Visual Basic

- Click **Macros in the Code group under the Developer tab.**
- Enter **the macro's name in the Macro name box.**

Note: The new macro actions will take the place of the built-in macro in Word if you give it the same name. Click Word Commands in the Macros in the list to see an inventory of built-in macros.

- Choose the template or document that you wish to store the macro in from the list of macros.

Make sure you click Normal. dotm to enable your macro in all documents.

- To launch the Visual Basic Editor, click **Create**.

You may want to know more about using Visual Basic for Applications after you launch the **Visual Basic Editor.** Press **F1 or select Microsoft Visual Basic Help** from the Help menu for additional information.

29.2 Advanced Macro Programming

About VBA

A component of Microsoft Corporation's (NASDAQ: MSFT) legacy Visual Basic software is Visual Basic for Applications (VBA). VBA is an internal programming language used by Microsoft Office (MS Office, Office) applications like Word, Publisher, Access, Excel, PowerPoint, and Visio. It is also used to write programs for the Windows operating system. Beyond what is typically possible with MS Office host applications, VBA gives users more customization options.

- Microsoft created and owns the computer programming language Visual Basic for Applications.
- With VBA, you can create custom forms, graphs, and reports as well as macros to automate repetitive word processing and data processing tasks.
- VBA is an integrated component of Microsoft Office applications; it is not a standalone program.
- In Excel, you can access VBA by pressing Alt + F11 when an Excel workbook is open.
- VBA makes statements recognizable by debugging processes by utilizing objects, variables, properties, projects, logical operators, and modules.

Since VBA is an event-driven tool, you can use it to instruct the computer to start a single action or a series of related ones. To accomplish this, you type commands into an editing module to create custom macros, short for macroinstructions. In essence, a macro is a string whose input is another string of characters (its output), which is used to perform particular computing operations. Because VBA is the version of Visual Basic that comes with Microsoft Office, you do not need to buy the VBA software.

With the use of VBA, you can do the following;

- **Write macros**: Financial professionals, including accountants, investment bankers, and commercial bankers, salespeople, traders, portfolio managers, clerks, and administrators, can quickly analyze and make adjustments to massive amounts of data thanks to macros.
- **Perform scenario analysis**: You can create a variety of investment and portfolio-management scenarios using Visual Basic for Applications. This involves sorting through various scenarios that could have varying effects on the results.
- **Organize information:** Additionally, you can use VBA to generate customer name lists or any other type of content, make forms, invoices, and charts, analyze scientific data, and control data displays for forecasting and budgeting.
- **Be unconventional:** You can use VBA to strike accelerator keys, change cell styles across a workbook, and copy and paste values. You can carry out routine tasks, but you can do them more easily and automatically.
- **Prompt action**: You can communicate with users using VBA. For instance, to enter a user's first and last name on a form, you might need their input. VBA can be used to force this input from the user in an unavoidable manner.

Macro Security and Best Practices

A macro is a brief program that is frequently created in Microsoft Office applications to automate repetitive operations. In the past, macros have been used for a wide range of purposes, from individuals automating a portion of their work to organizations creating whole processes and data flows. The Office file contains macros that are written in Visual Basic for Applications (VBA). Although macros are frequently written with good intentions, hackers can also write them to compromise security measures like application allow lists, damage a system, or obtain access to it. Malicious macros can virtually perform any action that other malware is capable of on your computer, such as simulating ransomware, stealing data, and sending emails to your contacts. As the majority of attacks against Microsoft Office, malicious macros are not new; the underlying attack has not changed since the 1990s. However, malicious documents are now harder for traditional antivirus to detect due to obfuscation and dynamic content loading.

Campaigns using spear phishing or phishing frequently include macros. Through emails, the attacker tries to persuade the recipient to open the attached file and launch the malicious macro. Methods (like the ones Microsoft observed) effectively employ social engineering to deceive well-meaning users into permitting malevolent Office macros. Attacks that rely on macros are becoming less common as a result of modifications made to Windows Defender and the default settings in certain Office app versions. They are still very common, though, so action must be taken to further lessen the risk to your company. Microsoft has released more adaptable macro substitutes designed with the threat model of a networked world in mind. These are a combination of enhanced features found in Microsoft 365's cloud-native services and updated Office app versions. It is appropriate to treat macros as legacy features.

Getting your system protected from malicious macros

Office macros are still widely used in many organizations for routine business tasks, such as communicating with outside partners. Companies that continue to use macros ought to plan how to replace them. Since different organizations use macros in different ways, you will need to determine which combination of the mitigations listed below will cause the least amount of disruption for you if you are unable to turn off macros at this time.

Having said that, for every Microsoft Office installation, you should:

- Office macros should only be enabled for staff members who depend on them daily. Disable Office macros outside of the apps where they are necessary.
- If you use Windows, use an anti-malware program that interfaces with the Anti-Malware Scan Interface (AMSI).

When you automatically apply the most recent security updates to the Office Apps and the underlying operating system, such as Windows or macOS, your organization is always best protected.

Disable macros where they are not being used

If macros are not used by your organization, they ought to be completely disabled. If you are unable to turn off macros at this time, you should endeavor to replace the ones that are essential to your company's operations so that eventually you will be able to do so completely. Bigger organizations ought to think about enabling macros only for the teams or groups that need them. As a result, training can be more effectively targeted and focused for these smaller user groups, assisting them in comprehending social engineering tactics and coming to sensible precautionary measures.

Take note of the following;

- The macro engine is enabled by default in currently supported versions of Microsoft Office for macOS and Windows; however, some more recent iterations of the program make an effort to prevent macros that originate from the Internet, as detailed below. Prompts that ask the user to click a button before any macros can begin operating shouldn't be relied upon as mitigation because it is comparatively easy to trick the user into clicking this button.
- On Windows, macros are set up according to the application. You should disable macros in Office applications that you don't use if you use them in some but not in others. For instance, you can turn off macros in Word, PowerPoint, Visio, Access, and Publisher if your company only uses them in Excel. Keep in mind that OneNote does not allow macros.
- On macOS, macros are set up for the whole Office suite, so you should try to turn them off completely.

Reduce your dependency on macros

If you currently use macros, begin substituting them with safe, contemporary alternatives so that, in the long run, you can turn off macros entirely. Replace macros that don't work with the attack surface reduction (ASR) guidelines below priority.

Macro replacements in the modern office automation space include:

- automating data flows with contemporary no-code substitutes like Office Scripts and Power Automate
- creating bespoke web applications to assist your business procedures and utilizing Microsoft Graph to connect to Office 365 data

Disable high-risk macro capabilities

Windows

It is possible to set Windows Defender attack surface reduction (ASR) rules to prevent malicious macros from performing certain functions. If all macro usage in your organization has been disabled, there's no need for you to set these. If you do permit certain macros to execute, you ought to try to activate every recommended mitigation. Initially, they will be executed in audit mode, which enables you to verify that the macros utilized by your organization will function as intended. ASR rules must be tested before being widely implemented in organizations that depend on third-party Office plugins because they also have an impact on how other Office features, like add-ins, behave.

macOS

Office for macOS limits the harm that a malicious document can do by utilizing the sandbox feature of the platform. We advise implementing preferences to fortify the Office sandbox's default setup to further lessen the effects of executing malicious macros.

Disable macros except if they are in trusted files

Additionally, Office for Windows can be set up to only permit macros when a file is loaded from a reliable source, like a particular folder, file share, or website. That list of reliable locations must be established by your organization. It is advisable to restrict the execution of macros to a reliable source, like a network share that is accessible only by trusted administrators. Since many organizations use macros that behave similarly to malware, the antivirus integration mentioned above does not automatically apply to macros in trusted files. It is advised that you change this default as mentioned above to ensure that all trusted files are examined for potentially harmful activity.

Block macros from the Internet

With Office on Windows, an organization can now prevent macros from running in files downloaded from the Internet, except files bearing a publisher's digital signature that the organization has decided to trust. This increases the difficulty of tricking users through social engineering to ignore the warning. This option has been automatically enabled in the Microsoft 365 versions of Office Apps since 2024. Verify if you have deployed version 2206 or a later version. Keep in mind that the setting is not activated by default in Office LTSC or other perpetual versions.

Use an anti-malware product to detect malicious behavior in macros

By using an anti-malware program that offers behavioral analysis for Office documents with macro functionality, you can lessen the likelihood that a malicious macro will infect a user. It might be a function of the anti-malware program installed on the user's device, or it might be a part of your email service. Even if the malicious intent is deceitfully concealed, organizations that use antivirus software that leverages Microsoft's AMSI interface—as advised by the

NCSC's device security guidelines for Windows—will be able to identify malicious macros. As the feature by default only scans documents that Office has recognized as coming from the Internet, you should set it up to scan all documents.

Activity

1. What are Macros and how do they work?
2. Following the illustrations about macros in this book, attempt writing a macro code.
3. Run a simple macro
4. What are macro security and best practices?

CHAPTER 30

ADVANCED TIPS AND TRICKS

30.1 Power User Keyboard Shortcuts

Take some time to become familiar with a few MS Word keyboard shortcuts if you frequently create or edit Word documents. Several of these shortcuts also function in other Microsoft Office programs, such as PowerPoint and Excel.

Learn the Alphabet: Ctrl/Command + A to Z

- Ctrl + A: Select all.
- Ctrl + B: Bold.
- Ctrl + C: Copy to clipboard.
- Ctrl + D: Modify the formatting of characters. This gives us access to effect options such as Subscript, Superscript, Double Strikethrough, and Strikethrough. It can also be used to convert text from lowercase to uppercase or small caps. It can also be used to alter the selected text's font, style, and size.
- Ctrl + E: Align center.
- Ctrl + F: Find.
- Ctrl + G: Go to.
- Ctrl + H: Replace.

Together, these three keyboard shortcuts are very helpful when working with lengthy documents. The Navigation pane may open when using the Find keyboard shortcut rather than the dialog box below. There are more options in the dialog box than in the navigation pane. You can always open the Find and Replace dialog box by using the keyboard shortcuts Ctrl + G or Ctrl + H. Each function in the box—finds, replace, and go to—has its tab.

- Ctrl + I: Italics.
- Ctrl + J: Justify.
- Ctrl + K: Insert hyperlink. This isn't limited to email addresses and web page links. Links to different sections of the same document or to separate documents can be made. Word even allows you to use it to create a new blank document that you can link to and edit at a later time.
- Ctrl + L: Left align.
- Ctrl + M: Indent paragraph.

- Ctrl + N: New document.
- Ctrl + O: Open document.
- Ctrl + P: Print.
- Ctrl + Q: Remove paragraph formatting. Imagine that you have used one of the tools below to format a paragraph. The paragraph formatting will be erased if you place your cursor inside the paragraph and hit Ctrl + Q, regardless of how long ago you applied the formatting.
- Ctrl + R: Right justify.
- Ctrl + S: Save.
- Ctrl + T: Create hanging indent (tab).
- Ctrl + U: Underline.
- Ctrl + V: Paste.
- Ctrl + W: Close document.
- Ctrl + X: Cut.
- Ctrl + Y: Redo previously undone action.
- Ctrl + Z: Undo an action.
- To increase or decrease the font size, press **Ctrl/Command + [(Left Bracket) and Ctrl/Command +] (Right Bracket).** One-point changes in font size can be made quickly with these two key combinations. The selected text's font size can be changed by using **Ctrl + [to make it smaller or larger.**
- **Click/Press Ctrl + Enter to Add a Page Break.** Adding a page break is as simple as hitting **Ctrl + Enter.**
- For Ribbon Keyboard Shortcuts, Use Alt.

This is a Windows-only set of shortcuts. By itself, pressing the Alt key will bring up Key Tips, which are keyboard shortcuts to various Ribbon tools. You can see shortcuts to the various Ribbon tabs by pressing Alt. Next, to access a particular Ribbon tab, you can use Alt in conjunction with the tab shortcut. To exit selection mode, press the **Esc key at any moment.** To close a task pane, use the **Ctrl + Spacebar shortcut.** To see the Key Tips for the Ribbon's tabs, for instance, press Alt. Next, combine Alt with the tab-specific shortcut. The Insert tab can be accessed by pressing **Alt + N.** The Key Advice for the options on the Insert tab will then be visible to you. Just type the desired tool or option's letter(s). You can also choose to change the document's zoom magnification without ever taking your hands off the keyboard. You will use it constantly once you have mastered it. Toggle the **Alt key.** Next, hit **W, followed by Q.** Next, pick the desired value by using the **Tab key** to move around the Zoom dialog box. Click the **Enter key to choose the OK button.**

Navigate the Document with Ctrl key shortcuts

Most likely, you're already navigating your document with the End, Home, Page UP, and Page Down keys. End advances the pointer to the end of the line it is currently on. Home advances the pointer to the start of that line. Page down and Page up move the document left or right.

For more precise document navigation, use the Ctrl key combination.

- Ctrl + End moves the cursor to the end of the document. Command + End on a Mac and Command + Fn + Right arrow on a MacBook.
- Ctrl + Home moves the cursor to the beginning of the document. Command + Home on a Mac and Command + Fn + Left arrow on a MacBook.
- Ctrl + Page up will move the cursor to the top of the previous page. Command + Page up on a Mac and Command + Fn + Up arrow on a MacBook.
- Ctrl + Page down will move the cursor to the top of the next page. Command + Page down on a Mac and Command + Fn + Down arrow on a MacBook.
- Ctrl + Left arrow key will move the cursor one word to the left. Option + Left arrow on Macs.
- Ctrl + Right arrow key will move the cursor one word to the right. Option + Right arrow on Macs.
- Ctrl + Up arrow moves the cursor up one paragraph. Command + Up arrow on Macs.
- Ctrl + Down arrow moves the cursor down one paragraph. Command + Down arrow on Macs.

Use Ctrl to choose Graphics and Text

You can also use the Ctrl key to select text and images. To make choices, use it in conjunction with Shift and the arrow keys.

- Ctrl + Shift + Left arrow key will select the word to the left of the cursor. Shift + Option + Left arrow key on a Mac.
- Ctrl + Shift + Right arrow key will select the word to the right of the cursor. Shift + Option + Right arrow key on a Mac.
- Ctrl + Shift + Up arrow key will select from where the cursor is positioned to the beginning of that paragraph. Command + Shift + Up arrow on a Mac.
- Ctrl + Shift + Down arrow key will select from where the cursor is positioned to the end of that paragraph. Command + Shift + Down arrow on a Mac.

Customizing Keyboard Shortcuts

Keyboard shortcuts, also known as shortcut keys, can be personalized by linking them to a command, macro, font, style, or frequently used symbol. Moreover, keyboard shortcuts can be eliminated. Using a mouse or just the keyboard, you can add or remove keyboard shortcuts.

Make use of a mouse in assigning or removing a keyboard shortcut

- Select **File > Options > Ribbon Customization.**
- Choose **Customize from the bottom of the Customize the Ribbon and keyboard shortcuts pane.**
- Choose **the template or current document name that you wish to save the keyboard shortcut modifications in from the "Save changes in" box.**
- Choose the category from which the command or other item you wish to add or remove a keyboard shortcut is located in the Categories box.
- Choose **the name of the command or other item that you want to add or remove a keyboard shortcut from the Commands box.**
- The Current keys box, or the box beneath the label Currently assigned to, displays any keyboard shortcuts that are currently associated with that command or other item.
- **To assign a keyboard shortcut just do any of the following;**

  o Commence keyboard shortcuts with the use of the Ctrl or a function key;
  o Press the key combination you wish to assign in the Press new shortcut key box. To use a key, for instance, press **CTRL plus the desired key.**
  o To check if a key combination is already assigned to a command or other item, look at Current keys (or currently assigned to). Enter a different combination if the one you're using is already taken.

Important: If you reassign a key combination, its original purpose will no longer be possible to use. For instance, selecting text becomes bold when **CTRL+B** is pressed. You cannot use **CTRL+B** to make text bold if you reassign **CTRL+B** to a new command or other item. Instead, you must select Reset All at the bottom of the Customize Keyboard dialog box to return the keyboard shortcut assignments to their original configuration.

o Choose **Assign**

Remove a keyboard shortcut

- Choose **the keyboard shortcut you wish to delete from the Current keys box.**
- Choose **Remove.**

Use just the keyboard to assign or remove a keyboard shortcut

- To bring up the Word Options dialog box, press **ALT+F, T.**
- To select **Customize Ribbon**, press the **DOWN ARROW key.**
- Tap the Tab key in a repeated manner until Customize has been chosen at the lower part of the dialog box, and then touch the **Enter key.**
- To assign or remove a keyboard shortcut from a command or other item, select the category containing it by pressing the **DOWN or UP ARROW keys** on the keyboard.
- To access the Commands box, press the **TAB key.**
- To choose the name of the command or other item you want to add or remove a keyboard shortcut from, press **DOWN ARROW or UP ARROW.** The Current keys box or the box beneath the label "Currently assigned to" both display any keyboard shortcuts that are currently linked to that command or item.
- **Do the following to have a keyboard shortcut assigned;**

    o Start keyboard shortcuts with Ctrl or a function key
    o When the cursor appears in the Press new shortcut key box, keep pressing the **TAB key.**
    o To assign a key combination, press the desired key combination. To use a key, for instance, press **CTRL plus the desired key.**
    o To check if a key combination is already assigned to a command or other item, look at Current keys (or currently assigned to). Enter a different combination if the one you're using is already taken.
    o To select the Save changes in the box, keep pressing the **TAB key.**
    o To save the keyboard shortcut changes, highlight the name of the current document or template by pressing DOWN ARROW or UP ARROW, and then hit ENTER.
    o Once Assign is selected, keep pressing the **TAB key** until it appears, and then hit **ENTER.**

The key combination CTRL+ALT+F8 may already be set aside for starting keyboard programming if you use a programmable keyboard.

To remove a keyboard shortcut

- To select the Save changes in the box, keep pressing the **TAB key.**
- To save the keyboard shortcut changes, highlight the name of the current document or template by pressing **DOWN ARROW or UP ARROW, and then hit ENTER.**
- When the cursor appears in the Current keys box, keep **pressing the SHIFT+TAB key.**
- Using the **DOWN or UP ARROW keys**, choose **the keyboard shortcut you wish to delete.**
- Once Remove is selected, keep pressing the **TAB key** until you see it, and then hit **ENTER.**

30.2 Efficiency Hacks for Word

Streamlining Your Workflow

Success in the fast-paced world of today depends on maintaining efficiency and organization. It's essential to have tools that can help you stay on top of your tasks and streamline your workflows because work demands are always growing. Microsoft Office Word for PC is one such tool that has become standard in offices all over the world. This section will go over the features and advantages of Microsoft Office Word for PC, as well as how using it can improve productivity and help you stay organized. With its extensive feature set, Microsoft Office Word for PC is a potent word processing program that makes it easy to create, edit, format, and share documents. Word has all the features you need to create documents quickly and easily, whether you're writing a report, a business proposal, or just taking notes. Word's user-friendly design and intuitive interface make it easy to navigate through all of its features. Word has everything you need for formatting, from basic options like font styles and sizes to more complex features like inserting tables, charts, and images. Additionally, the program provides a variety of customizable templates that you can use to save time and effort when creating documents that look professional.

Collaboration Made Easy

The smooth collaboration features of Microsoft Office Word for PC are among its best qualities. The days of having numerous people work on separate drafts of the same document or exchange endless email attachments are long gone. Teams can now collaborate in real-time on a single document using Word's real-time collaboration feature. With the help of this feature, several people can edit the same document simultaneously and instantly see each other's changes. Team members can discuss edits or offer feedback using the chat feature without ever leaving the document. In addition to saving time, this guarantees that everyone agrees, fostering better teamwork and increased output.

Enhanced Organization and Efficiency

Apart from its capabilities for creating documents and collaborating with others, Microsoft Office Word for PC provides a range of tools that can assist you in maintaining organization and enhancing productivity. The ability to create and manage headings, subheadings, and content tables is one such tool. This saves you important time when looking for specific information by making it simple to navigate through lengthy documents or reports. The capability of Word to create hyperlinks inside of your documents is another helpful feature. This removes the need for manual searches and window switching by enabling you to link pertinent data or external sources directly within your document. Word allows you to quickly access related content or additional resources, which help you stay, focused on the task at hand and streamline workflow.

Seamless Integration with Other Office Suite Applications

Word for PC with Microsoft Office easily interacts with PowerPoint and Excel, among other Office suite programs. Data can be easily transferred between documents with this integration, maintaining data integrity and formatting. For instance, you can easily import tables from Excel into Word or incorporate PowerPoint presentations into your writing. This degree of integration guarantees consistency between files while also saving time. It makes it unnecessary for you to constantly switch between different software programs, which improve your productivity. Microsoft Office Word for PC can help you with any type of report creation, including data analysis from Excel and the incorporation of PowerPoint visuals.

Advanced Find and Replace Techniques

Occasionally, after typing a report, presentation, or letter, you realize that there are a few frequent spelling mistakes in the Word document. It shouldn't take long to make a few changes if the document is brief. However, you can quickly accomplish that by using Word's Find and Replace feature. While the Replace feature lets you replace words, the Find feature lets you find every instance of a particular word. Here's how to make use of both functions.

Find Text

You can use a keyboard shortcut to quickly access the Find function in Microsoft Word's Navigation panel. This is how it operates:

- Open the document in Microsoft Word.
- To open the Navigation pane, simultaneously press the **CTRL and F keys.**
- Enter the text you're looking for in the **"Search document" text box.**

- In the Navigation pane, you will see the related matches when you press Enter to carry on with your search. All of the matching words in the text—even the ones that only partially match—are highlighted by the tool.
- Use the arrows next to the text box to navigate between results. Additionally, you can **edit any result directly by clicking on it.**
- You can use the Headings tab to search your document if it has headings. To use headings to navigate your document, go to the Navigation pane and **select any heading.**

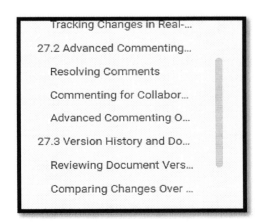

- To search by page, select the **Pages tab from the Navigation page**. When you do, the document's pages will all appear as thumbnails. Locate the text by **clicking on the desired page.**

After making changes to the document, you can close the Navigation Pane, in which case the highlights will vanish. The next method can be used to search for special characters in a Word document using the find feature.

Find Text with special characteristics (Advanced Find)

When searching for more precise words or phrases, the Advanced Find feature is useful. Special characters only complete words, or a unique style or font are a few examples. You can easily track these words or phrases with the aid of Advanced Find.

To learn how follow the instructions below:

- Open the **document in Microsoft Word.**
- Click the **drop-down menu under Editing on the Ribbon.**
- To open the Find and Replace dialog box, click **the drop-down arrow next to Find and select Advanced Find.**

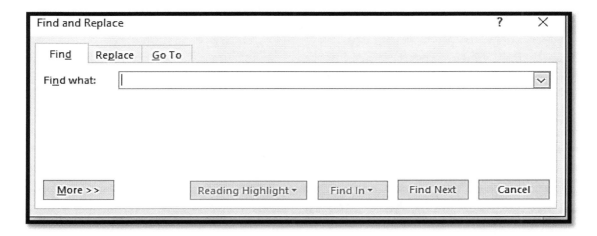

- To open the Find and Replace dialog box, simultaneously press the **CTRL and H keys on your keyboard.**
- Click **More** to further customize your search.

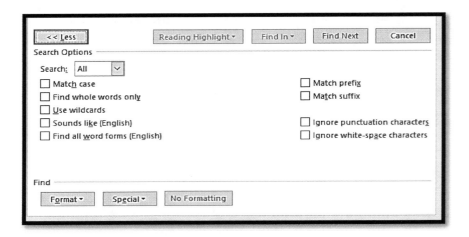

You'll be able to access additional advanced search options after doing this. Any of the following options can be chosen:

- ○ Match case
- ○ Use wildcards
- ○ Find whole words only
- ○ Sounds like
- ○ Match prefix
- ○ Match suffix
- ○ Find all word forms
- ○ Ignore white-space characters
- ○ Ignore punctuation characters

Replace Text

Using the Replace Text feature is one way to change a particular word or phrase. The steps below will walk you through how to accomplish this:

- Open **the document in Microsoft Word.**
- Click the **drop-down menu under Editing on the Ribbon.**
- To open the Find and Replace dialog box, click the **drop-down arrow next to Find and then select Replace.**
- Two fields ought to be visible in the Find and Replace window. Put the new word or phrase in the Replace with box and the word or phrase you wish to replace in the Find what box.

- Click **Replace** if you want to change a specific search result. Choose **Replace All**, though, if you want to change every search result.

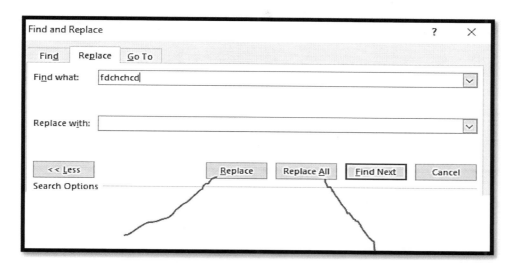

Replace Text with Special Characteristics

This function and the previous Advanced Find option are extremely similar. It lets you select text and swap out characters, sentences, or words with punctuation, capitalization, or a particular style or font.

You can use this option by following these steps:

- Open the **Microsoft Word document.**
- Click the drop-down menu under **Editing on the Ribbon.**
- To open the Find and Replace dialog box, click **the drop-down arrow next to Find and then select Replace.**
- Two fields ought to be visible in the **Find and Replace window**. Put the new phrase or word in the Replace with box and the special word or phrase you wish to replace in the Find what box.
- To further personalize your search, select **More** and check the appropriate boxes for your Replace feature.

30.3 Integrating Word with Other Microsoft Apps

Seamless Integration with Excel, PowerPoint, and Outlook

Excel

In a Word document, insert any portion of an Excel worksheet:

- To view the worksheet, open the Word document.
- To link the data in an Excel worksheet to a Word document, open the worksheet.
- To include a range of cells, select **it in Excel and copy it**. If adding additional rows or columns to the worksheet, choose **the complete worksheet.**
- Move the cursor to the desired location in the Word document to insert the linked table.
- Choose **Insert > Link then ensures you Keep Source Formatting or Link & Use Destination Styles** with a right-click.

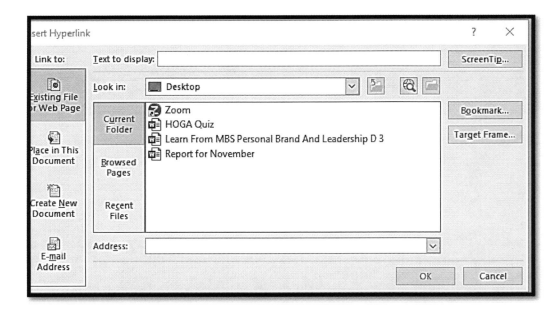

Note that Destination Styles makes use of Word's default table formatting, which typically yields a more aesthetically pleasing table. The Excel workbook's formatting is used when using the "Keep Source" format. Wherever the cursor is, the Excel data pastes right into the Word document. The Word document automatically updates with modifications made to the source Excel file.

What happens when you link Excel to Word

When you link an Excel file to a Word document, any changes made to the Excel file's data will also be reflected in the Word document. The linked Word document receives the updated Excel data through a one-way link feed. Because the data does not save to the Word document, linking an Excel worksheet also helps to keep your Word file small.

- The link to the Word document must be reestablished if the Excel file moves.
- The Excel file needs to be transported if you intend to use it on a different computer or transport the Word document.
- Data editing must be done in the Excel worksheet. Unless you need different spreadsheet formats in the Word document, it shouldn't be an issue.

How to Embed an Excel Spreadsheet in Word

Linking to an Excel worksheet is not much different from embedding an Excel worksheet in a Word document. Although it does take a few more clicks, it imports not just the selected range but all of the worksheet's data into your document. Word offers two options for embedding an Excel worksheet. The worksheet should first be embedded as an object. The insertion of a table is the second. Please be aware that Word applies the formatting from the Excel worksheet when you embed a worksheet. Verify that the worksheet's data appears in the Word document the way you intend it to.

- **Embedding an Excel worksheet as an object;**
    - Launch the **Word document.**
    - Locate the **insert tab.**
    - Choose **Insert > Object.**

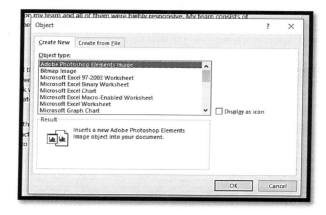

- Choose the **Create from File tab** in the Object dialog box.
- Choose the **Excel worksheet** that has the data you would like to embed after you have chosen **Browse.**
- Choose **OK.**
- The Excel worksheet is then embedded in the Word document.
- Embedding an Excel Spreadsheet Table. Inserting the Excel worksheet as a table is an alternative. The worksheet is inserted using this method in an object-like manner. The distinction is that you can fill out a blank Excel worksheet by opening it. If you haven't yet created the Excel file, use this method.

Follow the set of instructions below to insert an Excel worksheet as a table in Word;

- Launch a **Word document.**
- Position the cursor where you would like to put the Excel worksheet.
- Locate the **Insert tab**, and then choose **Table.**
- Choose **Excel Spreadsheet.**
  - This menu item launches an Excel spreadsheet that is empty and ready for data entry. You can either paste data from another spreadsheet or add new data. You have an Excel file that you can update at any time when you insert and complete a new worksheet in Excel. The Word table's data automatically updates to correspond with the Excel file's data.

PowerPoint

You have undoubtedly noticed by now the similarities in how Microsoft apps integrate. The Microsoft suite is particularly well-suited for both traditional office buildings and collaborative workspaces because of this important feature. At all organizational levels, communication and teamwork are made easier by the simplicity with which Word and Excel, Excel and PowerPoint, and PowerPoint and Word can be integrated. Using an integrative suite like Microsoft can be beneficial for both small and large businesses. This section is dedicated to Word and PowerPoint. This integration can be especially helpful when creating materials for meetings or presentations where having information available may be necessary. In addition to a slideshow presentation that supplements the meeting discussions, this information may be provided as a Word document or handout. Presenting the slideshow content on the handout or including a link to a Word document within a PowerPoint can be helpful at times. Integrating Word and PowerPoint allows you to use many of the methods you discovered in this and earlier chapters on the subject. As with other integrations, the first thing to decide on when integrating the two apps is whether to link or embed. If you are certain that you won't need access to the source files and that the original document won't change, then go ahead and embed it. Select linking if you want to be able to access the source document in case you need it and you anticipate updates.

Follow the steps below to add Microsoft Word documents to Microsoft PowerPoint slides;

- Make **a fresh presentation**. Alternatively, you could open a previous presentation or work from a template instead of starting from scratch. (These subjects were discussed in the chapters on PowerPoint.)
- Choose **the slide on which you want the content from the Word document to appear in the presentation**. The data from the source file will be displayed at the cursor location, just like in other applications. Go to the **Text command group, then to the Insert tab, and finally to Object.** The function window looks like other Microsoft programs, but on the left side, there are option buttons to select from rather than separate tabs for **Create New and Create from File.**
- Locate the Word file by using the **Browse button**. Make sure to check the **Link box if you want to create a link between the Word and PowerPoint files**. A picture of the information will be added to the slide when the Word document is linked. Double-clicking the image will launch Word, allowing you to make any necessary edits to the document. The content from the Word document will be embedded into the slide rather than linked if you do not select the Link box. (Ensure that the monthly report document is closed; an error message will show if it is.) Click **OK** when you are finished. The slide will now display the report's contents.

Follow the steps below to integrate Microsoft PowerPoint slides into Microsoft Word documents;

Let's say you decide that people who are unable to attend the monthly sales meeting in person should have access to the PowerPoint slides. Sending several files, though, is not what you want to do. Rather, the presentation should be incorporated into the document you already created to also present. The first thing you must do is choose whether to include all of the presentation's slides or just a select few in the Word document. It is preferable to use the cut-and-paste techniques you studied in a previous chapter if you want the user to be able to view every slide in the Word document without having to double-click on the inserted object. If you wanted to see every slide in the Word document, you would have to cut and paste each slide separately. You can allow the user to access any or all of the presentation's slides by linking or embedding them, but unlike copying and pasting, they won't show up on the screen individually. When using linking and embedding, the user will only see a single slide's image; to access the other integrated slides, they must double-click on that image. Depending on whether you anticipate updates to the source file, decide whether linking or embedding is better for your purposes. Next, decide whether you want to integrate all of the slides or just some of them. Choose the **Object function to embed or link the PowerPoint file to your Word document** if you wish to incorporate the complete presentation. To do this, select the **Insert tab, then the Text command group.** After copying the slides you want to use, you'll need to use Paste Special if you just want to include a few of them. Choose **a slide from the presentation from the PowerPoint file's** preview thumbnail to get started. You will need to use Ctrl or Shift when you click on the additional slides to select multiple slides. As usual, to select a slide on a Mac, press the **Command key rather than the Ctrl key.** If you would like to pick slides 1, 3, and 5 separately, or if the slides are not consecutive, use **Ctrl to select each one separately.** Click the first slide, hold Shift, and click the last slide in the grouping you want to select to choose a set of contiguous slides. Move the pointer to the desired location in the Word document to insert the chosen slides into it. In the Clipboard command group on the Home tab, select Paste Special from the Paste drop-down menu. Click **OK** once you're prompted to select **Microsoft PowerPoint Presentation Object.** The Word document will contain embedded slides. Since you are only including a few chosen slides and not the complete file, you are not able to link the PowerPoint file in this scenario. The user can view the other embedded slides in the Word document by double-clicking on the slide image. You can scroll through the slides to view the remaining ones once they open on a PowerPoint view screen. Be aware that when inserted into a Word document, embedded PowerPoint slides can occasionally appear hazy. This is typical; their translations are not always accurate. **By performing a right-click on the slide image, you can also access the other embedded slides. To view the remaining slides,**

- Select **Presentation Object and Show Next**. With this option, the first embedded slide appears full screen. To view the next slide, press **the keyboard's Page down key.** Alternatively, right-click to view all embedded slides and select Next or View All Slides. You can use the keyboard shortcut ESC to return to the Word document. If you want to return to the Word document, you can also right-click and select End Show. Edit, Open, and Convert is further available options. You can edit the slides in a PowerPoint environment inside the Word document by using the **Edit function.**

Selecting **Open** will cause PowerPoint to open the item. Lastly, you can change the object's file type by using Convert. Using the **Add Comment tool** located in this menu, you can also invite your readers to add comments to the PowerPoint. Without sending separate files, this can be a great way to promote feedback and teamwork on your PowerPoint file.

Outlook

Your Word documents' contents can be sent as an email message. Outlook converts formatting to HTML when a message is sent, so Word gives you more formatting control when composing a message than Outlook does.

- You must first set up your email in Microsoft Outlook before you can send an email from Word. You also need to manually add the email button to the Word ribbon. All you need to do to send email from Word is click the **"Send to Mail Recipient"** button once Outlook is configured.
- In Microsoft Outlook, navigate to **"File"** and then "Account Information," then click **"Add Account"** to add a new email account. Outlook only allows you to link to an already-existing email address; it cannot be used to create new ones.
- Include your name, email address, and password in this field. Press "Next." You must install Microsoft Outlook Connector if your email address is from Hotmail or MSN (hotmail.com or msn.com).
- Make sure it connects correctly. If the automatic setup doesn't work, you may be asked to manually enter the server information. Verify in the documentation provided by your provider whether POP3 or IMAP can be used with your email address.

Add email button to Word

- In Microsoft Word, select **"File" and then "Options".** Navigate to the "**Quick Access Toolbar."**
- Click on the "**Choose Commands From"** list and choose "**All Commands."**
- Verify that it connects properly. You might be prompted to manually enter the server information if the automatic setup fails. Check whether POP3 or IMAP can be used with your email address by consulting the documentation that your provider has provided.

Data Sharing and Collaborative Workflows

Giving digital files; Microsoft Word documents—to other people is known as document sharing. It allows multiple users, no matter where they are, to access and collaborate on the same document at the same time. This implies that it will be simple to track changes, make comments, and make edits in real-time. These days, businesses and organizations have to have document sharing. Colleagues can work together on projects without having to worry about time zones or distances thanks to this perfect method. Electronic document sharing improves productivity and efficiency while streamlining communication. A Microsoft Word document can be efficiently and without difficulty shared. Multiple users can work together and edit simultaneously. Here are a few methods for sending your document to friends, clients, or coworkers.

Using Word's built-in sharing feature is one way.

- To collaborate, just click the **"Share" button** in the upper-right corner of the screen and enter the email addresses of the individuals you want to work with. Additionally, you can indicate that they have only view or edit rights.

Using cloud storage services such as Google Drive or Microsoft OneDrive is another way to share Word documents. To create links that can be shared and used for collaboration, upload your document. When sharing large files or when someone doesn't have Word, this is helpful. Use password protection or limit access permissions for greater control. Assign each recipient a password or restricted editing rights. This works well for working with small groups or sensitive information. Working together on Microsoft Word documents enables several people to edit the same document at once, increasing efficiency and productivity. Through the use of Microsoft Word's collaboration features, users can share documents with ease, make edits in real-time, and seamlessly track changes. Apart from sharing features, Microsoft Word offers several tools for collaborative editing. The ability for multiple users to edit the same document at once makes it possible for teams to collaborate effectively. Everyone involved can see real-time updates instantly, doing away with the need for manual change merging and frequent document transfers.

There are many benefits to sharing a Microsoft Word document. You can work together easily, exchange ideas instantly, and edit and review with precision and few errors. It can also be accessed simultaneously by multiple users. Additionally, version control makes it easy to track changes made by various contributors. Improved team communication leads to increased productivity and more efficient workflows. Decisions can be made more quickly because feedback can be given promptly. Additionally, it easily integrates with other Office programs like PowerPoint and Excel, enabling improved analysis and presentation creation. Document sharing facilitates creativity and problem-solving.

Follow the steps below to be able to adequately share a Microsoft Word document with ease;

- Launch the **Word document that needs to be shared.**

- In the upper left corner of the screen, select the **"File" tab.**
- From the drop-down menu, choose **"Share."**

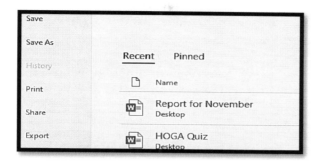

- Select your favorite sharing technique, whether it is creating a sharing link or sending an email invitation.
- Either copy the sharing link or enter the recipients' email addresses.
- If necessary, adjust each recipient's permissions before clicking "**Share.**"

Working together on projects with Microsoft Word documents provides a smooth and effective method of collaboration. **To have a view of the genuine advantages and features of working together on Microsoft Word documents, see the table below:**

Benefits	Description
Real-time collaboration	Allows more than one user to simultaneously modify and make comments on a document.
Track changes	Ensure it keeps track of modifications created by each collaborator giving way for a very easy review.
Version History	Enables users to gain access to former versions of the document and bring back the changes that were made.

Comments	Help with the facilitation of communication and feedback among team members
Co-authoring	Offers support to editing and also encourages writing simultaneously with other people.

To adequately collaborate on a document, follow the steps below;

Step 1: Opening a shared document

- Open **Word.**
- Select **File > Open.**
- Select **"Shared with Me**" from the menu on the left.
- Select t**he required shared document.**
- After clicking **Open**, you're all set to go!

Additionally, keep in mind that you can view real-time changes made by other collaborators and engage in dialogue through comments when you open a shared document. Always use Word's collaboration features and save your work.

Step 2: Editing and making changes

When working together on Microsoft Word documents, editing and making modifications is essential.

To ensure everything goes as planned, follow these five easy steps:

- **Launch the document:** Obtain it via a file-sharing website or email.
- **Monitor Changes:** Maintain a log of every alteration that is made. This enables team members to evaluate each other's edits.
- **Include remarks:** Make comments or recommendations for particular sections. This facilitates the editing procedure.
- **Accept or reject the modifications:** Before incorporating any changes into the final version, give them careful thought.

- **Conserve and distribute:** Save the document and distribute it to others for additional assessment and editing.

Step 3: Commenting and providing feedback

Collaborative work necessitates comments and feedback on Microsoft Word documents. Use this function to quickly and easily share your thoughts, opinions, and concerns. Boost the caliber of the document! **These three actions will help you provide effective feedback:**

- To leave a comment, select the **text or document section.**
- On the toolbar's **"Review" tab, select "New Comment."**
- Enter your feedback and click outside the box to save it.

This approach helps you focus on your ideas and makes them more comprehensible. You can also respond to previous remarks made by other team members. This removes confusion and keeps everyone's feedback organized. Never has teamwork gone so smoothly!

Step 4: Resolving conflicts and version control

Get your work organized! To indicate edits and suggestions make use of tools like track changes, comments, and highlighting. Talk to each other! Maintain communication with your partners. Reach a consensus by talking about the changes. Manage iterations! Keep track of revisions to the document and go back to earlier iterations as necessary. When resolving disputes and conflicts, initiative is crucial. Improve cooperation and steer clear of issues.

Activity

1. Name powerful shortcuts that can be used in Microsoft Word for easy navigation.
2. Streamline your workflow.
3. Make use of the find-and-replace technique.
4. Integrate Microsoft Word with Excel, PowerPoint, and Outlook.

CHAPTER 31

EQUATIONS AND FORMULAS IN WORD

31.1 Introduction to Mathematical Equations and Symbols

Inserting Basic Mathematical Equations

Equations

Worksheets for students or financial reports are just two examples of math-related documents that many professionals create. Equations may be needed in these documents to illustrate mathematical concepts and assist the reader in completing calculations. You can efficiently insert formulas and maintain the formatting of your documents by using Word's equation feature. In this section, you will learn about inserting math equations and symbols in Word.

Inserting an equation in Word using preset options

The program includes the Pythagorean Theorem and the area of a circle formula, among other common equations you can use in your documents. Here's how to use Word's preset options to insert an equation.

- Access any given document.
- To make the equation appear in the desired area of the document, click on it.
- Make a click on the **"Insert" tab.**
- Either choose **"Equation" from the "Symbols" group** or use the keyboard shortcuts "Alt" and "=".
- Click **"Equation" in the "Tools" group of the "Design" tab.**

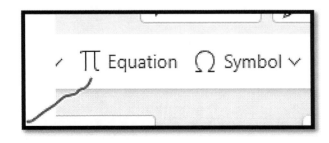

- To view more equations, either click **"More equations from Office.com" or browse the options in the drop-down list.**
- Choose the equation you want to use.

Inserting an equation in Word manually

Although there are a good number of pre-made equations in the program, you might want to make your own. Here's how to manually enter an equation in Word:

- Click the equation's insertion point when your document is open.
- Navigate to the **"Insert" tab.**
- Locate the "Symbols" group and select **"Equations."**
- To construct your equation, select the **"Design" tab.**
- Type common characters and symbols like "+," "=," and "with your keyboard.
- To enter more complex expressions, use the icons found in the "Symbols" and "Structures" groups.
- To finish your equation, click outside the box.

Insert an equation in Word with the use of Ink Equation

Using Word's "Ink Equation" feature, insert an equation as follows:

- To place the equation where you want it, click **on the desired area of the document.**
- Navigate to th**e "Insert" tab.**
- Within the "Symbols" group, select **"Equation".**
- Choose **"Ink Equation"** from the **"Tools"** category.

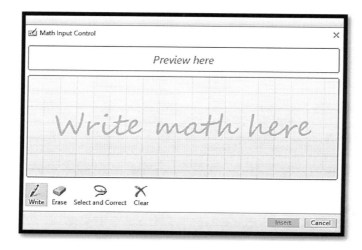

- If you're on a desktop, use your mouse to write your desired equation in the yellow box; if you're on a mobile device, use your finger or stylus pen.
- Check the **"Preview here"** box to make sure the program is reading your handwriting correctly.
- To carry out these tasks, press the **"Erase,"** "Select and **correct,"** **and "Clear"** buttons.
- To complete your equation, click **"Insert"**.

Saving an equation in Word

You might want to store the equation you create for later use. This is a particularly helpful feature if you intend to use the equation a lot.

To save an equation in Word, follow these steps:

- Get your document open.
- The equation you wish to save can be clicked.
- In the lower right corner, click **the down arrow.**
- Select **"Save as New Equation."**

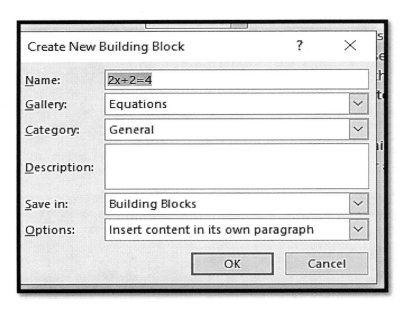

- Give the equation a name in the **"Create New Building Block"** dialog box.
- Click "**Equations"** from the list of galleries.
- Press **"OK."**

As an alternative, you can select the

- **Equation** by clicking on the insert tab first. In the "Symbols" group, select **"Equations"**. Choose **"Equation" from the "Design" tab**. Go to the drop-down menu and choose **"Save Selection to Equation Gallery."** As with the previous method, by clicking **"OK,"** you can give the equation a name and save it to the gallery list.

Editing an equation in Word

To edit an equation in Word, follow these steps:

- Toggle the equation.
- Navigate to the **"Design" tab.**
- To modify an equation, use your mouse to click on its various parts.
- Use the keyboard's back arrow to remove components.
- You can add components by clicking the symbols and structure icons or by using your keyboard.
- To complete edits, click **outside of the equation box.**

Equations saved that you do not need again can be deleted with ease, follow the steps below to delete the equation;

- Launch **the document.**
- The equation you wish to remove can be clicked.
- On your keyboard, hit the **"Delete" key.**

Symbols

Inserting a special character, fraction, or other symbol into Microsoft Word is a simple process. The font you choose is crucial when inserting symbols, fractions, special characters, or foreign characters. This is the most important thing to realize. Not every font contains the same characters. Verdana, for instance, contains fractional characters, whereas Elephant does not. Consequently, it's critical to select the appropriate font to locate the desired symbol or character. Move the pointer to the desired location in the file to insert the symbol.

- Go to **Symbol under Insert.**
- Select an **icon or click on More Symbols.**

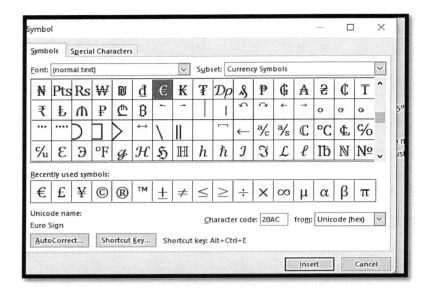

- To find the symbol you want to insert, scroll up or down. The most widely used symbols are found in the Segoe UI Symbol font set, though other font sets frequently contain different symbols as well. To choose the font you wish to peruse, use the Font selector above the symbol list.
- Double-click the desired symbol once you've located it. Your file will contain the symbol.
- Choose **Close.**

Inserting special characters

- To insert the special character, click or tap the desired location.
- Selec**t Insert > Symbol > Additional Symbols.**
- Access Special Characters.
- Double-click **the desired character to insert it.** Shortcut keys are connected to many of the special characters. To insert that unique character once more in the future, simply hit the shortcut key. You can insert the Copyright symbol (©) by pressing ALT+CTRL+C.
- Choose Close.

Inserting fractions

When you type certain fractions, like 1/4, 1/2, and 3/4, they automatically change to a fraction character, like ¼, ½, or ¾. However, some do not (1/3, 2/3, 1/5, etc.), so you will need to use the insert symbol procedure if you wish to insert those as symbols.

- Wherever you wish to insert the fraction, click or tap.
- Select **More Symbols** under **Insert > Symbol.**
- Select Number Forms using the Subset dropdown menu. Not every font has a subset of number forms. You will need to use a different font, like Calibri; to insert the fraction character if your font does not have the number forms subset available.
- Pick **Close.**

There are very few common fractions that have a substitute symbol. You can get close to the symbol for more uncommon fractions, like 8/9, by placing the denominator as a subscript and the numerator as a superscript.

Inserting international characters

You should think about changing your keyboard layout to the language you plan to type in frequently if you type in other languages. Office virtually always has keyboard shortcuts for one-off characters.

As an illustration:

- CTRL+SHIFT+ALT+? inserts a ¿
- CTRL+SHIFT+~ followed immediately by "a" will insert ã.
- CTRL+SHIFT+: followed immediately by "u" will insert ü.

Inserting a symbol with the use of a keyboard with ASCII or Unicode character codes; The symbol's character code can also be used as a keyboard shortcut. Either ASCII or Unicode codes are used to insert symbols and special characters. If you check the character's code, you can determine which is which.

- Select **More Symbols under Insert >Symbol.**
- To find the desired symbol, scroll up or down the list; keep in mind that you may need to adjust the font or subset to find it.
- There are boxes for a form and a character code towards the bottom right. You can enter this symbol from the keyboard using the character code, and the from: indicates what kind of character it is. It is a Unicode character if the source specifies "Unicode (hex)". It is an ASCII character if from: states "Symbol (Decimal)".

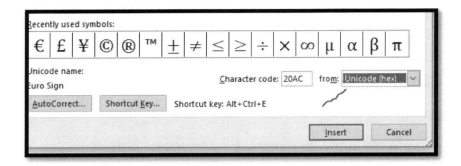

- **ASCII Characters;** Instead of typing the numbers across the top of your keyboard, use the numeric keypad with Num Lock enabled to enter ASCII numbers. Every ASCII character code consists of four digits. Add zeros to the beginning of the code to make it four digits if the desired character's code is less than four digits.
  - Navigate to the Home tab and select Wingdings (or another font set) from the Font group.
  - On the numeric keypad, type the character code while holding down the ALT key.
  - Once the symbol is inserted, return to your original font.

Unicode Characters

- Wherever you want to insert the Unicode symbol, type the character code.
- To change the code to a symbol, press **ALT+X.**
- Before pressing **ALT+X**, select only the code if you're placing your Unicode character right after another character.

Available symbol sets

You can find the following sets of mathematical symbols in Word's Symbols group. To view each grouping of symbols, click the menu at the top of the symbols list after selecting the More arrow.

Symbol set	Subset	Definition

Basic Math	None	Commonly used mathematical symbols, like > and <.
Greek Letters	Lowercase	Lowercase letters from the Greek alphabet
	Uppercase	Uppercase letters from the Greek alphabet
Letter-Like Symbols	None	Symbols that look like letters
Operators	Common Binary	Symbols that act on two quantities like +
	Common Relational Operators	Symbols that express a relationship between two expressions like = and ~
	Basic N-ary Operators	Operators that act across a range of variables or terms
	Advanced Binary Operators	Additional symbols that act on two quantities
	Advanced Relational	Additional symbols that express a relationship between two expressions.

	Operators	
	None	Symbols that show direction
	None	Symbols that express a negated relationship
Scripts	Scripts	The mathematical Script typeface
	Frakturs	The mathematical Fraktur typeface
	Double-struck	The mathematical double-struck typeface
Geometry	None	Commonly used geometric symbols

Creating Simple Algebraic Expressions

In mathematics, an algebraic expression consists of variables, constants, and algebraic operations (addition, subtraction, etc.). Terms comprise expressions. It takes more than just typing basic keyboard characters and numbers to write algebraic expressions. What about fractions alone, radicals, exponents, and mathematical characters? Thankfully, Microsoft Word comes with a unique set of equation tools that make it easy for you to form algebraic expressions. Use the equations tab on the Ribbon, which gathers all the characters, symbols, and functions you need to create even complex, advanced expressions, instead of sifting through the vast Symbols menu in search of math characters and then manipulating text boxes, format buttons, and various font attributes.

- To write the algebraic expression where you want it to appear, click anywhere in the text.

- On the Ribbon, select the **"Insert" tab.**
- On the Ribbon, select the **"Equation" button,** which is symbolized by the "Pi" symbol. You can form the algebraic expression in a new equation field that Word creates.
- Using the number keys on your keyboard, enter any number you wish in the expression. To add unique mathematical symbols, use the characters found in the Ribbon's Symbols menu. To create more complex expressions, such as those involving radicals, fractions, exponents, or other operators, click the icons in the Structures section of the Ribbon.
- When you're done, click outside the expression to shut the equation tools.

31.2 The Equation Editor

Accessing the Equation Editor

When calculating the area of a circle or using the Pythagorean Theorem, it can be laborious to enter some frequently used equations into Word. Nevertheless, MS Word has supplied some equations as a workaround. To use those equations, just edit them. Here is a comprehensive guide on how to enable the equation editor in Microsoft Word if you're wondering how to get access to it. Don't worry; it's not an impossible task. All you need to do is turn on the equation editor. After that, solving your math problem will be as simple as adding the values you already have. Now that you know that, let's get Microsoft Word open and see how to display the equation editor within Word. Word is software that is used by a wide range of users. Therefore, you're probably using Microsoft Word and Excel whether you're a student trying to finish your homework or an accountant trying to figure out your clients' taxes. You can use Word's built-in equation editor to perform calculations and streamline your work. To obtain the desired symbol, you won't need to continuously enter formulas or try to figure out strange key combinations. For Mac users, enabling the equation editor is incredibly easy.

Here's how to go about it.

- Launch Word in Microsoft. Next, click the Insert option located in the upper toolbar.
- Select the **Equations tab** located on the page's right side.

There are two methods available to you for installing the equation editor on your document if you own Microsoft Word versions 365, 2024, 2019, or 2016. As previously mentioned, one adopts Mac's style. In case the equation editor cannot be displayed using the first method, we have provided you with an alternate method.

- Launch **Word in Microsoft. After that, choose Insert**.
- On the right side of the page, tap the **Equations tab.**

Don't worry if using the above methods doesn't allow you to locate the equation option. You can enable Word's equation editor by using the alternate method that follows.

- Launch Word. In the upper-left corner of the application, select **File.**
- Select your options.
- Click on **Customize Ribbon**. More choices ought to be visible now.
- Open the menu and select **Choose commands.**
- Select **Every Command by clicking on them**. You'll receive a list of every option as a result.
- Next, select **Symbols** from the tabs that are displayed on the right side of the display.

Designing Complex Mathematical Expressions

To design a complex mathematical expression, follow the steps below;

- Either choose **Insert > Equation or hit Alt + =.**
- Choose **Design > Equation** to utilize a built-in formula.
- Simply choose **Design > Equation > Ink Equation** to start creating your own.

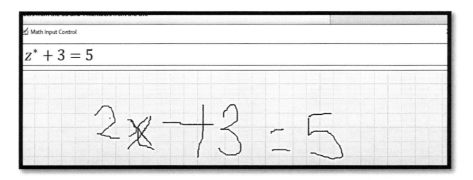

- Write your equation using your finger, a stylus, or a mouse.
- To insert your equation into the file, select **Insert.**

To start typing an equation from scratch, use the keyboard shortcut Alt +=.

OR

Insert > Equation > Insert New Equation.

- To write your equation, use a mouse, stylus, or your finger.
- For additional Structures and Convert options, view the ribbon.

For the addition of an insertion gallery, follow the steps below;

- Choose the equation you wish to include.
- With the down arrow selected, choose **Save as New Equation.**
- Enter a name in the **Create New Building Block dialog box for the equation**.
- Choose **Equations** from the list of galleries.
- Select **OK.**

31.3 Math AutoCorrect

Microsoft Word's AutoCorrect feature is designed to modify the way text is formatted and corrected as you type. The AutoCorrect dialog box will open when the user clicks the AutoCorrect Options button, allowing them to select which features to enable or disable. One feature that allows the user to customize where Math AutoCorrect replaces math terms in your Word document with math symbols is the Math AutoCorrect option under the AutoCorrect Options.

Follow the steps below to enable AutoCorrect for Math in Microsoft Word;

- Select the **File tab.**
- To access the backstage view, click **More > Options**.

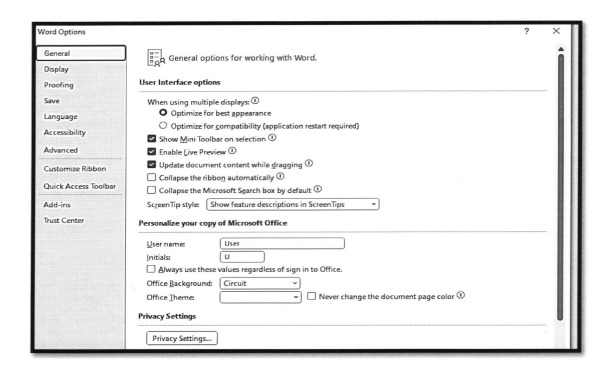

- Within the left pane, select **Proofing**.

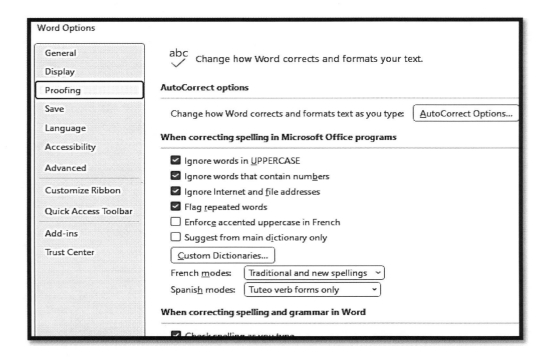

- Click the **AutoCorrect button** located under the AutoCorrect Options section.
- A dialog box for auto-correction will show up.
- Select the tab for **Math AutoCorrect**.

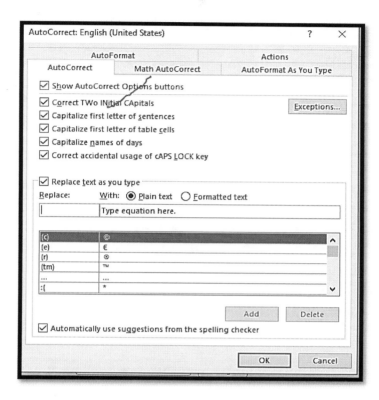

- Select the option to "Use Math AutoCorrect rules outside of math regions."
- Next, select **OK.**

Using AutoCorrect for Maths Symbols

These frequently used shortcodes can be used to quickly insert math symbols in Microsoft Word when the Math AutoCorrect feature is enabled.

- Does not equal sign (≠): \ne or \neq
- Approximately equal to (≅): \cong
- Less than or equal to (≤): \le or \leq
- Greater than or equal to (≥): \ge or \geq
- Almost equal to (≈): \approx

392

Use the backslash key (\) rather than the forward slash (/) key to insert these symbols correctly. When you enter the short code and press **ENTER**, Microsoft Office replaces your text with the appropriate symbol.

31.4 Writing and Editing Formulas

Creating and Editing Mathematical Formulas

Although Word seems like a strange choice when it comes to mathematical equations, Microsoft Word is a great option. Word allows you to enter and even modify equations, in addition to having a gallery of pre-built equations. Word is a good option if you need an equation editor. In addition to supporting equations, it also integrates with LaTeX and UnicodeMath.

Follow the steps below to insert your equation in Word;

The Word gallery contains a large number of equations, so you'll likely find what you're looking for there. When necessary, you can, however, enter your equation. Select Insert New Equation from the Equation dropdown menu by clicking **the Insert menu**. Alternately, hit Alt and =. Both will show a blank equation control. It can take some getting used to formatting at first, and it can take longer until you get used to Word's formatting capabilities. For example, you would use the Script dropdown in the Structures group on the contextual Equation tab to manually enter the Pythagorean Theorem. **To illustrate,**

- Select Superscript, the first script placeholder, by clicking Script.
- After choosing the variable frame, type a.
- Enter 2 after choosing the Superscript frame.
- Enter + after pressing the Spacebar.
- Make sure to save your equation by selecting **Save as New Equation** with a right-click on the control after entering it.
- You can name the equation; choose where to store it, which Category it belongs in, and other details in the dialog that appears. When you need to enter an equation, Word will store it in the equations gallery for easy access.

Now that you know how to input your equation in Word, in the section below are steps to editing equations in Microsoft Word. To see the contextual Equation Tools ribbon, select the equation control.

Changes are possible to the following elements:

- Utilize the symbols gallery to add symbols. To view additional symbols, click the **More button.**
- Select a **structure placeholder from the Structures group.**
- Select one of the following from the **Convert dropdown** to alter the equation's format: Professional, Linear, All Professional, or All Linear.

You should take your time exploring the many options so you are aware of what is available. You can write a mathematical equation on a touch screen device with your finger or a stylus. Use your mouse if you're not using a touch device; Word is forgiving, but I must admit that this is a challenging method.

To create an equation, take the following actions:

- Use **Alt and** = to enter a blank equation control.
- Click the **Ink Equation button** located in the **Tools group of the contextual Equations ribbon.**
- In the dialog that appears, **sketch your equation and select Insert.**

Word does a good job of translating a handwritten equation into its actual form. It might be misinterpreted, though, because it isn't flawless. Fortunately, it's simple to correct any error. You may find that entering an equation this way is simpler than using Word's structures, even though you may misinterpret some characters. Additionally, by verifying the preview before inserting it, you can prevent misunderstandings. Use the tools at the bottom to make the drawn elements correct if the preview isn't accurate.

Inserting Subscripts and Superscripts

In text bodies, superscripts and subscripts are two distinct ways to display unique numbers, letters, or symbols. A subscript shows up beneath the text, and a superscript appears above another piece of text. Creating an accurate and aesthetically pleasing document can be facilitated by becoming familiar with these Word scripts. Additionally, Text can be formatted to appear above another piece of text by using a superscript. Superscript is typically located above the larger text and is smaller in size than the surrounding text. Depending on the typeface and formatting, superscript's distance from the related text varies. When a particular font or typeface is incompatible with superscript, for example, writers and designers can utilize bolding to make the superscript stand out more clearly.

Any character that is printed beneath the text and is half the height of the standard text is called a subscript.

- Select **'Home' from the ribbon tab.**
- Place **your cursor** where you want the superscript or subscript to be inserted in the text. As an alternative, you can choose the text to format directly as superscript or subscript.
- Depending on your requirements, selec**t the superscript or subscript button** from the 'Font' group. When the formatting feature is enabled, the button becomes a deeper shade of gray than the rest of the ribbon.

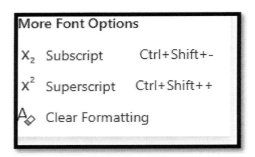

- Input the desired text to be shown as either superscript or subscript. If you are using pre-existing text, you can omit this step.
- To turn off the formatting, select the superscript or subscript button once again.
- To save the updated superscript or subscript text, save the file.

Additionally, you can enable superscript or subscript numbers in Word using the dialogue box—this is helpful for things like mathematical formulas. Because symbols are a component of the font file, the kinds of symbols that are available as scripts here vary based on the typeface you use. This feature is available for many font types, such as Verdana and Arial.

The steps below can be used to insert subscripts and superscripts using the dialogue box:

- Point the pointer where in the text you wish to add the superscript or subscript.
- Select the **'Insert' tab from Word's command ribbon at the top.**
- From the 'Symbols' group, choose **'Symbol'.**
- From the drop-down menu, select **'More Symbols'.**

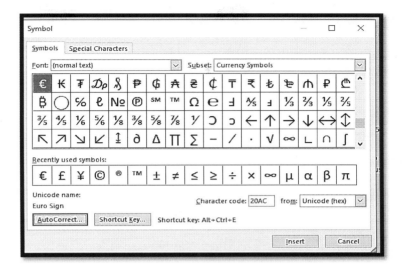

- Verify that the dialogue box's **'Symbols' tab** is visible to you.
- To ensure that the superscript or subscript aligns with the font you're using, select **'Normal Text' from the 'Font' menu.**
- From the 'Subset' drop-down list, select **'Superscripts' and 'Subscripts'.**
- Select the **desired superscript or subscript.**
- Select the **'Insert' button.**
- From this point on, you can keep the 'Symbol' dialogue box open by moving your cursor to other areas of the Word document to add more superscripts or subscripts.
- To exit the 'Symbol' dialogue box, click the **'Close' button**.
- To insert the new superscript or subscript into the Word document, save the file.

There are several circumstances where using superscript or subscript formatting is helpful.

Examine the following scenarios to gain an understanding of when to use these formatting styles:

- **Trademark and copyright symbols:** To indicate that something is intellectual property, it can be helpful to use trademark and copyright symbols when writing a body of text. To indicate that a good, service or other entity is intellectual property, the superscript format is usually used. It's useful to include a symbol to indicate that certain things, like product names or company branding, are usually trademarked in a body of text. It can be more difficult to read the content if these symbols are included in regular text size, which is why superscript is useful here.

- **For endnote and footnote numbers:** Additional information can be included in endnotes and footnotes without having to be included in the text's body. This contains information that is typical of academic writing, such as references or source citations. When adding a footnote or endnote to a document that would benefit from more information, you can use superscript formatting. For instance, the reader is aware that the number four in a sentence indicates the fourth footnote or endnote in the document if it appears in superscript.
- **Chemical symbols:** Chemical symbols are typically displayed in scientific writing using superscript or subscript formatting. This increases readability by aiding in the separation of the chemical symbols from the main text. When writing mass numbers for elements or compounds, for example, superscript formatting is frequently used in scientific writing to indicate different chemical symbols.
- **Mathematical Functions**: Another common use of superscript and subscript formatting to make content more readable is in the writing of mathematical formulas. One useful way to indicate an exponent or a number to the power of another number is to use superscript formatting. This covers operations like cubing and squaring numbers. Because of the formatting, it's also helpful for very large numbers because smaller text is still readable.
- **Ordinal numerals:** Numbers in a list, group, or sequence can be categorized using ordinal numerals. For instance, designating the first and second items in a list with the letters 1st or 2nd. Superscript formatting frequently causes the two letters to appear smaller than the surrounding text. Because some style guides prefer not to use superscript formatting for ordinal numbers, it's a good idea to review those particular guides.

31.5 Advanced Math Formatting

Aligning and Justifying Equations

In mathematical writing, the ability to align and justify equations is helpful because it makes lengthy equations and sequences easier to read, which would otherwise be unintelligible. Some users align objects using the spacebar; however, this can lead to unexpected outcomes. Even though it appears to be aligned correctly on your screen, students may not see it that way because different devices and file conversations display spaces differently. Learning how to align equations correctly will help to ensure that content is displayed to all readers consistently and will also help to prevent odd characters from appearing when they go through an Ally conversion to PDF (to make the document more accessible). This is especially important if you are writing your content in Word and then uploading these documents.

Equations must be aligned correctly, so we must combine them into a single paragraph as opposed to several lines.

To do this:

Enter the first line of your equation in the equation editor by selecting Insert > Equation > Insert New Equation in your Word document.

- Once you've typed your first line, do not hit return. To go to a new line, use the keyboard shortcuts **SHIFT and ENTER.** A new line is created without starting a new paragraph when you use SHIFT and ENTER. In case you inadvertently hit the backspace key, just click on the final line of your equation, then hit **SHIFT and ENTER.**
- To go on to the next line, type it and hit **SHIFT and ENTER.**
- To create your equation, repeat step 3. You will align your equation after you have finished typing it completely.
- Select the **first equal sign in your equation with a right-click.** There will be a drop-down menu available.
- Select **Align at this Character from the drop-down menu**; even though it might not appear to have changed, press on.
- Apply the same procedure to the second line by performing a right-click in front of the first equal sign and selecting **Align at this Character from the drop-down menu.** Repeat for every line. Now your equation ought to be correctly aligned.

You might want to add some spacing to your equation to make it easier to read. To increase the distance between lines:

- Choose **the entire equation.**
- To access the Paragraph options pop-up menu, select the arrow located under the **Paragraph options section of the Home tab.**
- Select the **desired line spacing on the Indents and Spacing tab; in this case, 1.5 lines.** Now your equation should be spaced and aligned correctly.

Adding Equation Numbers and Captions

If your thesis or any other scientific paper you are working on has a large number of equations, you must include equation numbers. Writing your manuscript in latex would likely be the best and most convenient option for you if your paper contains a lot of equations. It can be done effectively and smoothly with latex. However, Microsoft Word has several features that make it superior to latex, such as a spelling and grammar checker and the ability to write quickly without having to remember codes for various tasks. The goal of collaboration is the most crucial of all. A small percentage of our collaborators are familiar with latex, whereas almost everyone is familiar with Microsoft Word. Microsoft Word has rapidly changed. One of my main complaints with older versions of MS Word is that it is not very responsive for longer documents. Fortunately, it has improved with time and now allows equations to be inserted into the latex syntax. With time, they keep adding new features.

Follow the steps below to add the caption;

- Choose the equation and then locate **the references tab.**
- Choose **Insert Caption** choice and then choose the label as an equation. Note that you can choose to exclude the label from the caption if need be.

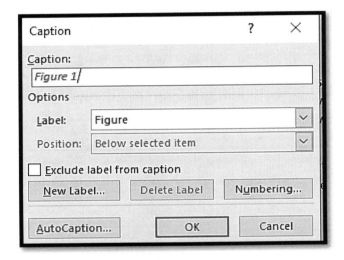

- In the next step, you can choose to modify the numbering format. You can also choose to add the chapter number just where the chapter commences with heading 1 numbering and also employ the use of the separator as "period".
- You can choose to cut and paste the equation and the equation number in the second and third columns of your equation if need be.
- Once you have done this, you can then proceed to align everything. Get this done by choosing the table, locating **the layout tab, and then choosing the align center.**
- Now you should have an equation and its number added to it. You can write as many equations as you like by simply making use of the copy-and-paste approach. You also can choose to right-click and update the field to get the ordered numbering of equations.

You can always save the equation to the equation gallery for much later use as in a template. Follow the steps below to get this done;

- Highlight the equation table.
- Choose **Insert > Equation > Save Selection to Equation Gallery**.

Formatting Equations in Tables

To carry out computations, you can add formulas to Word tables. Basic operators and functions like SUM and AVERAGE can be used in these formulas. Since you are inserting fields when you insert formulas in Word tables, the fields will need to be updated whenever the data in the table changes. Generally, it's best to create formulas in Excel that update automatically for more complicated calculations. Word table formulas and functions are limited to working with numbers. It is not possible to generate text or do text calculations. Each column and row in a Word table is identified and given a cell reference, just like cells in an Excel worksheet. The first cell in a Word table would be designated as A1 since column A would be the first column and row 1 would be the first row. As a result, you can write computations that make use of cells (like =A1+A2). **The same fundamental operators are available in both Word and Excel:**

- addition (+)
- subtraction (-)
- multiplication (*)
- division (/)

Word table formulas typically refer to a range and are made using standard functions like SUM, AVERAGE, MIN, MAX, or COUNT. The equal sign (=) must come first. When using ABOVE, LEFT, RIGHT, or BELOW as the arguments for functions, you can refer to ranges of cells. The formula to use if you want to add up the cells at the bottom of a column is =SUM (ABOVE). Additionally, you can combine these arguments. A formula like =SUM (ABOVE, LEFT) would, for instance, add up all the cells that are above and to the left of that particular cell. Additionally, functions may make use of cell references, like in =SUM (C1:C10). Individual cells can also be referred to, for example, as =SUM (B1, C1, and D5). Word tables can also use the IF function with the syntax =IF(test, true, false) to carry out more intricate computations. For instance, if orders are less than 1000, the shipping cost of 50 could be determined using =IF (A5>=1000, 0, 50). The IF function can also be used with the AND and OR functions. **Follow the steps below to insert a formula in a table;**

- Wherever you wish to enter a formula, click **in the cell.**
- In the Ribbon, select the **Table Layout or Table Tools Layout tab.**
- In the Data group, choose **Function (fx). A dialogue window opens. Usually, Word will add arguments and a function to the Formula box.**
- Click **OK** to confirm that you want to use the suggested formula. Click in the **Formula box and type a new formula (beginning with =)** if you wish to modify the existing one. The Paste Function drop-down menu offers additional functions for you to select from.
- Choose **a format from the Format drop-down menu if required.**
- Press **OK.** Word shows the results and inserts the formula as a field.

To modify a table's formula:

- To fix the formula or error, right-click. There's a drop-down menu.
- Choose the **Edit field option.**
- Make the appropriate adjustments.
- Press **OK.**

31.6 Math Accessibility Features

Making Math Content Accessible / Accessible Math Editor

Students of today have access to digital or online learning resources. Districts have embraced technology wholeheartedly or are making efforts to integrate it into all classes, including math classes. According to best practices, math should be taught to students initially through tactile graphics and braille. But students also need to learn how to access and finish digital math assignments in this digital age. To access digital math, many students prefer to use a braille display in conjunction with a screen reader-equipped device. This allows the student to access the refreshable braille while simultaneously listening to the math expression.

Current digital math options

Math markup languages have been used for decades by professionals and college students with visual impairments to access and create digital math expressions. Two well-liked math languages are MathML and LaTeX. Higher math can be accessed effectively by using markup languages, but there is a learning curve because these math languages need extra symbols to be added to the math expression. Few K–12 students are learning markup languages before attending college, and the majority of TSVIs are not familiar with them. Math editors are more recent options that work with editable text boxes to allow you to type in the math expression and have it automatically translated. You can enter the equation just like normal and don't need to add any extra symbols! The integrated Braille Math Editor feature was made available by JAWS, and Pearson is developing the Accessible Equation Editor. Although they both have limitations that are being adjusted, these math editors are functional. Another tool for accessing and creating digital math is the braille notetaker BrailleNote Touch (or BrailleNote Touch Plus). The BrailleNote interprets math input from Nemeth or UEB using KeyMath software.

Microsoft Word: Accessing math expressions

Teachers can easily create accessible math worksheets using Word's powerful math editor, and students can easily finish these digital worksheets. Educators and professionals use this potent mainstream tool, which can be accessed via paired braille displays and screen readers. Better yet, Word's math editor is so easy to use that even non-techies and/or non-math experts can use it!

Microsoft Word: Create accessible math expressions

Since this is a Microsoft Word tool, Word documents are required. The classroom teacher, TSVI, paraprofessional, or transcriber must recreate the document in Word if it is in PDF format. The math editor in Word can be used by students who use a screen reader or braille display to complete the math assignment or to create math expressions.

Use the equation text box to create a math equation:

- Launch a Word document.
- Optionally, choose Insert > Equation from the ribbon or you can choose to use the keyboard shortcut Alt + = (Windows) or Control + = (Mac) to access the menu.
  - Enter the desired math expression in the text box that appears on the screen.

Equation or the arrow next to Equation can be selected to show a variety of math symbols that can be chosen and added to the expression in the math toolbar.

Using Screen Readers with Mathematical Elements

Narrator scan mode

You can use the Narrator scan mode to browse your document's content by elements.

- Press the SR key and the Spacebar to activate the scan mode.

When the scan mode is activated, you can cycle between paragraphs, other elements, areas, and landmarks in your document by using the keyboard shortcuts and the Up and Down arrow keys.

Navigation pane

The Navigation pane allows you to quickly move between document elements, such as headings and graphics.

- Press Alt+W, K to open the Navigation pane. You will hear: "Navigation, search document, edit box."
- **Take one of the following actions:**
  - To navigate through the document's headings, hit the Tab key until you hear "Heading tab item," then hit the key again until you hear the desired heading, and finally hit **Enter.** The start of the heading row in the document body is now the center of attention.
  - When you hear the phrase **"Search, split button,"** press the **Tab key** to navigate by specific elements in your document, like symbols. Then, press the Alt+Down arrow key to expand the menu. To select an element, for example, "Symbol," press the Down arrow key until you hear it. Then, press Enter. The next result button comes into focus. To navigate through the results, keep pressing **Enter.**
- To close the Navigation pane, tap **Alt + W, K.**

Read Mode

With features like Read Aloud, Read Mode is intended to make text reading more **comfortable.**

- For Read Mode to be enabled, press **Alt+W, F.**
- **Perform a few or all of the following:**

- Press **Alt** to bring up the Read Mode toolbar. Next, press **Tab** to hear the name of the menu you want to select, and then press **Enter.** To navigate through the list of available options, press the **Down arrow key**. Then, press **Enter** to choose an option.
- Just hit **Alt+W, R** to activate Read Aloud. Press the **Tab key** until you find the option you want, and then press **Enter** to select it to access the reading controls.
- Tap the **Esc button** to leave the **Read Mode.**

Immersive Reader View

You can read scanned texts more easily, sharpen your focus, decode complex symbols, and organize the equations you're reading with Immersive Reader.

- To activate Immersive Reader, hit **Alt+W, L, and**
- Press **Alt** to bring up the **Immersive Reader ribbon and settings**. It says, "Immersive, Immersive Reader, tab." To navigate between the options on the ribbon, press the Tab key. Then, press **Enter** to pick an option.
- Use Alt+W, L, 2 to turn off Immersive Reader.

Focus Mode

You can reduce distractions and focus on writing, creating, and working with others in Word by using the Focus mode. In the Focus mode, only the Word document is visible; the ribbon and status bar are hidden.

- Press **Alt+W, O to activate the Focus mode.**
- Press **Esc to exit the Focus mode.**

Search

Use the search text field to find an option or to quickly complete an action.

- Choose the item or location where you want to execute an action in your spreadsheet, presentation, or document.
- Press **Alt+Q to open the Search text field.**
- Enter the search terms related to the desired action. Type a comma, for instance, if you wish to add a comma in between symbols or an equation.
- To peruse the search results, use the **Down arrow key.**
- When you've located the desired outcome, hit **Enter** to pick it and carry out the action.

Navigate between floating shapes

- To rapidly shift the focus to the first floating shape (such as a chart or text box), hit **Ctrl+Alt+5**.
- Use the **Tab or Shift+Tab keys** to switch between the floating shapes.
- Using **Esc** will return you to the standard navigation.

Activity

1. Insert basic math symbols in your document.
2. Access and make use of the equation editor.
3. Make use of the AutoCorrect for Math symbols.
4. What are subscripts and superscripts? Insert them in your Word document.
5. Align and Justify equations in Microsoft Word.
6. Format equations in tables in Microsoft Word.
7. Make math content accessible.
8. Employ the use of screen readers in getting to mathematical elements with ease.

Conclusion

Word Text document creation, editing, formatting, and printing are the main uses for Microsoft Word 2024. It gives users access to a robust word-processing platform that facilitates the creation of a variety of documents, from straightforward memos and letters to intricate reports and research papers. With its simple and intuitive graphical user interface, Microsoft Word enables users to start creating documents right away. Newer versions feature an interface called Ribbon that provides streamlined access to several features and tools. Many text formatting options, such as font styles, sizes, colors, and effects, are available in Microsoft Word. Users can make lists with bullets or numbers and change the paragraph alignment, spacing, and indentation. It also allows you to customize documents with different fonts, styles, and themes. A sizable library of pre-made templates for frequently used document types, including resumes, flyers, brochures, newsletters, and more, is included with Microsoft Word. Users can easily create documents with a professional appearance and save time by using these templates. Spell check and grammar check features are also integrated into Microsoft Word to assist users in finding and fixing mistakes in their writing. Additionally, it can offer recommendations for better word choice and sentence construction. Multiple users can work on a document at once with MS Word's collaborative features, which facilitate teamwork and colleague collaboration on projects. Comments, edit merging, and change tracking are all possible for users. It also combines with other Microsoft Office programs like Outlook, PowerPoint, and Excel with ease. Users can incorporate objects, tables, and charts from these programs into Word documents thanks to this integration. With every new version, Microsoft Word adds features that meet the demands of evolving user needs and technological advancements. It is still a useful and important tool for managing written content in a variety of personal and professional contexts.

INDEX

C

416

M

N

O

424

425

Y

Your Familiar Commands, 40
YouTube, 289, 345
YouTube or Vimeo video, 289

Z

zoom possibilities, 34